T0323869

"Any book on Jewish ethics that includes so many elements – classical and modern texts, theological and secular ethics, Maimonides and contemporary feminist thought – would be impressive. This book introduces all of these things and more, while remaining highly readable, concise, and generous in its analysis."

– **Emily Filler**, Washington and Lee University

JEWISH ETHICS

THE BASICS

Jewish Ethics: The Basics demonstrates how ancient and contemporary ideas have shaped and reshaped Jewish traditions about how to act toward others. Readers are introduced to foundational questions, controversies, and diverse ethical conclusions developed by Jewish thinkers throughout the ages. Topics addressed include:

- Assumptions about Authority
- Love, Compassion, Justice and Humility
- Human Rights, War, Land and Power
- Gender and Sexuality
- Personal and Social Ethics
- Environmental and Animal Ethics
- Bioethical Issues

Concise, readable, and engaging, this is the ideal introduction for anyone interested in religious ethics, secular traditions, Judaism, and the field of Jewish ethics.

Geoffrey D. Claussen is Lori and Eric Sklut Professor in Jewish Studies, Professor of Religious Studies, and Chair of the Department of Religious Studies at Elon University, USA.

THE BASICS

The Basics is a highly successful series of accessible guidebooks which provide an overview of the fundamental principles of a subject area in a jargon-free and undaunting format.

Intended for students approaching a subject for the first time, the books both introduce the essentials of a subject and provide an ideal springboard for further study. With over 50 titles spanning subjects from artificial intelligence (AI) to women's studies, *The Basics* are an ideal starting point for students seeking to understand a subject area.

Each text comes with recommendations for further study and gradually introduces the complexities and nuances within a subject.

For a full list of titles in this series, please visit www.routledge.com/The-Basics/book-series/B

JEWISH ETHICS

THE BASICS

Geoffrey D. Claussen

LONDON AND NEW YORK

Designed cover image: Geoffrey D. Claussen

First published 2025
by Routledge
4 Park Square, Milton Park, Abingdon, Oxon OX14 4RN

and by Routledge
605 Third Avenue, New York, NY 10158

Routledge is an imprint of the Taylor & Francis Group, an informa business

British Library Cataloguing-in-Publication Data
A catalogue record for this book is available from the British Library

Library of Congress Cataloging-in-Publication Data
Names: Claussen, Geoffrey D., 1979- author.
Title: Jewish ethics : the basics / Geoffrey D. Claussen.
Description: New York : Routledge, 2025. | Includes bibliographical references and
index.
Identifiers: LCCN 2024028410 (print) | LCCN 2024028411 (ebook) | ISBN
9781032221540 (hardback) | ISBN 9781032221533 (paperback) | ISBN 9781003271338
(ebook)
Subjects: LCSH: Jewish ethics.
Classification: LCC BJ1285.2 .C545 2025 (print) | LCC BJ1285.2 (ebook) |
DDC 296.3/6–dc23/eng/20240924
LC record available at https://lccn.loc.gov/2024028410
LC ebook record available at https://lccn.loc.gov/2024028411

ISBN: 978-1-032-22154-0 (hbk)
ISBN: 978-1-032-22153-3 (pbk)
ISBN: 978-1-003-27133-8 (ebk)

DOI: 10.4324/9781003271338

Typeset in Bembo
by Taylor & Francis Books

CONTENTS

ACKNOWLEDGMENTS

I am grateful to have had the opportunity to work with Rebecca Clintworth and the rest of the Routledge staff on this book. I am also grateful to my anonymous reviewers for their helpful feedback, and to Emily Filler for encouraging me to take on this project and for her feedback on the manuscript. Thank you to Elon University for the sabbatical leave that made my writing possible, to my colleagues at Elon for their support, and to Lori and Eric Sklut for their generous support through the Lori and Eric Sklut Endowed Professorship in Jewish Studies. Thank you to my family, including my mother Eileen, Hillary, J, Lahav, Abir, Rayah, Michael, Suzette, Max, Chelsea, Mason, Cole, Nikki, Jonny, Erin, and Sami. Above all, thanks to my daughters Eliana and Talya and my wife Jessica for their boundless love and support, and special thanks to Jessica for her wisdom, incisive editing, and the incredible blessings of her loving partnership.

WHOSE VOICES ARE INCLUDED IN JEWISH ETHICS?

What counts as Jewish ethics? And who decides what counts? Jews—people who identify as Jewish—often disagree with each other about these questions. One can find Jews advancing nearly every ethical position imaginable and claiming that their views represent "Jewish ethics," "Jewish values," "Jewish teachings," or "Jewish wisdom." Some assert that they, as individuals, can decide what counts as Jewish ethics. Others explain how authentic Jewish ethics is determined by certain authority figures, certain texts, the majority view within certain Jewish communities—or by God, whose will some believe to be expressed by those authorities, texts, or communities.

Many Jews view ethics as central to their Jewish identities and so care especially deeply about what counts as Jewish ethics. Many assume that Jewish ethics offers clear teachings that fit with their senses of what it means to be Jewish. For example, Jews with strong commitments to liberalism often see Jewish ethics as clearly supporting liberalism. Jews with strong commitments to Zionism often see Jewish ethics as clearly supporting Zionism. Jews with strong ethical commitments on any number of issues may see Jewish ethics as clearly supporting those commitments. People with perspectives like these may be troubled by representations of Jewish ethics that veer from the message they are sure Jewish ethics upholds.

People who do not identify as Jewish also sometimes care very deeply about what counts as Jewish ethics. Given the ways that Christian and Islamic identities developed with reference to Jews, large swaths of the world's population have historically defined

DOI: 10.4324/9781003271338-1

their identities in relationship to Jewishness (Nirenberg 2013). In particular, many Christians have historically defined their ethics in opposition to what they have defined as Jewish approaches, viewing Christian ethics as an improvement on inferior Jewish ethics. More recently, other Christians have viewed Jewish ethics in stereotypically positive terms. People with perspectives like these may also be troubled by representations of Jewish ethics that veer from the message they are sure Jewish ethics upholds.

For reasons including these, many people in the world are deeply attached to certain ideas about what "Jewish ethics says." For people with such attachments, it can be challenging to embark upon the critical study of Jewish ethics, which involves encountering the very diverse ways in which Jewish ethics has been imagined.

In this book, I introduce readers to the critical study of Jewish ethics. I do not seek to provide ethical guidance but rather to promote understanding of how Jewish ethics has been imagined. I work from the critical premise that there is no singular entity that can be identified as "Jewish ethics" that says one thing about a given subject, though there are many people who claim that there is such an entity. I argue that the most basic thing to understand about "Jewish ethics" is that it has been constructed in different ways by different people in different contexts and for different reasons.

This is no different from the way that other forms of ethics have been constructed by other human groups. Just as there is no singular "Jewish ethics" that "says" something, there is no singular Christian ethics or Islamic ethics, Chinese ethics or British ethics, Yoruba ethics or Navajo ethics that proclaim singular ethical teachings. Large groups of people who see themselves as distinct political entities, nationalities, cultures, or religions are seldom unified in their approaches to ethics. The ethical ideas that emerge from any diverse group are necessarily diverse and, rather than generalizing about large groups, it is always best to identify who in the group is constructing or following a particular approach.

When I say that forms of ethics are "constructed," I employ a metaphor of building commonly used by scholars to emphasize that traditions, ideas, and ways of acting are not timeless but are developed in particular locations by particular people for particular reasons. One may not be able to tell how and when a structure was built, and people may claim that it is an unchanging part of a given landscape, but structures have histories that are valuable to understand. When seeking to understand traditions of ethics that influence many people's lives, critical scholars believe that it is valuable to understand the histories of these traditions. Traditions may be depicted as offering a clear message and unchanging essence, but those depictions are built by people in particular historical contexts seeking to lend authority to those ideas.

When I speak here of critical study and scholarship, I do not mean "critical" in the sense of being inclined to find fault or judge negatively. Rather, I refer to an approach to inquiry that seeks to uncover how diverse ideas are constructed and their underlying assumptions, functions, consequences, and limitations. The critical approach taken in this volume especially seeks to understand how Jewish ethics means different things and has different functions for different people. This volume offers a critical introduction to the diversity of Jewish ethics, exploring some of the ways in which Jews have developed very different ideas of how ethics might be shaped by Jewish tradition, experience, history, or identity.

WHAT IS JEWISH ETHICS?

In this volume, I understand Jewish ethics broadly: ideas developed by Jews, shaped by Jewish tradition, experience, history, or identity, about how humans should live, especially in relation to others. In the paragraphs below, I will seek to explain what I mean by each of these phrases—how they lead this book to consider a relatively broad range of ideas and also how this framework limits what appears in this book.

I focus on ideas developed by Jews as that term is commonly used, including people who identify as "Jewish," or as "Jews," "Hebrews," or "Israelites," or as part of the "Jewish people," "the people of Israel," or, simply, "Israel," or by similar terms in a range of languages. Though I use these terms interchangeably in this volume, I often use the words "Jews" and "Jewish" because of their common usage in contemporary English, even though that word was seldom employed by members of the group under discussion until recent centuries (Baker 2017: 3).

The only people who would be included by my general standard but whose ideas I am consciously excluding are people with a

particular devotion to the figure of Jesus of Nazareth—people generally referred to as Christians—who have often used some of these
terms (especially invoking the term Israel) to refer to themselves; I
think that the ethical ideas of such people, however, are sufficiently
addressed in introductions to Christian ethics.

Even with this limitation in place, the varieties of people who
identify as Jews or with related terms is astoundingly broad,
including Jews in locations throughout the entire world over a
span of over three thousand years. Israelites first seem to have
emerged as a subgroup of Canaanites in the land between the
Jordan River and the Mediterranean Sea, in the second millennium BCE, and the differences between those early Israelites and
later Jews are significant. So are differences among Jews even
within the same time and place, where one will frequently find
Jews not recognizing other Jews as part of the same people. Today,
few Jews would recognize *all* others who self-identify as Jewish,
Israelite, or Hebrew as Jewish. But this book takes a broad
approach, as my goal as an author is to promote understanding of
the diversity of Jewish ethics rather than curtail that diversity by
siding with particular groups of Jews.

That having been said, this short book can only contain so much
diversity, and I am focusing on Jewish ethics as it has been developed by modern Jews, with an eye to premodern sources that have
been of great interest to the modern Jews who have constructed
the category of Jewish ethics. While I seek to consider ideas from a
considerably diverse group of modern Jews, I limit my focus
among premodern Jews to the authors of these particularly influential sources: the authors of "classical" Rabbinic literature in the
first millennium CE; the authors of the Zoharic literature produced
in the early second millennium CE; and the twelfth-century CE
philosopher Moses Maimonides.

I further limit what counts as "Jewish ethics" in this book by
limiting my focus to ideas about ethics that reference Jewish tradition, experience, history, or identity or that are otherwise clearly
shaped by Jewish tradition, experience, history, or identity. Ideas
developed by people who happen to be Jewish but whose Jewishness does not seem to inform their ethics are not included.
Jewish tradition, experience, history, or identity, however, include
a broad range of possibilities; I understand "Jewish ethics" more

broadly than scholars who define Jewish ethics solely with reference to, say, "tradition," and who do not include ethical claims that draw on other aspects of Jewish experience.

Finally, this book understands ethics broadly as referring to ideas about how humans should live, especially in relation to others. This includes ideas about moral character—for example, ideas about compassion, humility, or courage—as well as ideas about conduct.

Ethics further includes general ideas about how to be and act, practical ideas of how to act in specific situations (applied ethics), and also theoretical ideas about the nature, justifications, and meanings of ethics (meta-ethics). It includes what is commonly referred to with the word "morality," a word that I use synonymously with "ethics" (rather than following any convention of distinguishing the two terms).

Ethics also includes ideas that may be viewed as "philosophical" or "non-philosophical," ideas about conduct and character in more private contexts as well as in social and political contexts, and ideas about law.

In contrast to scholars who may define ethics more narrowly as distinct from law and politics, or as a branch of philosophy that requires following certain conventions of philosophical inquiry and argument, I include a wide range of Jewish ideas, considering those that seem more or less political, more or less legally-oriented, and more or less philosophical. I keep my focus, however, on Jewish ideas about how one *should* live (normative ethics), rather than on descriptions of how people *have* lived.

I also keep my focus in this volume on ideas about how humans should live in relation to *others*, including other humans, non-human animals, and the broader non-human environment. In doing so, I follow a widespread convention of defining ethics as pertaining to our relationships with others; actions that seem to only affect oneself are not in the category of ethics. This is a difficult distinction to make, however, as even private rituals or personal comportment may affect others and so may be seen as a matter of ethics in that sense. Issues of relating to other persons may also be distinguished from relating to God, where the former is viewed as "ethics" and the latter is viewed as "theology," but the distinction here is often blurry as well. While I do focus on ethics in this volume as a matter of relating to human beings above all, and non-human animals or the environment to some extent, I recognize that ethics may include an even wider range of ideas about character and conduct.

THE ETHICS OF "JUDAISM"?

My framework for what counts as Jewish ethics is intentionally broad compared to many other presentations of Jewish ethics. It is more typical, in introductory works, to describe Jewish ethics as the ethics of "Judaism."

Judaism is a term, however, that is often misleading. It is a term that has only come into use among Jews in recent centuries (Boyarin 2019). The English language suffix -ism implies a commitment to a certain kind of belief or approach, and the term Judaism or equivalent terms in other languages is often used by those who want others to think of Jewish tradition as embracing a particular belief or approach.

Asserting that a particular approach is the approach supported by "Judaism" has been a regular feature of Jewish discourse about ethics in the modern era. One rabbi trumpeting a certain approach to ethics and human nature asserts that "Judaism views humans as being basically prone to evil behavior" (Wein 2007), and another asserts that "Judaism has … maintained an unshakable faith that the good of human nature outweighs the evil" (Heinze 2004: 223–4). One claims that "Judaism is certainly against discriminatory treatment of any section of the population" (Petuchowski 1966: 163), and another claims that Judaism "distinguishes and discriminates between Jew and non-Jew" (Kahane 1990: 162). All such assertions rely on the claim that there is an entity called "Judaism" that clearly stands for one approach.

Jews have taken many different approaches that they have claimed are the approach of "Judaism," and they have built many different "Judaisms" that align with these approaches. The use of the term Judaism may be useful for convincing others that a vast tradition supports their particular view and that contrary views are not part of the authoritative tradition. One who asserts that Judaism opposes discrimination will assure you that views favoring discrimination are not part of authentic Judaism; one who asserts that Judaism favors discrimination will assure you that views opposing discrimination are not part of authentic Judaism.

As the goal of this book is to promote understanding of the diverse ways that Jewish ethics has been imagined, I will not take sides on questions such as these about what views should count as authentic or authoritative Judaism. This book may help you to see, however, how the term "Judaism" may be deployed in different ways by different people seeking to mark the boundaries of what should count as Jewish ethics. Rather than claiming that "Judaism" supports some particular approach, this book encourages readers to consider how different Jews have used ideas about "Judaism" to construct Jewish ethics.

ARE THERE CERTAIN IDEAS THAT ARE ESSENTIAL FOR JEWISH ETHICS?

Even without making claims about "Judaism," other Jews seeking to advance certain ethical ideas often assert that these ideas are "essential," "fundamental," or "foundational" to Jewish ethics. Contrary ideas, then, cannot be seen as part of Jewish ethics. This approach is "essentializing"—taking one part of a diverse group of ideas and portraying it as essential for being a part of the group at all. Essentializing Jewish ethics as fundamentally committed to some particular idea often serves as a way to mark certain ideas as authoritative and exclude other ideas from the history of Jewish ethics.

The remainder of this chapter will focus on how modern Jews have sought to center certain perspectives and exclude other perspectives as they have constructed the category of "Jewish ethics." Notably, the term "ethics" in the broad sense is seldom found in extant premodern Jewish literature, especially in Hebrew, a language commonly used in Jewish literature. (While the Hebrew term *musar* is sometimes used to mean something like "ethics," it generally referred only to matters of character and virtue, rather than other issues involving conduct.) The term "Jewish ethics" emerged only in the nineteenth and twentieth centuries.

One group who began to use the term "Jewish ethics" and to set its boundaries by defining its essence were liberal non-Orthodox rabbis and scholars in the late nineteenth and early twentieth century, especially in the United States and Western and Central Europe. Much of their discourse sought to affirm that authentic Jewish ethics was in line with liberal ideas about monotheism and the equality of all human beings (Newman 1998b: 5).

To take one example, an influential early twentieth-century guide to teaching Jewish ethics champions the idea that "the foundation of Jewish ethics" is belief in God, conceived in certain ways: "all Jewish ethical teaching therefore must be based on the unquestionable, undebatable assumption that God, the Supreme and Perfect Being, is the Author of all Moral Law" (Richman and Lehman 1914: 11). In this framing of Jewish ethics, ideas shaped by Jewish tradition, experience, history, or identity that are not based on such ideas about God cannot qualify as part of Jewish ethics and should not be studied as part of the history of Jewish ethics.

The present volume, by contrast, while giving ample attention to such theological framings of Jewish ethics, will also include ideas that are not based on such assumptions about God or that reject such assumptions. When we look at the diversity of Jewish ethics, we can find constructions that are grounded in such ideas about God, but we can also find constructions that are not.

Similarly, an influential Jewish encyclopedia published in the early twentieth century sees the essence of Jewish ethics in its commitment to the equality of all human beings: "The fundamental idea of Jewish ethics is accordingly that of true humanity, without distinction of race or creed" (Kohler, Hirsch, and Broyde 1903: 250). For this source, ideas shaped by Jewish tradition, experience, history or identity that do not recognize the equal humanity of all human beings cannot qualify as part of Jewish ethics.

This volume, by contrast, will include ideas that do not recognize the equality of all human beings; those are also part of the history of Jewish ethics.

Orthodox Jews, as well, have championed claims about the essence of "Jewish ethics" or "Jewish morality," seeking to draw the boundaries of what can count as part of authoritative tradition. The scholar José Faur, for example, referring to the idea of God's revelation of Torah (instruction) to the people of Israel at Mount Sinai and in the land of Moab, writes that "Jewish morality is essentially nomistic or legalistic: the Law of Sinai-Moab, and only that Law, determines good and evil" (1968: 44). For Faur, other ethical ideas developed by Jews that reject the legal tradition in question cannot be considered part of "Jewish morality."

This volume, by contrast, while giving ample attention to the idea of a revealed law, will also include sources that show no interest in the legal traditions to which Faur refers. Moreover, it will not define Jewish ethics as necessarily legalistic at all. Constructions of Jewish ethics have often incorporated laws, but they have sometimes focused on character and virtue rather than law, and sometimes rejected legal models in favor of a focus on general principles and values.

In these and in many other ways, modern Jews have made claims about the essence of Jewish ethics. Premodern Jews also employed related strategies for defining the boundaries of authoritative tradition, often invoking a term that is far older than "Judaism" or "Jewish ethics": "Torah," a Hebrew-language term referring to God's revealed instruction, a term that will be further explored in Chapter Two of this volume. As we consider both premodern and modern constructions of Jewish ethics, Judaism, and Torah, it will be valuable to consider who is drawing the lines that define the boundaries of terms such as these and why they are defining boundaries in those ways.

ARE CERTAIN TEXTS ESSENTIAL FOR JEWISH ETHICS?

Who does have the authority to draw the boundaries that define Jewish ethics? Must constructions of Jewish ethics grant authority to particular texts, individuals, or groups? Should those of us seeking understanding of Jewish ethics defer to certain claims about what has authority in shaping Jewish tradition?

Over time, many different Jews have made many different claims about where such authority lies. This volume will not side with any of them, but rather will acknowledge the diversity of claims. Rather than granting authority to particular texts, individuals, or groups, it will raise questions about people's claims and how those claims affect their presentations of Jewish ethics.

Modern presentations of Jewish ethics often point to particular works of Jewish literature and insist that Jewish ethics must be grounded in those works. For example, one influential book on Jewish ethics by the scholar Moritz Lazarus, published in Germany in the late nineteenth century, begins by ranking the most essential texts for Jewish ethics as follows:

> The Bible is the text-book of Jewish Ethics. Next rank the Rabbinical
> writings, that is, the Talmud, the Talmudic Midrashim, and the later
> Midrashim, and they, in turn, are followed by religious and philosophic
> works, which elaborate and continue the ethical thought of earlier times.
>
> (Lazarus 1900 [1898]: 1)

This list (the terms of which I will explain below) resembles lists
found in a number of other modern books introducing Jewish
ethics, though the ranking is sometimes different, as when some
Jews view the Talmud, rather than the Bible, as the primary "text
of Jewish Ethics."

What Lazarus calls "the Bible" (a term that I will also use in this
book) may also be referred to by a variety of other names: "the
Jewish Bible" or "Hebrew Bible"; in Hebrew, "Mikra" (scripture)
or "Tanakh" (Torah, Prophets, and Writings); and, among Christians, as "the Old Testament." The Bible is commonly viewed as
one volume, but it is an anthology of ancient Israelite texts written
over the course of hundreds of years by diverse individuals in
diverse cultural contexts throughout the land of Israel (Canaan),
mostly in the first millennium before the common era. Biblical
authors had a wide variety of ethical perspectives, including a wide
variety of political agendas. Significantly, though, many Jews have
viewed the contents of the Bible—and especially the contents of its
first five books, "The Torah" (Genesis, Exodus, Leviticus, Numbers, and Deuteronomy)—as revealed by God, expressing one
divine perspective rather than diverse human perspectives.

What Lazarus calls "the Talmud" is commonly known as the
Babylonian Talmud, edited in Sasanian-ruled Babylonia during the
sixth and seventh centuries CE. A product of the Rabbinic
movement, the Talmud itself incorporates an earlier Rabbinic
work, the Mishnah, which stems from the land of Israel (Roman-
ruled Palestine) at the start of the third century CE. Focusing on
rules or laws, the Mishnah is a document filled with the often
conflicting statements of scholars with the title of "Rabbi" from
the first centuries of the common era, especially from the period
following the destruction of the central Jewish Temple in Jerusalem. Many of the Mishnah's traditions are grounded in ideas
found in the Bible, but those connections are sometimes very
tenuous, and there are statements in the Mishnah that have no

connection at all or that contradict Biblical ideas. The Babylonian Talmud also includes a commentary (gemara) on the Mishnah, often probing the contradictory opinions of various Rabbis. While the Talmud describes the first five books of the Bible as the "Written Torah," it describes Rabbinic teachings as "Oral Torah," indicating that both Torahs were revealed to the people of Israel through the prophet Moses at Mount Sinai and that "Oral Torah" constitutes the authoritative explanation of God's will.

The Rabbinic movement of the first millennium CE produced many other works, including an alternative Talmud (the Palestinian Talmud), redacted in the land of Israel in the fourth or fifth century; and, as Lazarus notes, many "Midrashim," both those produced in the time periods in which the Mishnah and Talmud were produced ("Talmudic Midrashim") as well as later Midrashim. Midrashim is the plural of "midrash," a genre of Rabbinic literature which directly interprets Biblical texts. Midrash is contained not only within the Talmuds (alongside other material) but also in many other Rabbinic collections. All such midrash appears to have been viewed within the Rabbinic movement as part of the Oral Torah; even as many collections of midrash are filled with contradictory interpretations from various rabbis, the Rabbinic movement appears to have viewed them as authoritative understandings of divine revelation.

For Jews devoted to the legacy of the Rabbinic movement, these various texts constitute Torah, and later works gain authority only if they build on their precedents. As Lazarus puts it, authority is granted to later "religious and philosophic works, which elaborate and continue the ethical thought of earlier times"—but not to later works that do not build on those earlier sources. For Lazarus, the Bible and the Babylonian Talmud have particular authority, and their "fundamental" views determine the shape of later Jewish ethics. Among later Jewish thinkers, he writes, "none denies, or assails, or essentially modifies the fundamental thoughts, the opinions, the principles which close investigation discovers in Bible and Talmud" (Lazarus 1900 [1898]: 7).

From a critical perspective, however, the Bible and Talmud both anthologize a wide diversity of thoughts, opinions, and principles and do not clearly indicate which of those are most fundamental. And, in any case, many later Jewish thinkers have in fact denied, assailed, and modified Biblical and Talmudic ideas, and many have doubted that one or the other (or both) should serve as a primary textbook for Jewish ethics. Skepticism about the authority of the Bible, for example, is quite ancient: even some Rabbinic sources, including within the Talmud, caution Jews not to rely on written Biblical texts (Wollenberg 2023). Some modern Jewish thinkers have had more serious concerns, viewing the Bible as an all-too-human anthology that offers limited ethical guidance. Some have viewed the Bible in clearly negative terms: for example, Rabbi Sherwin Wine (1995: 137), the founder of the Society for Humanistic Judaism, describes the Torah as "a reactionary document" that "promotes a lifestyle that is morally offensive to most contemporary Jews." One can, of course, read such critics of the Bible out of the history of Jewish ethics by insisting that Jewish ethics requires a commitment to the Bible's authority. This volume, however, will not endorse any such efforts to limit the boundaries of what counts as Jewish ethics, though it will encourage understanding why some Jews make such efforts.

The authority of the Babylonian Talmud and other Rabbinic texts has also been called into question by Jews. One organized group of Jews who rejected the Rabbis' claims to authority was the Karaite movement, which rose to prominence in ninth-century CE Babylonia, Palestine, and elsewhere. The Karaite movement was distinguished by its focus on the Bible as the sole source of authority for Jewish tradition and its rejection of the Mishnah, Talmud, and other Rabbinic literature that claimed to be part of an "Oral Torah." Jewish leaders in Ethiopia, likewise, did not accept the authority of the Rabbis. Looking to the modern era, we find leaders of the Reform movement such as the nineteenth-century German rabbi Samuel Holdheim, who labeled the ancient Rabbis as "perverters and distorters" and declared that "the Talmud is not authoritative for us" (Harris 1995: 169; Philipson 1905: 663). One can read such critics of the Rabbis out of the history of Jewish ethics by insisting that authentic Jewish ethics must accept Rabbinic authority. But again, rather than taking sides in these debates, we will seek to understand why Jews make claims such as these.

WHO IS GRANTED AUTHORITY TO SHAPE JEWISH ETHICS?

Debates about questions of authority played a role in the development of many of the modern Jewish movements that remain prominent to this day, such as Reform Judaism, Conservative Judaism, and Orthodox Judaism. For example, Holdheim shaped Reform Judaism through his rejection of the teachings of the ancient Rabbis, whose ideas were out of step with what he saw as the standards of rationality. Holdheim insisted, however, that present-day rabbis like himself who were committed to reason did possess the authority to shape and reform Jewish tradition.

Holdheim's emphasis on the authority of certain rabbis to articulate new standards for the Jewish people was opposed by more conservative scholars such as Zacharias Frankel, often viewed as the forerunner of Conservative Judaism in nineteenth-century Germany. While Frankel believed that Jewish tradition changed over time, he cautioned against the Reform movement's reliance on rabbinic authority and insisted that changes to tradition must be guided by the consensus of "the people"—the Jews as a whole, or at least the Jews whom he thought understood "the spirit" of their people.

These approaches to authority were opposed by the nineteenth-century rabbi often regarded as the intellectual founder of modern Orthodox Judaism, Samson Raphael Hirsch. Hirsch insisted, contrary to Holdheim and Frankel, that true Judaism did not change, as it was "the gift and the word of God, an untouchable sanctuary which must not be subjected to human judgment nor subordinated to human considerations" (Hirsch 1956: 237). Hirsch argued that authoritative rabbis quoted in the Talmud were presenting the Torah revealed to Moses at Sinai, which could not be altered by reforming rabbis, popular consensus, or anything else.

These nineteenth-century European ideas about authority have continued to guide many presentations of Jewish ethics in the present day. Following the lead of figures such as Holdheim, some presentations of Jewish ethics insist on foregrounding Jewish ethical concepts that fit with contemporary standards of reason as understood by particular rabbis. Following the lead of figures like Frankel, some presentations of Jewish ethics foreground a vision of ethics that, they claim, captures the consensus of the Jewish people as a whole—or, at least, those with proper understanding. Following the lead of figures like Hirsch, some presentations of Jewish ethics insist that those who do not uphold certain Talmudic traditions are not part of the history of Jewish ethics at all.

While these frameworks for thinking about authority have been influential, other ideas about authority have also shaped constructions of Jewish ethics. For example, some presentations of Jewish ethics (especially within the Reform movement) stress the authority of the individual to decide ethical questions for themselves, rather than deferring to authority figures or communal consensus. Others have deferred to the authority of the State, stressing how the limits of Jewish ethical discourse are determined by State authority. The importance of accepting the laws of German states was, in fact, recognized by nineteenth-century German thinkers including Holdheim, Frankel, and Hirsch. Since 1948, it has also been common to find articulations of Jewish ethics that defer to the authority of the State of Israel, including by equating Jewishness with Zionism and labeling Jewish critics of Israel as "un-Jews" who have no right to claim their Jewish identities (Butler 2012; Magid 2021b, 2023b).

WHOSE IDEAS HAVE BEEN EXCLUDED FROM JEWISH ETHICS?

Claims about who has the authority to shape Jewish ethics also commonly depend on hierarchies related to gender, sexuality, disability, race, ethnicity, and class. Scholar Judith Plaskow has pointed to ways in which such hierarchies are linked, and she has critiqued "the essentialization of authority: the identification of authority with certain groups that are invested with power by virtue of their supposed nature," as when elite men are granted authority in Jewish communities because they are elite men (Plaskow 2005: 139). Plaskow's work seeks to dismantle oppressive structures that perpetuate sexism, racism, classism, and other forms of injustice, and calls for a Jewish community in which those who have been marginalized "find our voices and begin to speak" (Plaskow 1990: xvii).

A wide range of other scholars have critiqued structures that have silenced particular groups of Jews. Dena Davis (1991), Rachel Adler

(1998), Donna Berman (2001), and Esther Fuchs (2018) have joined Plaskow in demonstrating how Jewish ethics has been constructed on the basis of men's authority, especially through a reliance on Biblical and Rabbinic sources that filter all mention of women through the perspectives of men. Scholars including Rebecca Alpert (1997), Noach Dzmura (2010), and Noam Sienna (2019) have shown how openly LGBTQ Jews have been excluded from constructions of Jewish tradition. Scholars including Judith Abrams (1998) and Julia Watts Belser (2016) have pointed to ways in which Jews with disabilities have been disenfranchised in various contexts.

Scholars including Walter Isaac (2006), Marla Brettschneider (2010), Lewis Gordon (2018), and Amanda Mbuvi (2020) have pointed to ways in which Jewish traditions in the United States have been constructed by white Jews, excluding the perspectives of Black and other racialized Jews. Scholars including Ella Shohat (1988), Pnina Motzafi-Haller (2001), Atalia Omer (2013), and Devin Naar (2019) have shown how Sephardic Jews (who generally trace their ancestry or customs to Spain) and Mizrahi Jews or Arab Jews (who generally trace their ancestry to the Middle East or North Africa) have been excluded from Jewish public discourse, which has often been dominated by Ashkenazi Jews (who generally trace their ancestry to Central or Eastern Europe). Scholar Santiago Slabodsky (2014) points to the exclusion of Jews from the Global South. Scholars including Marla Brettschneider (1999), Dawn Robinson Rose (1999), and Judith Kay (2020) have pointed to the exclusion of poor and working-class Jews.

Despite these histories of exclusion, historically marginalized groups of Jews have made major contributions to Jewish ethical discourse. Reflecting on the prominence of modern Jewish approaches grounded in the experiences of women, scholar Susannah Heschel (2002: xvii) has argued that "Jewish feminists have brought about the most significant transformations of Judaism since the destruction of the Jerusalem Temple in the first century C.E." Scholar Max Strassfeld (2022b) has pointed out that "BIPOC, trans, intersex, feminist, and queer rabbis, activists, and artists have been reinterpreting and reinventing the tradition by reading from the perspectives of those who were deliberately excluded from it." Belser (2016: 113) has shown that "deaf Jews and Jews with disabilities have also claimed their own place as interpreters of the

tradition, as architects of new Jewish identities that reflect the
embodied experience and particular sensibilities of Jewish disability
culture." Jews of color and Sephardi and Mizrahi Jews have been
prominent advocates for justice and have played major roles in
shaping Jewish ethical discourse (Kaye/Kantrowitz 2007; Omer
2013, 2019; Isack 2023). For example, scholar Atalia Omer (2019:
93) has shown that "Mizrahi, Sephardi, and Jews of color participate centrally in rewriting Jewishness, its normative boundaries,
and thus also the meanings of self-love and liberation" while
engaging in Palestinian solidarity activism. Insights from Jews from
historically marginalized groups are entering "canons" of Jewish
ethics, especially through efforts to "recanonize"—"explicitly
naming sources as canonical and challenging boundaries of what
we consider normative" (Epstein-Levi 2023: 475).

Some may also believe that authoritative sources must be written
texts; but scholars of Jewish ethics have sought to expand canons
by including non-written sources alongside written sources
(Epstein-Levi 2023: 477). As scholar Michal Raucher (2016: 645)
has pointed out, "Making Jewish texts the sine qua non of Jewish
ethics means anyone who does not have access to those texts is not
part of the conversation," privileging only those with certain
resources, access, and educational backgrounds. Raucher (2016:
638) has argued that "ethics built on the power of elites is critically
flawed" and has called for Jewish ethics to center ethnographic work
that documents the range of ethical views among marginalized
populations.

While this volume often centers texts, it also seeks to point to
non-textual sources of Jewish ethics. Jews who have not written
texts also have ethical ideas that are important to consider when
we are seeking to understand the breadth of Jewish ethics.
Moreover, in contrast to presentations of Jewish ethics that
center only certain models of authority (e.g. only texts by elite
male rabbis) and only insights from Jews with certain characteristics (e.g. white, straight, cisgender, able-bodied Ashkenazi
men from the Global North), this volume seeks to include a
wider range of sources, as we are seeking to understand how
Jewish ethics has been constructed in different ways by different
people in different contexts.

IS JEWISH ETHICS A FORM OF RELIGIOUS ETHICS?

One term that has played a key role in limiting what counts as part of Jewish ethics is the word "religion."

Some Jews, and some scholars seeking to understand Jewish ethics, define Judaism as a religion and Jewish ethics as a form of "religious ethics." Even though only a small percentage of Jews over the course of history have defined Jewishness as primarily a matter of "religion" (not least because the concept is a modern invention), modern Jews who do define their identity with this term have often felt very strongly that religion is central to authentic Jewish ethics. And some scholars have been convinced that even if Jews themselves don't think of their ethical traditions as a matter of religion, authentic Jewish ethics should be defined in religious terms, and approaches to ethics that are not "religious" are not part of authentic Jewish tradition.

The very concept of "religion" was developed by modern European political thinkers (especially in the eighteenth and nineteenth centuries) who sought to distinguish the public sphere of "politics" from other traditions that they saw as best confined to the private sphere and which were defined as "religion." Religion was understood as essentially about private faith commitments that should be kept separate from politics (Martin 2017: 6–7). This concept was favored by those who sought to keep certain kinds of traditions out of the public sphere by labeling them as religious and defining religion as a private matter; the idea of defining Jewishness in this way became attractive to a number of Jews seeking political emancipation and integration as individuals into modern states. While seeing Jews as part of a nation did not seem compatible with integration into other nation-states, seeing Jewishness as a matter of private religion or faith provided a clear path for integration, allowing Jews to adopt other national identities and keep their Jewish identities private. Arguments like these helped to give rise to the invention of the idea that "Judaism is a religion" in the nineteenth century.

Those who conceive of Jewish tradition in these terms may think of Jewish ethics as above all a matter of private, personal faith or spirituality—and that perspectives that are overtly political, or insufficiently linked to matters of "faith" or "spirituality," are not part of, or at least not essential to, Jewish ethics. The early modern philosopher Moses Mendelssohn, who invented the idea that Judaism is a religion and is often regarded as the founder of modern Jewish thought, played an especially important role in defining the domain of Jewish moral teachings as a matter of religion separate from the realm of politics and coercive power. As the scholar Leora Batnitzky (2011: 19) has put it, for Mendelssohn "the state concerns power and coercion, while religion, properly understood, does not."

Others have defined the term "religion" in other ways—for example, to refer to a system that focuses on belief in God. Jews who see belief in God as central to their own Jewish identities have been especially motivated to argue that Jewish tradition constitutes a religion in this sense. We saw a teaching, along these lines above, in a textbook that saw belief in God as "the foundation of Jewish ethics"; as the textbook authors Julia Richman and Eugene Lehman (1914: 10) specified, this shows the indispensability of "religion" for Jewish ethics. Labeling Jewish ethics as a matter of religion thus supports claims that Jewish ethics requires belief in God. Constructions of Jewish ethics that reject belief in God are then not part of, or at least not essential to, Jewish ethics.

Others who define Jewish tradition in terms of religion have associated the term "religion" with a range of other ideas that can restrict what counts as "Jewish ethics." For example, some define religion as based on powerful experiences of "the sacred" that are noncognitive and that are unlike "ordinary" experiences; in the words of the scholar Mircea Eliade, religion is linked with "a primary religious experience that precedes all reflection on the world" (Newman 2005: 14). From this perspective, traditions that are not grounded in such an experience of the sacred cannot be described as "religious." If Jewish tradition is described as a religion under this definition, Jewish approaches to ethics that seem "ordinary," or that require a good deal of critical reflection, may be placed outside the boundaries of Jewish ethics.

Others associate "religion" not with unusual experiences but with ideas of social order and "civilization," ideas that have played an especially important role in the construction of religion in the United States, including among U.S. Jews. For example, the twentieth-century Jewish intellectual Will Herberg, amidst what he saw as a "crisis of Western civilization," emphasized the "social utility of religion for Western culture, especially in fighting Communism," understanding "religion" as forms of Judaism and Christianity compatible with U.S. politics (Herberg 1955: 73–4; Levitt 2012). Herberg pointed to U.S. President Dwight Eisenhower's recognition of "the indispensability of religion as the foundation of society," since Judaism and Christianity affirmed the "'spiritual ideals' and 'moral values' of the American Way of Life" (Herberg 1955: 98). Drawing on such ideas, Herberg edited a journal that promulgated the idea that Judaism and "Jewish ethics" should be viewed as "religious" rather than secular (Kavka 2021). From this perspective, Jewish approaches to ethics that are out of line with the "American Way of Life," including secular or communist approaches, would not be included within the boundaries of "Jewish ethics."

Religion, in all these cases, is a category constructed by particular people in particular contexts for particular purposes. Categorizing Jewish ethics as a form of religious ethics may serve many such purposes. When we encounter people categorizing Jewish ethics in this way, we may consider why and how they do so, seeking understanding of the approaches and agendas that may be at work.

IS JEWISH ETHICS POLITICAL, NATIONAL, OR CULTURAL?

We should bear in mind that premodern Jews never used the concept of religion to describe their traditions or ethical ideas. Many modern Jews, as well, have avoided the language of religion in such contexts, including when they have *embraced* ideas about God. God-centered Jewish approaches to ethics, just like other Jewish approaches, have sometimes been described by modern Jews not with the language of religion but with terms such as "political," "national," or "cultural." Although some modern people have sought to confine God to the realm of "religion" and keep God out of the realms of politics and culture, others have insisted that God fully belongs in such realms. After all, as Rabbi Tzevi Yehudah Kook put it in explaining the necessity for Jews to conquer the historic land of Israel, "The Master of the Universe has His own political agenda, according to which politics here

below are conducted" (Ravitzky 1996: 131). Others have stressed
the authority over all matters of politics and culture of the rabbis
who know God's will, bearing in mind that on all matters "God in
His lovingkindness provided us with guides, our sages, the scholars
of Torah," as Rabbi Eliyahu Eliezer Dessler wrote (Walzer et al.
2000: 300; Brown 2014: 281). In insisting that God is essential to
politics and culture, and not confined to the realm of mere "religion," thinkers such as these often point to texts such as the Bible
or Talmud, which develop structures for governing the life of a
community and clearly include what moderns might call "politics"
or "culture." It would make no sense, from their perspective, to
define Jewish ethics as merely "religious."

Jewish thinkers who *reject* God-centered models of Jewishness—
often described as "secular" thinkers—have also rejected the idea that
Judaism is a matter of religion, and often prefer to use the language of
nationality, politics, or culture. One movement in which such
rhetoric has flourished has been the secular Zionist movement, a
nationalist movement that emerged in the late nineteenth century
seeking to establish a homeland for the Jewish people in the historic
land of Israel. The early Zionist thinker Ahad Ha-Am, for example,
argued that all Jews were bound to follow what he described as the
authentic Jewish "national morality," which obligated them to center
Jewish "national interests" and support his Zionist program (Shapira
1990: 64). David Ben-Gurion, Israel's first prime minister, built on
this model with his claim that Judaism was "a national culture" that
served as the "ethical basis" of Zionism, especially grounded in the
Bible—which Ben-Gurion did not view as a "religious" text but as a
part of "national culture" and as a source of political guidance for a
sovereign Jewish State (Kedar 2013; Havrelock 2020).

Secular non-Zionist or anti-Zionist thinkers have also rejected the
language of religion to describe Jewish approaches to ethics. For
example, American feminist poet and writer Irena Klepfisz (1990:
196–7) grounded her work in a "secular tradition of *yidishkayt*
[Jewishness]" that is committed to social justice and secular Yiddish
culture. The philosopher Judith Butler builds on political theorist
Hannah Arendt's understanding of Jewishness as "a cultural, historical, and political category that characterized the historical
situation of populations that may or may not engage in religious
practices or explicitly identify with Judaism" (Butler 2012: 14).

Other anti-Zionists who are less easily labeled as "secular" have similarly rejected the category of religion in describing Jewishness. The historian Daniel Boyarin (2023), for example, argues that Jews should be understood not as members of a religion but as a nation—a nation that does not require, and should not seek, political sovereignty over a particular piece of land.

Concepts of nationality, politics, and culture, in all these cases, are categories constructed by particular people in particular contexts for particular purposes. Categorizing Jewish ethics in terms of nationality, politics, and culture may serve a variety of purposes. When we encounter people categorizing Jewish ethics in these ways, we may consider why and how they do so, seeking understanding of the approaches and agendas that may be at work.

Whether Jewish ethics is best defined as a matter of religion, nationality, politics, culture, or something else has been the subject of considerable debate among Jews. This book does not seek to take sides on such debates, but we will seek to understand how arguments on behalf of these different ideas have been made.

THE DIVERSITY OF JEWISH ETHICS

As modern Jews have created the category of Jewish ethics, they have drawn its boundaries in various ways and sought to exclude various ideas. As we have seen, some thinkers have drawn boundaries by making claims about "Judaism" or about the essence of Jewish ethics, seeking to exclude voices that don't share the beliefs or approaches that they view as foundational to Jewish tradition. Others point to works of literature such as the Bible or Talmud that they think are essential to Jewish tradition, excluding Jewish perspectives that do not engage with this literature. Others insist that certain rabbis, or certain communities, have the authority to define Jewish tradition, seeking to exclude those who do not defer to those rabbis or communities. Others defer to State authority and may seek to exclude critics of the State of Israel or other states. Others embrace hierarchies of gender, sexuality, disability, race, ethnicity, and class, excluding those who are not male, straight, able-bodied, white, Ashkenazi, or upper-class. Others believe that authority must come from written texts, excluding Jewish perspectives that are not found in writing. Others believe that Jewish

ethics must be seen as a matter of religion, or as a matter of
nationality, politics, or culture, excluding sources that don't fit
within their preferred categories.

Limiting what counts as Jewish ethics in these ways reflects a
wide range of agendas. We can see some of those agendas as we
critically consider whose voices are included and whose voices are
excluded from various constructions of Jewish ethics. This book,
however, will seek to define Jewish ethics broadly and consider a
wide range of ideas developed by Jews, shaped by Jewish tradition,
experience, history, or identity, about how humans should live,
especially in relation to others. Rather than seeking to provide
ethical guidance by quoting sources that I think are morally edify-
ing and that support my own ethical convictions, I am seeking to
introduce readers to the diversity of Jewish ethics.

As noted above, however, while this book showcases the diversity
of thought among modern Jews, it focuses on a smaller number of
premodern sources that have been particularly influential among
modern Jews. Chapter Two focuses on the classical rabbinic literature of the first millennium CE, including the Mishnah, Talmud,
and collections of midrash, and Chapter Three focuses on the *Zohar*
and the writings of Moses Maimonides. These two chapters give
particular attention to ethical approaches that relate to ideas about
God's creation, revelation, and redemption. Chapters Four and
Five return to the modern era and explore a broader diversity of
Jewish sources, with Chapter Four focusing on diverse modern
sources that are not framed in theological (God-centered) terms
and Chapter Five focusing on diverse modern sources that center
God and modern ideas of creation, revelation, and redemption.
The focus on creation, revelation, and redemption in Chapters
Two, Three, and Five allows readers to easily contrast the views
that appear in those chapters.

I also facilitate drawing contrasts between chapters by focusing
on a select set of ethical issues addressed in each of the following
four chapters. These include issues regarding authority, Jews and
Gentiles, gender, race, disability, sexuality, abortion, animals and
the environment, violence and war, settling the land of Israel,
political governance, the rights of refugees, strangers, and others in
need, and the development of compassion and other virtues.
Readers will see these issues surface in each of the chapters that

follow and will readily see how the same issues have been addressed differently by diverse Jews. Even considering this limited number of issues will make it clear that Jewish ethics has been constructed in different ways by different people in different contexts and for different reasons.

FURTHER READING

On the term "Jew," see Cynthia M. Baker, *Jew* (2017). On the term "Judaism," see Daniel Boyarin, *Judaism: The Genealogy of a Modern Notion* (2019).

On debates regarding authority, see Jay Michael Harris, *How Do We Know This?: Midrash and the Fragmentation of Modern Judaism* (1995); and Leora Batnitzky and Yonatan Y. Brafman, eds., *Jewish Legal Theories: Writings on State, Religion, and Morality* (2018).

On the equation of Jewishness and Zionism, see Judith Butler, *Parting Ways: Jewishness and the Critique of Zionism* (2012).

On the exclusion of women from Jewish ethical discourse, see Judith Plaskow, *Standing Again at Sinai: Judaism from a Feminist Perspective* (1990); and Rachel Adler, *Engendering Judaism: An Inclusive Theology and Ethics* (1998).

On the exclusion of LGBTQ perspectives, see Rebecca T. Alpert, *Like Bread on the Seder Plate: Jewish Lesbians and the Transformation of Tradition* (1997); and Noach Dzmura, ed., *Balancing on the Mechitza: Transgender in Jewish Community* (2010).

On the exclusion of Jews with disabilities, see Julia Watts Belser, "Judaism and Disability" (2016).

On the exclusion of Black Jews, see Walter Isaac, "Locating Afro-American Judaism: A Critique of White Normativity" (2006); and Lewis R. Gordon, "Afro-Jewish Ethics?" (2018).

On the exclusion of Mizrahi Jews, see Ella Shohat, *On the Arab-Jew, Palestine, and Other Displacements: Selected Writings* (2017).

On the value of centering ethnographic accounts rather than texts, see Michal S. Raucher, "Ethnography and Jewish Ethics" (2016).

For an introduction to Jewish ethics framed in terms of religion, see Louis E. Newman, *An Introduction to Jewish Ethics* (2005). For an introduction framed in theological terms without employing the concept of religion, see Alan Mittleman, *A Short History of Jewish Ethics: Conduct and Character in the Context of Covenant* (2012).

On debates regarding whether to understand Jewish traditions in terms of religion, nationality, politics, or culture, see Leora Batnitzky, *How Judaism Became a Religion: An Introduction to Modern Jewish Thought* (2011); and Daniel Boyarin, *The No-State Solution: A Jewish Manifesto* (2023).

CLASSICAL RABBINIC ETHICS

Between the third and tenth centuries CE, a group of men who described themselves as "the Rabbis" or "the Sages" produced a vast literature that is filled with ethically significant stories, rules, and discussions of values and virtues. Their movement, the Rabbinic movement, was small and diffuse and had limited influence for many centuries after it first emerged in Roman Palestine. Throughout the first millennium, relatively few Jews looked to the Rabbis or their literature when considering their ethical obligations. But the literature produced by the Rabbis—often called "classical Rabbinic literature," "ancient Rabbinic literature," or, simply, "Rabbinic literature," the term I will use in this chapter (using a capital R to reference these "classical" Rabbis, as opposed to later Jews holding the title of "rabbi")—eventually gained significant influence, such that many contemporary Jews regard it as essential to Jewish tradition, including Jewish ethics. Even more than Biblical literature (the other body of literature commonly viewed as authoritative in presentations of Jewish ethics), Rabbinic literature is regularly depicted by contemporary Jewish thinkers as authoritative and foundational (Filler 2015: 154). This volume does not claim that Rabbinic literature should be viewed in these terms, but I am giving special attention to this literature given its centrality to many contemporary constructions of Jewish ethics.

The Rabbinic literature discussed in this chapter includes the following:

1   The Mishnah, redacted in Roman-ruled Palestine (the land of Israel) in the third century CE, largely consisting of rule/law-based statements of Rabbis from the first centuries of

DOI: 10.4324/9781003271338-2

the common era. As noted in Chapter One, these teachings often relate to themes in the Bible, but the connections are often very tenuous, and some statements in the Mishnah have no connection to or contradict Biblical ideas.

2   A variety of collections using the genre of "midrash," the direct interpretation of Biblical passages, compiled between the third and tenth centuries CE. The Rabbis quoted in these collections commonly interpret Biblical passages in light of their assumption that Biblical texts contain messages from God that, while often cryptic, are relevant to the present day (Kugel 1997: 17–23). Collections cited in this chapter include *Mekhilta de-Rabbi Yishmael* (on the Book of Exodus), *Sifra* (on Leviticus), and *Sifrei Devarim* (on Deuteronomy), which all seem to have been redacted in third-century Palestine; later Palestinian midrashim including *Genesis Rabbah* and *Leviticus Rabbah* (likely both fifth century), *Pesikta Rabbati* (fifth or sixth century) and *Ecclesiastes Rabbah* (from between the sixth and eighth centuries); and two works likely redacted by the ninth or tenth century (in uncertain locations), the *Alphabet of Ben-Sira* and *Exodus Rabbah*.

3   Two collections known as "Talmuds": the Palestinian Talmud ("PT" in citations below; also known as the Jerusalem Talmud), redacted in Roman/Byzantine-ruled Palestine in the fourth or fifth century CE; and the Babylonian Talmud ("BT" in citations below), redacted in Sasanian-ruled Babylonia during the sixth and seventh centuries CE. These texts are organized as commentaries (gemara) on the Mishnah, and include a good deal of midrash alongside rules, stories, and other teachings. Because the Babylonian Talmud has had particular influence on later Jewish constructions of ethics, I give it particular attention in this chapter.

Although this classical literature is often treated as a cohesive whole, it spans many centuries and a range of social contexts, and each of the particular works mentioned here contains a wide range of perspectives, often conflicting with each other. While the classical Rabbinic movement was united in certain ways, Rabbinic literature also contains a good deal of disagreement. This chapter introduces some of the central ethical ideas found across Rabbinic literature as well as some of its diversity, by focusing on ideas connected with three different theological claims that are central to that literature: that God created the world; that God revealed instruction (in Hebrew, Torah) to the people of Israel (a term I am using interchangeably with "Israelites" and "Jews"); and that God has redeemed, and will again redeem, the people of Israel from slavery and oppression.

Scholar Louis Newman has argued that classical Jewish approaches to ethics are closely related to ideas about creation, revelation, and redemption that permeate classical Jewish thought. "Questions of moral value," Newman writes, "are explored in the context of the grand divine-human drama that moves from creation through revelation to redemption" (2005: 40). In this chapter, I will build on Newman's insight by highlighting how the Rabbis came to diverse conclusions about the ethical implications of these central narratives. Looking at common Rabbinic motifs regarding creation, revelation, and redemption can help us to see the diverse ways that the Rabbis developed ethical ideas in relation to these concepts. Ideas about the revealed Torah are especially central to the construction of ethics in Rabbinic literature, and so I begin by giving sustained attention to Rabbinic concepts of Torah and how it was revealed to the people of Israel. In the latter part of the chapter, I consider ideas related to concepts of creation and redemption. I illustrate my discussions of revelation, creation, and redemption primarily with examples that show tensions within Rabbinic literature or that stand in tension with the Jewish perspectives discussed in later chapters.

I THE REVELATION OF TORAH

THE REVELATION OF WRITTEN AND ORAL TORAH

The idea that God revealed Torah to the collective people of Israel pervades Rabbinic literature. This idea is often grounded in the Bible's narratives about revelation to the people of Israel, which begin in the Biblical Book of Exodus. According to that book, just after liberating the Israelites from slavery in Egypt, God revealed instructions to the prophet Moses and the people at Mount Sinai. The Biblical narratives that follow include the Israelites' illicit worship of a golden calf and God's eventual forgiveness; the continued revelations of commandments, recounted in the books of Exodus, Leviticus, and Numbers; and then, in the Book of Deuteronomy, Moses' extended speeches in the land of Moab, transmitting and recounting God's instruction. While these Biblical sources were written by diverse authors, Rabbinic literature generally treats them as a harmonious text stemming from God and views the commandments they record as incumbent upon subsequent generations of the people of Israel.

At the same time, some Rabbinic traditions complicate or challenge the commandments and narratives found in the Bible, including the narratives about divine revelation itself.

One idea not found in the Bible that is central to Rabbinic literature is the idea that multiple "Torahs" were revealed to Moses at Sinai. God is often described as having revealed two Torahs: the Written Torah—the Biblical books of Genesis, Exodus, Leviticus, Numbers, and Deuteronomy—and also an Oral Torah, which was not written down but was orally transmitted from teachers to students through the generations.

The idea that God revealed an Oral Torah alongside the Written Torah might suggest that God's revelation could not be fully captured in fixed words. Indeed, some ancient Rabbis were adamant that the Oral Torah must be passed down from teacher to student through the generations without ever being written down: "teachings that are oral are not permitted to be recited from writing," as one put it. Another warned that "those who write down the [oral] laws are like those who burn the Torah." But others permitted writing down the Oral Torah, which they saw as justified "so that the Torah is not forgotten by the people of Israel" (BT *Temurah* 14b). Rabbinic texts beginning with the Mishnah seem intended to represent "Oral Torah" in written form.

The tractate of the Mishnah known as *Avot* ("Fathers"; also called *Pirkei Avot*, "Chapters of the Fathers" or "Ethics of the Fathers") begins by tracing the Oral Torah back to Sinai, imagining Torah as passed down through the generations in these terms:

> Moses received Torah at Sinai and transmitted it to Joshua, Joshua to the elders, and the elders to the prophets, and the prophets to the Men of the Great Assembly ... Simeon the Righteous was one of the last of the

> men of the Great Assembly ... Antigonus, a man of Sokho, received [Torah] from Simeon the Righteous ... Yosi ben Yoezer, a man of Tzeredah, and Yosi ben Yohanan, a man of Jerusalem, received [it] from them ...
>
> (Mishnah *Avot* 1:1–4)

This list continues with the names and key teachings of prominent early Rabbis of the first centuries of the common era. The teachings of these Rabbis, the text implies, can be traced back to Sinai; the Rabbis possess authority because they received the Oral Torah through a chain of transmission that goes back to God's revelation to Moses. Unlike the Bible, however, the Mishnah does not attribute its teachings to God, or to Moses; rather, it attributes each teaching to particular Rabbis.

A REVELATION OF DISAGREEMENTS?

Sometimes these teachings are at odds with each other, as with two different teachings in the first chapter of *Avot* about foundational values "upon which the world stands." Simeon the Righteous, the high priest at the central Jewish Temple in Jerusalem before its destruction in 70 CE, teaches that "the world stands upon three things: on the Torah, on the service, and on the bestowal of lovingkindness" (Mishnah *Avot* 1:2). "The service," here, seems to refer explicitly to animal sacrifice at the Jerusalem Temple. At the end of this chapter of *Avot*, the second-century sage Rabban Simeon ben Gamaliel teaches, by contrast, that "the world stands upon three things: on justice, on truth, and on peace" (Mishnah *Avot* 1:18). While those who assume that teachings in *Avot* (and in Torah more generally) are in harmony with each other can find many ways to reconcile these statements, many readers have seen a disagreement. Rabban Simeon ben Gamaliel, or at least the editor of this chapter of *Avot*, may be asserting that Temple sacrifices can no longer be a pillar upon which the world rests; a new list of key values must be formulated (Schwartz 2014: 58–9).

Still, disagreements in *Avot*, focusing mostly on broad ethical principles and virtues, can often be reconciled. Less easily resolved are the disagreements found within other tractates of the Mishnah that focus on halakhah—rules or laws for specific situations. In matters of halakhah, the disputes between Rabbis often lead to very different outcomes. For example, we might consider the controversial texts regulating how Jews must keep their distance from Gentiles (non-Jews), whom the Rabbis commonly assume are inclined to harm Jews (Wasserman 2017: 75). For example, may a Jew accept the services of a non-Jewish barber, given the dangerously sharp implements the barber will use? The Mishnah (*Avodah Zarah* 2:2) records a disagreement: "We should not have our hair cut by them in any place—these are the words of Rabbi Meir. But the Sages say: it is permitted in a public place, but not when they [the barber and client] are alone." In the view of Rabbi Meir, the (Oral) Torah prohibits ever accepting the services of a non-Jewish barber, but the majority of Rabbis ("the Sages") think the Torah only prohibits the riskier behavior of a private haircut. This is just one example of how the Rabbis seem unified in some ways—no Rabbi questions the assumption about the dangers that Gentiles pose or the prohibition of more intimate encounters with Gentiles—while divided in others.

Another disagreement about acceptable risks when alone with others is noted when the Mishnah deals with situations that may lead to illicit sex. May two unmarried Jewish men sleep together, perhaps naked, under the same sheet? The Rabbis see sex between men as prohibited, and one of them quoted in the Mishnah seems to think that unmarried men may be tempted by sex with other men. The Mishnah quotes Rabbi Judah as thus ruling that "two unmarried men may not sleep together under the same cover. But the Sages permit it" (Mishnah *Kiddushin* 4:14). For Rabbi Judah, the (Oral) Torah prohibits sleeping under the same cover, but the majority of Rabbis seem to think that Jewish men sharing a bed would not be tempted by intercourse with other men (Satlow 1995: 208–9; Peskowitz 1997: 60). Again, the Rabbis are unified in key respects—no Rabbi questions the prohibition on sex between men—while divided in other ways. The Mishnah, like Rabbinic literature generally, records many disagreements, though these disagreements only go so far.

But if the Mishnah is a record of God's authoritative revelation, why does it include any disagreements about what God revealed? The Mishnah most directly addresses this question in another of its tractates, *Eduyot*, a tractate perhaps added to the Mishnah at a late stage to address the halakhic disagreements the Mishnah presents. Strikingly, that source itself presents a disagreement:

> Why do they record the words of an individual [dissenting Rabbi] among the majority, inasmuch as the halakhah must follow the words of the majority? So that if a [Rabbinic] court should approve the opinion of the individual [dissenting Rabbi] it may rely upon him … [But] Rabbi Judah said: "… So that if a person shall say, 'Thus have I received [the tradition],' one may say to him, 'You heard it [only] as the [refuted] opinion of that particular individual.'"

> (Mishnah *Eduyot* 1:5–6)

According to the first view stated—an anonymous view, seemingly representing the majority of Rabbis—future Rabbinic courts may in fact decide to follow the dissenting opinion of an individual Rabbi. The dissent must be preserved so that it can be revived, at least under certain circumstances (as the rest of the teaching, not printed here, discusses). From this point of view, God's revelation may include uncertainty and multiple approaches, in line with a dictum that appears throughout Rabbinic literature (e.g. BT *Eruvin* 13b) as a response to disputes: "these and those are the words of the living God" (Simon-Shoshan 2021).

Rabbi Judah disagrees, suggesting that dissenting opinions are preserved only so that it can be made clear that the dissent lost out and should not be revived. Strikingly, the position that is less charitable towards dissenting opinions is preserved as an individual dissent (Halbertal 1997: 52). This view does, however, seem to align with a perspective found elsewhere throughout Rabbinic literature that idealizes an earlier time when "disagreement did not proliferate among the people of Israel" (e.g. BT *Sanhedrin* 88b).

The principle that "the halakhah must follow the words of the majority" of Rabbis, in any case, raises other tensions and questions. What rules govern the formation of the group of Rabbis out of which a majority can emerge? What authorizes such a majority to determine the content of God's Torah? Are there limits on their authority? The latter questions are addressed by a Talmudic story about a halakhic dispute (regarding the purity of an oven, though that detail is not important here) between Rabbi Eliezer and the majority of Rabbis who opposed him:

> On that day, Rabbi Eliezer offered every imaginable argument, but [the Rabbis] did not accept them from him. [Finally] he said to them, "If the

halakhah agrees with me, let this carob tree prove it!" The carob tree was uprooted from its place one hundred cubits, and some say four hundred cubits. They said to him, "No proof can be brought from a carob tree." He then said to them, "If the halakhah agrees with me, let this stream prove it." The stream flowed backward. They said to him, "No proof can be brought from a stream." He then said to them, "If the halakhah agrees with me, let the walls of the house of study prove it!" The walls inclined to fall ... He then said to them, "If the halakhah agrees with me, let Heaven prove it!" A Divine Voice came forth [from Heaven] and said, "What do you have against Rabbi Eliezer? The halakhah always agrees with him."

But Rabbi Joshua stood up and exclaimed: "It is not in heaven" (Bible, Deuteronomy 30:12).

What does it mean, "It is not in heaven"? Rabbi Jeremiah said, "We pay no attention to a Divine Voice, since the Torah was already given at Mount Sinai, and at Mount Sinai you already wrote in the Torah: 'Incline after the majority'" (Bible, Exodus 23:2).

Rabbi Nathan encountered [the prophet] Elijah and asked him, "What did the Holy Blessed One do at that time?" [Elijah] said: [God] laughed, saying, "My children have defeated me, My children have defeated me."

(BT *Bava Metzia* 59b)

In this story, not only a series of miracles but even God's direct verbal revelation from Heaven confirm that Rabbi Eliezer is correct in his position. But Rabbi Joshua and the other Rabbis assert that their ruling—the ruling of the majority—stands, and that even God's revelation will not override their decision. Notably, the Rabbis support their claim to authority by pointing to the Bible—the Written Torah, which God is said to have revealed at Mount Sinai. The Written Torah teaches, in this interpretation, that God's Torah "is not in heaven" (Deuteronomy 30:12): God has authorized the Rabbis to interpret it, relying on their own reasoning rather than giving heed to other divine messages; and while this is not what Deuteronomy 30:12 means in its original Biblical context, that is how the Rabbis interpret that Biblical verse. Moreover, the Written Torah teaches, in this interpretation, that the law follows "the majority" (Exodus 23:2)—God has authorized a certain procedure and agreed that God's own voice need not be followed; and while this is quite contrary to what Exodus 23:2 means in its original Biblical context, that is how the Rabbis interpret that Biblical verse (Boyarin 1990: 35–6).

The words of the Written Torah thus play an important supporting role in the story, but it is the Rabbis' understanding—the Oral Torah, determined by the majority—that ultimately wins out. Moreover, God plays an important supporting role in the story but does not have the direct power to determine how the Oral Torah should be understood. And yet God—as the prophet Elijah reports to Rabbi Nathan—appears to be happy to defer to the Rabbis and for them to ignore what God directly reveals.

This story can be read as celebrating how the Rabbis uphold the rule of law and the authority of reason, which is valued over miraculous revelations. The continuation of the story beyond what is printed above, however, makes it clear that the story's final editors see little to celebrate. Rabbi Eliezer is excommunicated, seemingly because he has refused to accept the authority of the majority. Rabban Gamliel, the Rabbinic leader who authorizes the excommunication, justifies his decision as carried out for God's honor and so that "disagreement will not proliferate among the people of Israel." But Rabbi Eliezer is portrayed by the Talmud as having been unfairly shamed and verbally mistreated, and his anguish leads to Rabban Gamliel's death at God's hands. (This is also a rare Talmudic story in which a woman—Rabbi Eliezer's wife Ima Shalom—is noted for her insight, as she points out the seriousness of verbal mistreatment.) The entire story is told as part of a commentary on a Mishnah which prohibits harming others with words; prior to the appearance of this story, the Talmud describes verbal mistreatment as causing injuries that can never be fully redressed and likens causing shame to murder. It is, the Talmud notes just before the story of Rabbi Eliezer and his colleagues, "better for a person to throw oneself into a fiery furnace than to humiliate one's fellow in public" (BT *Bava Metzia* 59a). Within this context, as the scholar Jeffrey Rubenstein (1999: 48) has argued, the entire story warns sages not to cause pain with their words, even if they are motivated by well-intentioned interests in honoring God, honoring legal processes, or ensuring unity: God will not accept such worthy principles "as justification for verbal wronging and causing pain."

THE AUTHORITY OF THE ORAL TORAH

The insistence that principles regarding Rabbinic authority ("it is not in heaven," "incline after the majority") can actually be found in the Written Torah—even when the words of the Written Torah do not seem to support such principles—is part of a broader tendency among the Rabbis to simultaneously engage with the Written Torah while also asserting their independence from it.

The Babylonian Talmud sometimes insists that its ethical principles are part of God's revelation of the Written Torah to Moses, even as it indicates that those principles are not actually supported by the Written Torah's words. For example, the Talmud refers to a prohibition on *tza'ar ba'alei hayyim*—"suffering caused to animals," generally understood as "*unnecessary* suffering caused to animals." In one passage, the fourth-century sage Rava states "it can be learned that the prohibition on suffering caused to animals comes from the Written Torah" (BT *Bava Metzia* 32a–b). The discussion engages Biblical commandments to assist fallen animals (Bible, Exodus 23:5, Deuteronomy 22:4), but rather than provide a convincing proof that the verses prohibit causing suffering, the discussion repeatedly challenges that possibility, leaving the Biblical derivation of the prohibition uncertain. Why don't the editors of the Talmud instead provide support for Rava's argument? One possibility is that the Talmud's editors use the phrase "from the Written Torah" to mean that it is "a serious concern" but want their readers to recognize that Rava could not easily derive this principle from the Biblical text (Berkowitz 2018: 111–2).

We can see an even stronger assertion of Rabbinic authority in the way that Rabbinic literature treats the issue of corporal punishment. The Bible authorizes legal authorities to engage in acts of violent corporal punishment in response to bodily injuries caused to others: "If anyone maims his fellow, as he has done so shall it be done to him: fracture for fracture, eye for eye, tooth for tooth. The injury he inflicted on another shall be inflicted on him" (Bible, Leviticus 24:19–20). The Mishnah, however, rather than adopting this system, offers the following set of guidelines for monetary compensation for non-lethal injuries: "One who injures one's fellow is liable [to compensate] on five counts: for damage, for pain, for medical costs, for loss of income, and for causing indignity" (Mishnah *Bava Kamma* 8:1). There is no implication whatsoever in the Mishnah that one should consider the words of the Torah that ordain corporal punishment. The Oral Torah as recorded in the Mishnah appears to completely override the teaching of the Written Torah.

Commenting on this Mishnah, the Talmud (BT *Bava Kamma* 83b–84a) seeks to find a Biblical verse that might support the Rabbinic system of monetary compensation, but while it fails to find any Biblical proof, it also does not challenge the authority of the Mishnah. The teaching of the Mishnah stands, and all that the Talmudic discussion has done is show how it cannot be supported by the Bible. As the scholar David Kraemer (1996: 48) has argued, the Talmud seeks to show that Biblical verses do not have ultimate authority, but rather that "the law will ultimately follow the Oral tradition (in this case, the Mishnah), regardless of the simple meaning of the Written text [of the Bible]." The change may well reflect ethical concerns with the Bible's system of corporal punishment (Fonrobert 2013: 60).

Some Rabbinic texts seem to imagine that later innovations were in fact part of what was revealed to Moses at Mount Sinai. But other Rabbinic texts show a clear awareness that Torah may change over time. In one story, Moses sees a vision of the future where the first-/ second- century sage Rabbi Akiva is teaching his students. Moses "did not understand what they were saying," but he hears Rabbi Akiva teach that the unfamiliar teaching under discussion is "a halakhah given to Moses at Sinai" (BT *Menaḥot* 29b). If Moses received the Oral Torah from God and passed it down in a chain of transmission that eventually reached Rabbi Akiva, one might assume that this Oral Torah would be familiar to Moses. This text suggests that some Rabbis were aware that conceptions of "Torah" do change over time.

WHAT ARE THE OVERARCHING PRINCIPLES OF TORAH?

In addition to the guidelines that the Rabbis saw themselves as enacting, one passage in the Talmud (BT *Makkot* 23b–24a) counts six hundred and thirteen commandments revealed to the people of Israel in the Written Torah—and then immediately goes on to list how the Torah's commandments can be summed up by smaller numbers of commandments. What commandments sum up the

Torah? Are some commandments more important than others? Are there certain principles that override other principles or rules?

The passage in *Makkot* culminates by referring to Biblical passages that seem to sum up God's message in short phrases. God asks the people of Israel, "only to do justice, and to love kindness, and to walk humbly with your God" (Micah 6:8); to "observe what is right and do what is just" (Isaiah 56:1); to "Seek Me and live" (Amos 5:4); and God proclaims that "the righteous shall live by his faith" (Habakkuk 2:4). Any one of these phrases might offer the overarching principles by which people might live.

Another Talmudic passage brings a debate between Rabbis who point to other Biblical verses that might serve as overarching "great principles of the Torah":

> "You shall love your fellow as yourself" (Bible, Leviticus 19:18)—Rabbi Akiva says, "That is a [the?] great principle of the Torah."

> Ben Azzai says: "This is the book of the descendants of the human being: [in the day that God created the human being, God made him in the likeness of God]" (Bible, Genesis 5:1)—this is a greater principle than that.
>
> (PT *Nedarim* 9:3)

A story about two earlier Rabbis, Hillel and Shammai, invokes an Aramaic paraphrase of the commandment to "love your fellow as yourself"—"that which is hateful to you, do not do to your fellow"—as Hillel's summation of the whole Torah:

> Once there was a [prospective] convert who came before Shammai and said to him: Convert me—on the condition that you can teach me the whole Torah on one foot. Shammai pushed him aside with the measuring stick he was holding. [The prospective convert] then came before Hillel, and Hillel converted him, saying: "'That which is hateful to you, do not do to your fellow'—this is the whole Torah. And the rest is commentary, go and learn it."
>
> (BT *Shabbat* 31a)

Other passages name other commandments that are said to be equal to all other commandments combined: for example, the commandment to study Torah (Mishnah *Peah* 1:1), the commandment to give money (*tzedakah*) to those in need (BT *Bava Batra* 9a), the commandment to put a blue fringe (*tzitzit*) on the corner of one's garment (BT *Menaḥot* 43b), the commandment of male circumcision (BT *Nedarim* 32a), or the commandment to live in the land of Israel (*Sifrei Devarim* 80:4).

Commandments are also sometimes described in Rabbinic literature as overriding other commandments. For example, the obligation to save another's life, linked with the biblical verse to "not stand idly by the blood of another" (Bible, Leviticus 19:16; BT *Sanhedrin* 73a), is said to override prohibitions such as the prohibition to observe the Sabbath. Notably, however, Rabbinic literature consistently rules that a Jew is obligated to desecrate the Sabbath to save the life of someone who is Jewish, but not to save the life of a Gentile (Ophir and Rosen-Zvi 2018: 221). The Mishnah also rules that "the man takes priority over the woman with reference to saving a life" (Mishnah *Horayot* 3:7). The Mishnah does, however, elsewhere show concern for protecting the lives of women when threatened; for example, it gives precedence to a woman's life over that of a fetus before childbirth:

> If a woman is having trouble giving birth, we cut up the offspring in her womb and remove it limb by limb, because her life takes precedence over its life. But if most of it [or, some manuscripts read, most of the head] has emerged, we do not touch it, because we do not set aside one life for another.

> (Mishnah *Oholot* 7:6)

These are just some of the commandments and principles that are named in Rabbinic literature as summing up the Torah or carrying particular weight so as to override other obligations. But the literature as a whole offers no clear system for how to navigate conflicts between most of these overarching norms. Rabbinic literature contains the voices of hundreds of individuals living in various contexts over hundreds of years, and it contains a range of ideas about which obligations are of the utmost importance.

THE REVELATION OF PRINCIPLES, RULES, AND VIRTUES

Rabbinic ethical discourse, like other forms of ethical discourse, often includes broad principles or values, as well as more specific rules that can be followed and character traits that can be internalized. Our chapter thus far has included many broad principles or values that are identified within Rabbinic literature as part of God's Torah, including general obligations such as "love your fellow as yourself" that might be understood in many different ways. But we have also seen more specific rules or laws that offer directives for how to act in concrete situations, such as the Mishnah's directive for how to act in a case of difficult childbirth. We have seen fewer references to character traits—that is, the embodiment of values as dispositions that people possess, including virtues (positive character traits) and vices (negative character traits)—although some of the broad commandments listed above might be understood as referring to character. The commandment to "love your fellow as yourself," for example, may require not only certain behaviors but also a disposition to be loving towards others.

More explicit ideas about moral character are found throughout Rabbinic literature (Barer 2023). In some cases, Rabbis do point to commandments to cultivate certain virtues. Thus, for example, one midrash explains the commandment "to walk in all [God's] ways" (Bible, Deuteronomy 11:22) as a commandment to emulate the traits of mercy that God (according to the Bible, Exodus 34) revealed at Mount Sinai:

> "To walk in all [God's] ways": these are the ways of "The Lord! the Lord! a God compassionate and gracious, slow to anger, abounding in kindness and faithfulness, extending kindness to the thousandth generation, forgiving iniquity, transgression, and sin, and cleansing ..." (Bible, Exodus 34:6–7). As God is merciful, so should you be called merciful; as the Holy Blessed One is called gracious, so too should you be gracious ...
>
> (*Sifrei Devarim* 49:1)

Some Rabbis also depict the virtue of humility as at the heart of God's Torah and as "greater than all" other virtues (BT *Avodah Zarah* 20b). The requirement to be "exceedingly humble" (Mishnah *Avot* 4:4) is sometimes linked with a recognition of human mortality and the lowly place of human beings in creation, as discussed below. Such a stress on humility, though, also sits in tension with Rabbinic claims about the lofty place assigned to the people of Israel, and especially men—and, above all, the Rabbis themselves—who saw themselves as chosen to receive the Torah revealed at Mount Sinai.

WHO RECEIVED GOD'S REVELATION?

Who, after all, is included in the "people of Israel" to whom Torah, with all of its rules, principles, and virtues, was revealed? Rabbinic texts often imagine the "people of Israel" as consisting only of free adult men. One midrash notes that when God tells Moses to "speak to the people of Israel," additional words would be needed to show that women and slaves are included (*Sifra* Kedoshim 4; Cohen 2005: 123). Such teachings imagine God as speaking above all to the free men who are the subject of most of the commandments; those of subordinate status may also be included, as many of the commandments apply to them as well, but they are not God's primary audience.

Some Rabbinic texts do highlight that women were present at Sinai, but in a limited way. One midrash interprets the language of the Bible, Exodus 19:3, where God tells Moses: "Thus shall you say to the house of Jacob and declare to the people of Israel." Why does God mention both "the house of Jacob" and "the people of Israel," which appear to refer to the same people? Rabbinic interpreters saw a cryptic meaning here: while "the people of Israel" refers to men, women were also included by the phrase "the house of Jacob." And a different sort of revelation was given to each of them:

> "Thus shall you say to the house of Jacob"—the women,
>
> "and declare to the people of Israel"—the men....
>
> "Thus shall you say to the house of Jacob"—gently give the women the basic ideas;
>
> "and declare to the people of Israel"—speak in detail to the men.
>
> (*Mekhilta de-Rabbi Yishmael* 19:3)

While the authors of this text clearly imagined that women stood at Sinai, they did not see women as included within the true "people of Israel" or given access to the full revelation of Torah at Sinai to which men had access.

Rabbinic literature is remarkably consistent in teaching that those who were not a part of the people of Israel—Gentiles—were not present at Sinai. The Torah, in the Rabbis' view, is the exclusive property of one, chosen nation. One midrash imagines that God did first offer the Torah to other nations but that these nations turned down the opportunity to receive it, as they could not accept even its most basic commandments prohibiting murder, theft, and forbidden sexual relations (*Mekhilta de-Rabbi Yishmael* 20:2). Other texts emphasize the exclusivity of God's revelation in even starker terms. One passage in the Talmud sees God's revelation of Torah as purifying only Israel from the "filth" that has otherwise infected humanity since they were in the Garden of Eden:

> Rabbi Yoḥanan said: When the serpent had sex with Eve, it placed filth in her.
>
> If this is so, then Israel too [should have this filth in them]!
>
> But when Israel stood at Mount Sinai [and received the Torah], their filth ceased.
>
> But the filth of the Gentiles, who did not stand at Mount Sinai, has not ceased.
>
> (BT *Avodah Zarah* 22b)

According to Rabbi Yoḥanan, sex between Eve and the serpent in the Garden of Eden left a stain on humanity: as the context of the passage in the Talmud indicates, that filth may be understood as "lust," including a perverse desire for sex with non-human animals. Only divine grace—the giving of Torah at Mount Sinai—can save humanity from the consequences of Eve's original sin (the phrase "original sin" is not used in Rabbinic literature, but the idea here is remarkably similar to the way that concept is described in ancient Christian literature). Therefore, only the people of Israel were freed from these perverse lusts; Gentiles were not freed of them, which is why the Mishnah upon which the Talmud is commenting warns Jews to beware of Gentile bestiality (Wasserman 2017: 75–95). Notably, the Talmudic discussion warns that Jewish widows—that is, Jewish women who are not subject to the authority of a Jewish man—are also suspected of bestiality. As the scholar Mira Wasserman (2017: 105–12) has argued, the implication is that

women are only under the rule of Torah (which frees them from
their lusts) when they are under the authority of husbands or
fathers, the men who inherited the gracious protection of the
Torah revealed at Sinai.

II THE CREATION OF THE WORLD

COMMANDMENTS AT THE DAWN OF CREATION

If the Rabbis understood that the Torah revealed at Sinai was only
intended for the people of Israel, did they think that God also had a
message about ethical living for Gentiles? If so, how was that message
communicated? A number of passages in Rabbinic literature suggest
that God does have instruction for those who are not Jewish and that
this instruction was made available to humanity in the early days of
the world's creation (and its subsequent re-creation after the Flood),
long before there was a people of Israel and long before the revelation
of Torah at Sinai.

One discussion in the Talmud (BT *Sanhedrin* 56b) locates seven
commandments given to all humanity within the first commandment given to the first human being ("Adam") in the Garden of
Eden. Rabbi Yoḥanan understands the Biblical verse "And the
Lord God commanded the man, saying: 'Of every tree of the
garden you may freely eat'" (Bible, Genesis 2:16) as a cryptic
message filled with ethical guidance, teaching that seven of the
Hebrew words of the verse stand for seven commandments given
to Adam—and, through Adam, to all human beings: a prohibition
on idolatry; a prohibition on murder; a prohibition on robbery; a
prohibition on forbidden sexual relations (seemingly including
incest, bestiality, adultery with a married woman, and male anal
same-sex intercourse); a prohibition on blasphemy; a prohibition on
eating a limb from a living animal, and an obligation to establish law
(perhaps courts of law).

Rabbinic literature also includes variations on this formulation.
One alternative list of commandments intended for all humanity,
said to have been given to Noah and his descendants ("Noahides")
after the Flood and amidst the re-creation of the world some generations after Adam, does not include blasphemy or establishing law
but instead includes a prohibition on castration (likely of animals as

well as humans) and a prohibition on cross-breeding different species (likely both animals and plants) (BT *Sanhedrin* 56b). This list of "Noahide commandments" seems to have a particular interest in the treatment of non-human animals, and it is derived less from explicit Biblical commandments and, instead, largely from observations about the story of the Flood and the subsequent re-creation of the world (Steinmetz 2008: 25–33; Wasserman 2019: 58–63).

One might view these traditions as inclusive traditions, referring to commandments that are universally accessible and equally incumbent upon all human beings rather than differentiating between Jews and non-Jews. Rabbinic sources, however, tend to present the commandments in strikingly discriminatory terms. Discussing the prohibition of murder, the Talmud teaches the tradition that while a non-Jew who murders has committed a capital crime, a Jew who murders a non-Jew does not deserve capital punishment (BT *Sanhedrin* 57a). Rabbi Ḥanina teaches that a non-Jew should be killed even for striking a Jew (BT *Sanhedrin* 58b). The discussion of the prohibition on murder also yields a ruling that abortion, which does not appear to be prohibited for Jews, is in fact prohibited for non-Jews (BT *Sanhedrin* 57b). The Talmud ends up showing how each commandment should be applied differently to Jews and to non-Jews, in a discriminatory fashion. These commandments do not appear to be universally accessible "natural laws" that any human being could discover through reason alone (Hayes 2015: 356–70).

Claims that ethical insights are universally accessible are not easy to find in Rabbinic literature. A rare example of such a claim might be found in another teaching of Rabbi Yoḥanan: "If the Torah had not been given, we could have learned modesty from the cat, [the prohibitions of] stealing from the ant, forbidden sexual relations from the dove, and proper sexual mores from the rooster" (BT *Eruvin* 100b). This alternative tradition can be read as implying that even without commandments from God anyone can learn proper behavior from consideration of the natural world that God created (Newman 1998b: 127).

THE BODY'S CREATION IN THE IMAGE OF GOD

There are other ways, though, that Rabbinic literature suggests that ethics might be learned from "creation." In particular, many texts make claims about how to live by interpreting Biblical passages from the Book of Genesis that describe God's creation of the world, including God's creation of human beings.

Human beings are described in a number of Biblical passages as having been created "in the image of God" (e.g. Genesis 1:27, 9:6) or "in the likeness of God" (e.g. Genesis 5:1). What does it mean to be in the image or likeness of God?

Rabbinic literature generally understands the image and likeness of God to refer to a bodily form shared by God and humans. Human beings, in these sources, look like God. The Rabbinic leader Hillel makes this idea clear as he explains that washing in the bathhouse is "a commandment": just as the statues of kings must be washed and polished, how much the more is washing imperative for "I, who was created in the image and likeness of God, as it is written, 'For in the image of God He made man'" (*Leviticus Rabbah* 34:3). Here, it is precisely the bodily form that is in the image and likeness of God.

But do all human bodies resemble God's body? Some Rabbis believed not. One midrash teaches: "The first human emerged circumcised, as it is written: 'God created the human in His image'" (*Avot De-Rabbi Natan* A2). Adam, the first human being, is imagined as having been created with a circumcised penis, and his circumcision is the sign of his creation in God's image. This source may be suggesting that God has male genitalia, and it is not clear that those without circumcised penises (paradigmatically, those who are not Jewish men) reflect the image of God (Eilberg-Schwartz 1994: 182).

The question of whether Gentiles are created in God's image appears to be an issue on which the Rabbis were not united, however. At least one Rabbinic saying clearly affirms that non-Israelites are created in the image of God, though it hardly affirms the equality of Israelites and non-Israelites.

As Rabbi Akiva is quoted as saying: "Beloved is the human being [*adam*], who was created in the image [of God]." We can tell that the Hebrew word *adam*, here translated as "the human being," refers to human beings in general rather than the people of Israel specifically because the statement goes on to offer a contrast with the people of Israel, who are "beloved" in a different way: "Beloved are Israel, for they are called the children of God" (referring to the Bible, Deuteronomy 14:1, where the people of Israel are addressed as "the children of the Lord your God"). The implication is that all human beings are created in God's image but that it is only Israel who may be considered "God's children." And, as the teaching from Rabbi Akiva concludes, "Beloved are Israel, to whom was given the precious vessel. It was an act of still greater love that it was made known to them that they were given the precious vessel with which the world was created" (Mishnah *Avot* 3:14)—the Torah, which was, according to this tradition, the primordial blueprint that God used in creating the world. All human beings are beloved, in this teaching, but Israel is especially beloved, as the nation chosen to receive the Torah and enter into a covenant with God.

WHO IS FULLY HUMAN?

Are there Rabbinic texts that teach that all humans were created equal? There is one text, found in some manuscripts of the Mishnah, that offers a message of equality as part of a warning to witnesses testifying in capital cases:

> The human [*adam*] was created alone, to teach you that whoever destroys a single soul is deemed by Scripture as if he had destroyed a whole world. And whoever saves a single soul is deemed by Scripture as if he had saved a whole world. And it was also for the sake of peace among people, so that someone should not say to his fellow, "My father is greater than your father."

But many manuscripts of the Mishnah include the word "Israelite" in the first part of the text, indicating that the discussion concerns only killing or saving the lives of members of the people of Israel:

> The human [*adam*] was created alone, to teach you that whoever destroys a single Israelite soul is deemed by Scripture as if he had destroyed a whole world. And whoever saves a single Israelite soul is deemed by Scripture as if he had saved a whole world ...

> (Mishnah *Sanhedrin* 4:5)

Some versions of the Mishnah, then, assume that the story of the first human being's creation teaches about the equal protection due to all human beings, while other versions assume that the creation story teaches about the special protection due to the people of Israel, who uniquely possess the dignity of the first human.

Other sources also indicate that the meaning of the term "human" was a subject of debate among the Rabbis. One statement, quoted three times in the Babylonian Talmud (*Yevamot* 61a, *Keritut* 6b, *Bava Metzia* 114b), teaches that those who are not Jewish do not deserve to be called by the title of "adam"—i.e. "human being." In these instances, the Talmud quotes a biblical verse: "And you My sheep, the sheep of My pasture, are human [*adam*]" (Ezekiel 34:31), meaning, the Talmud explains: "you [the people of Israel] are called human [*adam*] but Gentiles are not called human [*adam*]." But in two of the three instances where this teaching is offered, the Talmud challenges it, pointing to instances in the Bible (Numbers 31:40, Jonah 4:11) where non-Israelites are indeed described with the word *adam*. The Talmud responds that Gentiles are called *adam* in these instances to make it clear that they are human rather than being non-human animals. The implication is that both Jews and Gentiles are part of the same species but that ordinarily Gentiles are not given the honorific title of "human," whereas Israelites are. One may understand, according to this line of thinking, that the first human being, Adam, was in fact an Israelite. Elsewhere, however, the Talmud uses the term "adam" more broadly, as with the statement that "even a non-Jew who is engaged in Torah is considered a high priest," which is supported by arguments that the word "adam" should indeed apply to all human beings (BT *Bava Kamma* 38a; BT *Avodah Zarah* 3a; BT *Sanhedrin* 59a) (Stern 1994).

GENDER AND THE IMAGE OF GOD

In any case, is it only men who are created in the image of God? The perspective quoted above, describing the image of God as linked with male circumcision, indicates that some Rabbis thought so. As the scholar Judith Baskin (2002: 49) has written, "the predominant view among the rabbinic sages was that man alone was created in the divine image and only later was a woman built from his body. The possibility that God simultaneously created two independent entities, a man and a woman, is never directly addressed in rabbinic exegesis."

The Rabbis do, however, consider the possibility that men and women were created at the same time as part of one being. This exegesis seeks to reconcile Biblical texts (Genesis 1:27 and 5:1–2) that describe the creation of the human being as "male and female" (using both singular and plural nouns) with the Biblical story (Genesis 2:21–22) that the first female human (Eve) was created from the first male (Adam). Attempting to combine these stories, and employing a motif also found in ancient Zoroastrian mythology (Secunda 2012), one Rabbinic interpretation imagines that the first human being was neither male nor female but, possessing both male and female genitalia, can be identified with one of the other physical genders often mentioned in Rabbinic texts, *androginos* (androgynous). A second interpretation, echoing a tradition found in ancient Greek literature (Boyarin 1993: 43), describes the first human as "two-sided" and then separated into a male and a female:

> Said Rabbi Yirmiyah ben Elazar: When the Holy Blessed One created the first human being, He created him *androginos*, as it is written (Bible, Genesis 5:2): "Male and female He created them."

> Said R. Shmuel bar Naḥman: When the Holy Blessed One created the first human being, He created him two-sided, then split him and made him two spines, a spine here and a spine there.

> (*Genesis Rabbah* 8:1)

The first interpretation, notably, even as it invokes binary gender, may also challenge the male–female binary, as it points to the primacy of a non-binary gender not named in the Written Torah but often mentioned in Rabbinic literature. As the scholar Gwynn Kessler has put it, this text "invites us to see the *androginos* as much a part of rabbinic gender as male and female" (Kessler 2020: 80). As such, it may be in line with other Rabbinic traditions that refuse to view the androginos as male or female but that instead describe the androginos as a "unique creation," as the sage Rabbi Yosi puts it (Mishnah *Bikkurim* 4:5; Kessler 2020; Strassfeld 2022a).

Alternatively, these interpretations of the creation story may seek to reify binary gender and show why heterosexual marriage is compulsory. As Baskin (2002: 62) has argued, this midrash serves primarily to teach "that only when the male and female are united are they truly *'adam*, that is truly human." This idea is elsewhere expressed in the dictum of Rabbi Elazar that "any man who does not have a wife is not a man, as it is stated: 'Male and female He created them ... and called their name Adam' (Bible, Genesis 5:2)" (BT *Yevamot* 63a). Another midrash stresses that being "in God's image" requires marriage: "'In our image, after our likeness' (Bible, Genesis 1:26): neither man without woman nor woman without man, nor both of them without the divine presence" (*Genesis Rabbah* 8:9, 22:2). Another stresses that men are obligated to procreate to be like God: he who does not marry "even impairs the 'likeness,' as it is written, 'For God made the man in the image of God' (Bible, Genesis 9:6)," followed by "'Be fruitful and multiply' (Bible, Genesis 9:7)" (*Genesis Rabbah* 17:2). Rabbinic literature is sometimes ambivalent about marriage for men, especially because marriage may distract men from Torah study (Boyarin 1993: 134–66), but even so it often views marriage and procreation as essential for being fully human.

COMMANDING MALE MASTERY

When Rabbinic sources discuss the first woman (Eve) as created out of the body of the first man (Adam), they occasionally treat her positively. One midrash sees God having "granted a woman greater understanding than that of a man" (BT *Niddah* 45b; *Genesis Rabbah* 18:1) though, as scholar Judith Romney Wegner (1998: 84) has pointed out, "understanding" here may be understood as on a lower level than other forms of intellect. Other midrashim are clearly negative, as with one that describes God seeking to create the first woman so that she would possess ideal female traits such as humility, sexual modesty, and passivity; instead, even at the very moment of her creation, the woman turns out to be inherently haughty, immodest, and a gadabout (*Genesis Rabbah* 18:2; Baskin 2002: 53). One midrash imagines that Eve's creation brought Satanic evil into the world: "when she was created, Satan was created with her" (*Genesis Rabbah* 17:6; Baskin 2002: 56). And one tradition sees male dominance over the woman as commanded not only after the couple's expulsion from the Garden of Eden, where God tells the woman that "he shall rule over you" (Bible, Genesis 3:16), but before any sins in the Garden. In this tradition, the commandment to "fill the earth and master it" (Bible, Genesis 1:28) should be read as "fill the earth and master *her*," addressing the man and commanding mastery over women (specifically, with the goal of keeping women out of public spaces): "the man must master his wife, that she not go out into the marketplace, for every woman who goes out into the marketplace will eventually come to grief" (*Genesis Rabbah* 8:12; Baskin 2002: 51–2).

Although Eve is often viewed in very negative terms in Rabbinic literature, there are also sources that imagine that another woman was created prior to Eve who was far worse. One midrash imagines that this first woman was named Lilith and that she was unwilling to accept Adam's claims to superiority—or his insistence on being on top during sexual intercourse:

> After God created Adam, who was alone, He said, "It is not good for man to be alone" (Bible, Genesis 28:18). He then created a woman for Adam, from the earth, as He had created Adam himself, and called her Lilith. Adam and Lilith immediately began to fight. She said, "I will not lie below," and he said, "I will not lie beneath you, but only on top. For you are fit only to be in the bottom position, while I am to be in the superior one." Lilith responded, "We are equal to each other inasmuch as we were both created from the earth." But they would not listen to one another. When Lilith saw this, she pronounced the Ineffable Name and flew away into the air.
>
> (*Alphabet of Ben Sira* 23a–b)

Lilith, the midrash goes on to explain, continues to exist as a demon. As Baskin (2002: 59) has put it, the lesson of the story is clear: "this narrative reflects rabbinic tradition in its certainty that mutuality cannot work in marital relations: the husband must be dominant." While one can find diversity in Rabbinic literature about many subjects, it is difficult to find Rabbinic sources that disagree with this conclusion. The Talmud offers no dissent to its ruling that Jewish men should praise God, daily, as the one "who did not make me a woman" as well as the one "who did not make me a Gentile" and "who did not make me an ignoramus" (or, some manuscripts say, "who did not make me a slave") (BT *Menaḥot* 43b–44a).

"DIFFERENT CREATURES": SKIN COLOR AND DISABILITY

The Talmud also rules that Jews should express gratitude for creation in a variety of other ways, including for seeing "beautiful creatures and beautiful trees": "Blessed is He who has such in His world." The text juxtaposes this with a ruling on the blessing to recite for seeing "different creatures": "If one sees a black person, a red person, a white person, a hunchback, a dwarf, or a dropsical person, he says: Blessed is He who makes different creatures" (BT *Berakhot* 58b). In this passage, the Talmud links "abnormal" skin color and disability together as two parts of God's creation that call for expressions of praise.

While skin color is not a major topic of interest in Rabbinic sources, this passage is instructive in showing how some Rabbis judged the different skin colors of God's creations. The Mishnah quotes Rabbi Ishmael as describing the people of Israel as colored "like boxwood, neither black nor white but of an intermediate shade" (Mishnah *Nega'im* 2:1), and the assumption that such an "intermediate shade" is normal—and beautiful—seems to be behind the discussion of colors in the Talmudic passage as well. Those whose skin is outside of this norm are affirmed as part of God's wondrous creation but, as the scholar Abraham Melamed has argued, are depicted as inferior. Black skin sometimes has a particularly negative valence in Rabbinic literature, as in traditions that view black skin as a punishment visited upon one of the progenitors of humankind, Noah's son Ham. In some texts, blackness is associated with ugliness and depravity. On the other hand, black skin is associated with beauty in one Rabbinic midrash, which describes Noah's son Shem (the ancestor of Israel) as "black and beautiful" (Melamed 2003: 71–121).

The Talmudic passage above also depicts those born with various disabilities as "different," viewing a variety of physical conditions as signs of inferiority, even if the differences (like different skin colors) provide a reason to praise God. As the scholar Julia Watts Belser (2018a: 172) has argued, this blessing practice preserves "a place for disability and difference within the bounds of sanctified creation," and yet "disability (like racial difference) becomes an object of fascination, a site through which the normative seer perceives and ritualizes the non-normative body as dissident and deviant." We should notice "the violence inherent in taking a body as an object of strangeness, fashioning the marginalized person as nothing more than an occasion for the dominant speaker to utter praise." But Belser (2018b) also points to ways in which, elsewhere in Rabbinic literature, those with physical disabilities are seen as possessing significant agency: for example, in narratives of how the disabled bodies of Rabbis mark resistance against Roman domination.

THE PLACE OF HUMAN BEINGS IN CREATION

The frailty of human bodies is a significant theme in Rabbinic texts, often linked with the idea that the first human being was created from dust (or dirt, as it can be translated) and told by God that "dust you are, and to dust you shall return" (Bible, Genesis 3:19). As the sage Rava put it, "I am dust in my life, all the more so in my death" (BT *Berakhot* 17a). Human beings (at least some) may be created in the image of God, but they also share the characteristics of more lowly parts of creation.

Some Rabbinic traditions view human beings as the most honored part of God's creation. A midrash explains that humans were created last in the sequence of creation by imagining that God was like a king holding a banquet in their honor: "he built palaces, furnished them, prepared a feast and afterwards brought in guests." An alternative view is that humans were created last so "if one becomes haughty, [God can] say to him: the gnat preceded you in the work of creation" (BT *Sanhedrin* 38a). In the view of some Rabbis, humans should not think all that highly of their species; in the view of others, they are the most honored of creations.

Would the world have been better off without human beings? The Talmud records a disagreement on this question between two rival Rabbinic schools:

> For two and a half years, the school of Shammai and the school of Hillel disagreed. These said: It would have been better had the human not been created than to have been created. And those said: It is better for the human to have been created than not to have been created. They voted and concluded: it would have been better had the human not been created than to have been created, but now that they have been created, let them examine their deeds.
>
> (BT *Eruvin* 13b)

Some traditions combine the sense that everything in the world is created for human beings with the concern that human beings are capable of great destruction, as in the following midrash:

> "Behold the work of God, for who could fix what he has marred?" (Bible, Ecclesiastes 7:13) When the Holy Blessed One created the first man, [God] took him to review all of the trees in the Garden of Eden and said to him: "Behold my works, how pleasant and praiseworthy they are. All that I created, I created for you. Pay heed that you not ruin and destroy my world, for if you do ruin it, there is no one after you who will fix it."
>
> (*Ecclesiastes Rabbah* 7:13)

As scholar Tanhum Yoreh has argued, this midrash may be connected with the Rabbinic prohibition on unnecessary destruction (*Bal Tashḥit*). Although in this midrash "all nonhuman creations were created for the sake of humans and for their utility ... God is the ultimate owner, implying that use is permitted, but wastefulness and wanton destruction are not." Elsewhere, the Rabbis refer to this prohibition in less anthropocentric terms: one midrash describes how a fruit-bearing tree, when cut down, cries a cry that can be heard across the entire world. Most Rabbinic texts view the prohibition in human-centered terms, however, and one prominent opinion in the Talmud justifies destructive human behavior such as cutting down trees in light of economic interests (Yoreh 2019: 246–50).

CREATION AND THE TREATMENT OF NON-HUMAN ANIMALS

Rabbinic teachings on the treatment of non-human animals are also sometimes framed with reference to creation. For example, the permission for humans to eat animals (though, for Jews, only a small number of species) is justified on the grounds that God abandoned God's requirement at the dawn of creation that humans be vegetarian:

> Rav Judah said in the name of Rav: the first human being was not permitted to eat meat, as it is written: "[I give you every seed-bearing plant that is upon all the earth and every tree that has seed-bearing fruit;] for you and for every animal of the earth they shall be for food" (Bible,

Genesis 1:29–30)—but the animals of the earth are not [food] for you. But when the children of Noah came, [God] permitted them [to eat meat], as it is stated: "[Every creature that lives shall be yours to eat;] as with the green grasses, I give you all these" (Bible, Genesis 9:3).

(BT *Sanhedrin* 59b)

Some Rabbis may have viewed vegetarianism as God's original ideal, fit for a world where death did not yet exist (Shemesh 2006: 146). But others may well have believed that even the first human beings were permitted to eat meat. After all, according to the teaching of Rabbi Yoḥanan discussed above, the prohibition on eating a limb from a living animal was given in the Garden of Eden; such a prohibition would seem to suppose that other forms of eating meat were permitted even there (Wasserman 2019: 49).

Some Rabbis evidently believed that non-human animals were created for the sake of human beings. "Were they not created only to serve me?" Rabbi Simeon ben Elazar asks (Mishnah *Kiddushin* 4:14). But other sources seem to challenge this idea. For example, the Talmud describes Rabbi Judah as punished for telling a calf that it was created for the sake of slaughter:

The sufferings of Rabbi [Judah the Patriarch] came due to an incident. What was it? Once there was a calf that they were bringing to slaughter. It went and hung its head in a corner of Rabbi [Judah]'s garment. And it cried. Rabbi [Judah] said to it, "Go. For this you were created." [The heavenly court] said: "Since he shows no compassion, let sufferings come upon him."

And these [sufferings] left as a result of an incident. One day, Rabbi [Judah]'s maid was sweeping the house. There were baby rats scattered there and she swept them up. [Rabbi Judah] said to her, "Let them go! It is written, '[God's] compassion is upon all of [God's] works'" (Bible, Psalms 145:9). They said: "Since he shows compassion, we will have compassion on him."

(BT *Bava Metzia* 85a)

It appears that Judah originally misunderstands how to think about creation; only after many years of suffering does he come to realize that all of God's creatures deserve compassion. As scholar Aaron Gross (2014: 167–70) has argued, this story also serves to elevate the value of the Rabbinic prohibition, discussed above, on causing unnecessary suffering to animals.

III THE REDEMPTION OF ISRAEL

ETHICS AND REDEMPTION FROM SLAVERY IN EGYPT

As we can see, the Rabbinic texts that engage and interpret stories of creation teach a wide variety of ethical lessons. The same is true of Rabbinic texts that engage and interpret stories about the redemption of the people of Israel from slavery and oppression. I conclude this chapter by exploring two kinds of Rabbinic discourse about redemption and ethics: discussion of the people of Israel's liberation from slavery in Egypt; and discussion of a future messianic redemption.

The story of how God liberated the people of Israel from slavery in Egypt teaches ethical ideas in a variety of ways, often through midrash on the first fifteen chapters of the Biblical book of Exodus, which narrates Pharaoh's enslavement of the Israelites, the resistance to his plans to kill all male Israelite babies, the emergence of Moses as God's prophet, and God's defeat of Pharaoh and liberation of the Israelites.

For example, midrashic texts expand on the Biblical account of the midwives Shifra and Puah, who worked against Pharaoh's efforts, often identifying Shifra with Moses' mother Yocheved and Puah with Moses' sister Miriam. One midrashic collection imagines that Miriam, as a young girl, speaks out in protest not only against Pharaoh but also against her own father, Amram, who divorces Yocheved and inspires the other Israelite adult males to divorce their wives in an effort to avoid Pharaoh's decree against male babies. Though Pharaoh does not listen to Miriam, Amram does, remarrying Yocheved, which leads to the birth of Moses (*Exodus Rabbah* 1:13). As the scholar Inbar Raveh (2014: 62–4) has argued, the midrash portrays Miriam showing exemplary audacity, modeling how to respond to injustices by confronting those who are responsible for them.

Rabbinic literature also shows admiration for a violent human response to oppression in Egypt, namely Moses' killing of an Egyptian taskmaster who is beating an enslaved Israelite (recounted in the Bible in Exodus 2:11–12). In the Talmud, Rabbi Ḥanina points to Moses' act as justifying the discriminatory standard discussed above, whereby a Gentile is liable to be killed for striking a Jew (though a Jew is not liable for striking a Gentile) (BT *Sanhedrin* 58b). But other Rabbinic texts seem to suggest that nothing practical should be learned from the example of Moses' deed, as they highlight Moses' uniquely prophetic power to see the particular depravity of the taskmaster and the depravity of all of his future possible descendants (*Exodus Rabbah* 1:28–29). Still other texts seem more critical of Moses, labeling him a manslaughterer or murderer (Sagi 1996: 74–5).

God frees the people of Israel from Egypt by unleashing violent plagues and punishments on the Egyptians and, according to some texts, on the many Israelites who were not worthy to be redeemed. A number of Rabbinic texts, however, warn that such violence is God's unique responsibility and not a human responsibility. One midrash imagines that when they were about to be liberated some Israelites declared their intention to fight Pharaoh's army: "Let us fight against them!" Moses responded: "The Lord will fight for you" (Bible, Exodus 14:14) (*Mekhilta de-Rabbi Yishmael* 14:13). "Israel only has prayer," another passage teaches, contrasting Israel with nations such as Edom (i.e. Rome), who "trust only in the sword" (*Mekhilta de-Rabbi Yishmael* 14:10). Such traditions seem to oppose the use of violence, trusting instead in God's deliverance, a posture that may have been especially compelling to some Rabbis after the failure of the second-century Bar Kokhba Revolt against Rome (Blidstein 2008).

The Biblical story of the exodus culminates with the drowning of Pharaoh and his army in the Sea of Reeds and the triumphant song of the Israelites (Exodus 15). Although the Talmud seems at first to affirm that it is right to rejoice in such deaths, in line with the verse "When the wicked perish, there is song" (Bible, Proverbs 11:10), it goes on to raise a question about doing so and presents a narrative in which God silences the angels who rejoice at the Egyptians' downfall:

"Does the Holy One, Blessed be He, rejoice at the downfall of the wicked?" … Rabbi Samuel bar Naḥman said in the name of Rabbi Jonathan: … [When Pharaoh's army drowned] the ministering angels wanted to sing a song before the Holy Blessed One. The Holy Blessed One said to them: "The works of my hands are drowning in the sea, and you are singing a song before Me?"

(BT *Sanhedrin* 39b)

However, an alternative version of the midrash tells a very different story about why the angels were silenced, imagining that God was concerned not about the downfall of the Egyptians at all but about the dangers faced by God's people, Israel: "My legions are in distress, and you are singing a song before Me?" (*Exodus Rabbah* 23:7). The Rabbis here teach sympathy not for the drowning Egyptian army but for one's own people.

Were there Egyptians who deserved to be saved from the destruction that God wreaked on Egypt? The Biblical text indicates that when the Israelites escaped from Egypt "a mixed multitude went up with them" (Exodus 12:38), which one Rabbinic tradition identified as Egyptians who could be trusted, and who seem to join the people of Israel (*Exodus Rabbah* 18:10). Other Rabbinic traditions, however, depict this "mixed multitude" as responsible for a variety of sins including the idolatrous worship of the golden calf. One midrash condemns Moses for showing inappropriate mercy to these foreigners and allowing them to join with the people of Israel (*Exodus Rabbah* 42:6).

HALAKHAH WITH REFERENCE TO REDEMPTION

One set of commandments in the Bible warns Israelites not to "oppress the stranger nor pressure him, for you were strangers in the land of Egypt" (Exodus 22:20) and to "love [the stranger] as yourself, for you were strangers in the land of Egypt" (Leviticus 19:34). The authors of these texts seem to have intended to protect non-Israelite strangers who lived among Israelites: Israelites should remember the experience of having been oppressed when they were non-Egyptian strangers in Egypt, and should therefore not oppress non-Israelite strangers living among their people.

Rabbinic texts are consistent, however, in understanding these commandments as protecting not non-Israelites who remain non-Israelites, but rather converts who join the people of Israel. In this understanding, it is the convert who is the most vulnerable stranger who lives among the people of Israel. As one passage in the Talmud claims, the convert is especially vulnerable because the convert's "inclination is evil": converts (such as the aforementioned "mixed multitude") are prone to problematic desires because of their Gentile origins. Those born Jewish, realizing that they (or their ancestors) had previously been in a "defective" condition of vulnerability themselves (as slaves in Egypt), are instructed not to make mention of the convert's condition:

> Rabbi Eliezer the Great says: For what reason did the Torah issue warnings in thirty-six places, and some say in forty-six places, with regard to a convert? It is because [a convert's] inclination is evil. What [is the meaning of that] which is written: "And you shall not mistreat a convert nor oppress him, because you were strangers in the land of Egypt" (Exodus 22:20)? We learned that Rabbi Nathan says: A defect that is in you, do not mention it in another.
>
> (BT *Bava Metzia* 59b)

Here, we see yet another example of how Rabbinic literature reinterprets a Biblical commandment—in this case, by narrowing its scope, focusing its attention on the people of Israel rather than on Gentiles.

Other Biblical commandments that refer to the experience of slavery in Egypt are explicit in their intent to distinguish the people of Israel from the Egyptians—as well as from the Canaanites in the land that they are promised. As part of a preamble to one list of sexual prohibitions in the Written Torah, God commands that "You shall not copy the practices of the land of Egypt where you dwelt, or of the land of Canaan to which I am taking you; nor shall you follow their laws" (Bible, Leviticus 18:3). One midrash understands this commandment as referring to Egyptian and Canaanite marriage practices, which are prohibited for the people of Israel. For example: "a man would marry a man, and a woman, a woman." While the Biblical chapter on which the midrash is commenting appears to forbid only anal intercourse between two men and does not speak of lesbian intercourse or marriage, we see here how some Rabbis sought to expand sexual or marital prohibitions, perhaps (ironically) mimicking Roman critiques of same-sex marriage (Berkowitz 2012: 88). Other Rabbis expand the halakhic prohibition on "copying practices" beyond sexuality and marriage to forbid all sorts of other practices that are marked as non-Jewish, ranging from attendance at theaters, circuses, and stadia to ways of dressing and hairstyling to methods of decapitation for certain capital crimes (Berkowitz 2012). Halakhah, in all of these examples, is shaped by ideas about the foreign practices of the land of Egypt from which Israel was freed, as well as ideas about foreign practices in the land of Canaan/Israel, where the Rabbis imagined ultimate redemption would be found.

FUTURE REDEMPTION IN THE LAND OF ISRAEL

According to the Bible's narrative, God liberates the people of Israel from slavery in Egypt so that they may settle in the land of Canaan, also called the land of Israel; and while the Bible narrates how the people entered this land and set up kingdoms there, it also tells of how the people were subsequently conquered and exiled by Assyrian and Babylonian armies. Some Biblical texts then see "redemption" in the return of exiles from Babylonia in the sixth century BCE, but centuries later Jews developed hopes for a more ultimate redemption in the future. Living under Roman rule, in the wake of the destruction of Jerusalem and the failure of revolts against Rome, the Rabbis often expressed hopes that God would bring about an ideal age ("the Days of the Messiah," "the messianic era," "the world to come," or "the future that will come") in which the people of Israel would live in peace and with devotion to God, in the land of Israel, under the rule of a "Messiah," a divinely chosen and anointed king.

In the view of some Rabbis, God would send the Messiah at a time of great wickedness; more common is the view that God would not send the Messiah until the people of Israel repented and turned to righteousness. "If the Israelites repent, they will be redeemed," Rabbi Eliezer is quoted as teaching. Rav teaches that "the matter depends only upon repentance and good deeds" (BT *Sanhedrin* 97b). Formulations like these place some power in the hands of the people, whose ethical choices may lead God to reward them with redemption. But, notably, even the sources that endorse this view avoid any implication that the people of Israel themselves could take political or military action to bring about the conditions associated with the messianic era. Just as the people trusted in God's deliverance at the time of the exodus from Egypt, they should trust in God's ultimate deliverance.

If the people of Israel would be brought to the land of Israel in the Days of the Messiah, did that mean that they could not settle there prior to that time? Rabbinic literature portrays the Rabbis disagreeing on this question. One passage in the Talmud on the subject begins with this teaching:

> The sages taught: A[n Israelite] person should always reside in the land of Israel, even in a city with a Gentile majority, and should not reside outside of the land, even in a city that is majority Israelite, for anyone who resides in the land of Israel is considered as one who has a God, and anyone who resides outside the land of Israel is considered as one who does not have a God, as it is stated, "to give to you the land of Canaan, to be your God" (Bible, Leviticus 25:38).
> (BT *Ketubot* 110b)

But the Talmud then counters this view with the teaching of Rav Judah, a Babylonian Rabbi who teaches that leaving Babylonia for the land of Israel before the Days of the Messiah would be a sin, violating God's commandment to remain there (which he understood as given in the Bible, Jeremiah 27:22); moreover, he suggests that living in Babylonia was no worse than living in the land of Israel ("Whoever dwells in Babylonia is as though he dwelt in the land of Israel."). He also imagines the people of Israel bound by an oath that they not move to the land of Israel before the time of redemption chosen by God: "I adjure you, daughters of Jerusalem, by the gazelles and by the hinds of the field, that you do not awaken or stir up love until it please" (Bible, Song of Songs 2:7).

Rabbi Zeira is then described as offering a sort of compromise between these positions, specifying that according to the terms of this oath it is permitted for *individuals* to move to the land before the Days of the Messiah but forbidden for Jews to move to the land of Israel *en masse* (BT *Ketubot* 110b–111a).

These views have much in common: none of them maintain that Jews should seek political control of the land of Israel in the present, and all imagine that God will eventually bring the entire people of Israel to that land to be ruled by a Messiah. But, prior to that time, they differ on how Jews ought to think about settling in the land (Firestone 2012: 90–5).

As Rabbinic sources describe the hoped-for messianic future, imagining what an ideal world would look like, they often teach ethical ideals with respect to a variety of other areas. For example, they imagine the land of Israel as filled with the joyous sounds of weddings, connecting their ideals of marriage between Jewish men and Jewish women with ultimate redemption (BT *Ketubot* 8a; Baskin 2002: 64). Other sources imagine that the sinful, sexual inclination will be eradicated at the end of days, pointing to Rabbinic concerns about difficult-to-control male sexual urges (BT Sukkah 52a; Kiel 2016). According to one opinion, except for the end of Israel's subjugation to other kingdoms, nothing will be different in the messianic age, and even poverty will persist; according to another opinion, however, the world will be substantially different (BT *Berakhot* 34b). Some Rabbis imagined other nations recognizing Israel's chosen status and submitting to the Messiah and God's judgment (BT *Avodah Zarah* 2a–3b). Some imagined the Messiah teaching the nations precepts that they needed to follow (*Genesis Rabbah* 98:9), while some imagined an initial Messiah "anointed for war," fighting enemy nations (*Genesis Rabbah* 99:2), and one source imagines other nations serving as slaves to Israel (*Pesikta Rabbati* 36). Many sources imagine the reinstitution of animal sacrifices at a rebuilt Temple in Jerusalem, even if one text imagines that sacrifices other than Thanksgiving offerings will be abolished (*Leviticus Rabbah* 9:7). And imagining that the bodily resurrection of the righteous would also occur at the time of redemption, some sources also emphasize the importance of bodily healing, including the reversal of disabilities (*Genesis Rabbah* 95:1)—though, as Julia Watts Belser (2015a: 305) has argued, some sources imagine that disabilities are reversed only after those with disabilities are recognized by their kin, demonstrating a Rabbinic sense of "disability as a powerful marker of human personhood." Rabbinic literature makes a wide variety of ethical claims with depictions of redemption such as these.

BEYOND THESE RABBINIC TRADITIONS

Rabbinic literature takes many other approaches in addition to those discussed in this chapter, including telling other sorts of stories about the Rabbis and interpreting Biblical stories that have nothing to do with revelation, creation, and redemption. But considering Rabbinic ethics through the lens of ideas about revelation, creation, and redemption has allowed us to see many of the central ethical ideas found in Rabbinic literature as well as some of the diversity of that literature.

We should remember, however, that the approaches discussed in this chapter represent just some of the many ancient approaches to Jewish ethics. Most ancient Jews did not recognize the authority of the Rabbis; and, in the medieval and modern periods, many Jews continued to dismiss the Rabbis' claims to authority. Many Jews today, even those who view the Rabbis as generally authoritative, would deny the authority of many of the ethical positions in this chapter. Modern Jews who hold strong commitments to universalism and egalitarianism (discussed in Chapters Four and Five) commonly deny that these ideas represent "Jewish ethics," especially when they seem ethnocentric, misogynistic, homophobic, racist, or ableist.

Still, the Rabbis' teachings did come to have significant influence among medieval and modern Jews. One reason for their prominence is that Rabbinic literature was viewed as authoritative by medieval thinkers including the philosopher Moses Maimonides and the authors of the *Zohar*, whose approaches to Jewish ethics were themselves deeply influential. These approaches are the subject of the following chapter.

FURTHER READING

On theoretical approaches to Rabbinic ethics and theology, see Louis E. Newman, *Past Imperatives: Studies in the History and Theory of Jewish Ethics* (1998).

On claims to divine authority and Rabbinic concepts of Torah, see David Charles Kraemer, *Reading the Rabbis: The Talmud as Literature* (1996); Christine Elizabeth Hayes, *What's Divine About Divine Law?: Early Perspectives* (2015); and Rebecca Scharbach Wollenberg, *The Closed Book: How the Rabbis Taught the Jews (Not) to Read the Bible* (2023).

On Rabbinic stories, see Jeffrey L. Rubenstein, *Talmudic Stories: Narrative Art, Composition, and Culture* (1999).

On approaches to virtue, see Jonathan Wyn Schofer, *The Making of a Sage: A Study in Rabbinic Ethics* (2004); and Deborah Barer, "Rabbinic Literature" (2023).

On constructions of Jewish/Gentile difference, see Beth A. Berkowitz, *Defining Jewish Difference: From Antiquity to the Present* (2012); Mira Wasserman, *Jews, Gentiles, and Other Animals: The Talmud After the Humanities* (2017); and Adi Ophir and Ishay Rosen-Zvi, *Goy: Israel's Multiple Others and the Birth of the Gentile* (2018).

On gender, see Miriam Peskowitz, *Spinning Fantasies: Rabbis, Gender, and History* (1997); Judith R. Baskin, *Midrashic Women: Formations of the Feminine in Rabbinic Literature* (2002); and Max K. Strassfeld, *Trans Talmud: Androgynes and Eunuchs in Rabbinic Literature* (2022a).

On sexuality, see Daniel Boyarin, *Carnal Israel: Reading Sex in Talmudic Culture* (1993); and Michael L. Satlow, *Tasting the Dish: Rabbinic Rhetorics of Sexuality* (1995).

On disability, see Julia Watts Belser and Lennart Lehmhaus, "Disability in Rabbinic Judaism" (2016).

On animals, see Beth A. Berkowitz, *Animals and Animality in the Babylonian Talmud* (2018).

On environmental concerns, see Tanhum Yoreh, *Waste Not: A Jewish Environmental Ethic* (2019).

On war and settling the land of Israel, see Reuven Firestone, *Holy War in Judaism: The Fall and Rise of a Controversial Idea* (2012).

TWO VERSIONS OF MEDIEVAL JEWISH ETHICS

This chapter considers two bodies of medieval Jewish literature that are often viewed as central to Jewish ethics: the writings of the philosopher Moses Maimonides in twelfth-century Egypt; and the literature known as the *Zohar*, written by a group of scholars—I will refer to them as "the Zoharic authors"—largely in thirteenth- and fourteenth-century Spain.

These two bodies of literature both proclaim the authority of the Rabbinic literature discussed in Chapter Two—the "Oral Torah," as put into writing in the Mishnah, the Talmuds, and collections of midrash. For the most part, both Maimonides and the Zoharic authors agree with the broad principles and practical conclusions about which Rabbinic literature was united. For example, neither Maimonides nor the Zoharic authors question the importance of deeds of lovingkindness, the value of cultivating qualities of mercy, or the Rabbinic model of compensation for injuries. Working from the understanding that these authors accept the validity of most of the ethical claims discussed in Chapter Two, this chapter focuses on some of the ways in which they depart from those claims or build on them in innovative ways. To facilitate comparison with the ideas discussed in Chapters Two and Five, I again focus on ideas about creation, revelation, and redemption, all of which are key categories for both Maimonides and the Zoharic authors.

I MAIMONIDES

MAIMONIDES ON GOD, ISRAEL, AND BEING FULLY HUMAN

Maimonides (Rabbi Moses ben Maimon, also known by the acronym Rambam) was born in Cordoba (Spain) in 1138. He fled

DOI: 10.4324/9781003271338-3

Spain after the Almohad conquest, lived in Morocco and the land of Israel, and settled in Egypt, where he served as a physician in the court of Saladin and a leader of Cairo's Jewish community. His writings include a commentary on the Mishnah (hereafter, *CM*); a systematic code of Jewish law, the *Mishneh Torah* (hereafter, *MT*); and a philosophical treatise, the *Guide of the Perplexed* (hereafter, *GP*).

Maimonides' thought was shaped not only by Rabbinic literature but also by philosophical writings from ancient Greece (the works of Plato and Aristotle) and medieval Baghdad (such as the writings of al-Farabi, a Muslim philosopher who himself drew on Aristotle and Plato).

Maimonides' view of God is particularly inspired by Plato's "idea of the good": an abstract ideal of perfect goodness that transcends any goodness in the world. Maimonides depicts God in these terms—as pure goodness or, to put it differently, pure intellect. But believing that God transcends human language, Maimonides argues that God can only truly be described by what God is not. Above all, he emphasizes that God is not a being. God does not have a body, a personality, or emotions, and God does not do anything that would require a body or emotions. God does not move things around in the world, nor does God speak, choose people, or fall in love with people. Any such claims about God are only metaphors. When, for example, the Bible says that God chose the patriarch Abraham to be the founder of a new people, what it really means is that Abraham, relying on his reason, chose God and then created a new community that would be devoted to God—to the good. Abraham's descendants—the people of Israel—are heir to Abraham's insights regarding God and above all to the insights of the Written and Oral Torah of the prophet Moses (Kellner 2006: 79–81).

For Maimonides, the Torah's insights provide the people of Israel with a superior path to achieving the good life and closeness to God. But there is nothing essentially different about the people of Israel that gives them a status inherently higher than other peoples, as all human beings are created in God's image and can therefore access God's goodness. Maimonides begins his *Guide of the Perplexed* by arguing that the "image of God" reflects a power of "intellectual apprehension" (*GP* 1:1). He sees the stories at the start of the Biblical book of Genesis not in historical terms but as teaching what it means to be human (Klein–Braslavy 2011: 80), including what it means to be in "the image of God":

> The intellect that God made overflow unto the human and that is the latter's ultimate perfection, was that which the human had been provided with before he disobeyed. It was because of this that it was said of him that he was created in the image of God and in His likeness ... Through the intellect one distinguishes between truth and falsehood, and that was found in the human in its perfection and integrity.
>
> (GP 1:2)

For Maimonides, those who are not Jewish can also reach the highest levels of intellect, even becoming prophets (Kasher 2019: 56). In identifying the intellect with the image of God, then, he rejects Rabbinic traditions that see only Jews as created in God's image.

Maimonides believes that women (at least exceptional women) can also reach the highest levels of intellect, and so he seems to also reject Rabbinic traditions that see only men as created in God's image. And in contrast to Rabbinic interpreters of the Garden of Eden story, Maimonides does not view the Garden of Eden story as involving human beings of different genders at all; rather, he understands it as an allegory about how human beings can go astray. The male character in the story (Adam) represents "form" (intellect), and the female character (Eve) represents "matter," in line with the gendering of form and matter that Maimonides attributes to Plato (GP 1:18). Drawing on the Rabbinic midrash describing the first human being as androgynous, Maimonides views the story as involving not two human beings but two different parts of the human being (intellect and matter), who can be tempted by imagination (represented by the serpent) (GP 2:30; Klein–Braslavy 2011: 147–60). Any human being, in this model, can resist temptation and follow the intellect—the true "form" of the human, and the image of God.

On the other hand, the allegory signals the superiority of the male over the female by using the male to symbolize the intellect and image of God and the female to symbolize the matter that should be controlled by the intellect (Kasher 2019: 48). This symbolism is in keeping with Maimonides' general tendency to view women as inferior to men. He describes women as "prone to anger, being easily affected and having weak souls," and follows the Rabbinic assumption that men should have authority over women (*GP* 3:48). Given their "natural" tendencies, Maimonides indicates that women will find high levels of intellectual achievement very difficult, though he also indicates that such levels are possible to attain—as shown by the figure of Miriam, who was a prophet, meaning that she attained the highest levels of intellectual virtue (Kasher 2019: 54).

Viewing intellectual attainment as necessary for being fully human, Maimonides also depicts people with intellectual disabilities as inferior (Belser 2016: 101). Moreover, following al-Farabi and other Muslim philosophers, he subscribes to a theory of climate according to which people from "extreme" climates—the far north, with its cold climate, or the far south, with its hot climate—are unable to develop the intellectual capacities that make human beings human. When Maimonides offers his Parable of the Palace, depicting God as a king within a palace and people located at various distances from him, he describes those from the far north and south as especially distant from God—in the parable, outside the king's city—because they lack the capacity for understanding foundational truths:

> Those who are outside the city are all human individuals who have no doctrinal belief … such individuals as the furthermost Turks found in the remote North, the Blacks found in the remote South, and those who resemble them from among them that are with us in these climes. The status of those is like that of irrational animals. To my mind they do not have the rank of men, but have among the beings a rank lower than the rank of man but higher than the rank of apes. For they have the external shape and lineaments of a man and a faculty of discernment that is superior to that of the apes.

> (*GP* 3:51)

Being fully human appears linked not just with geography but with skin color, as Maimonides views black people from sub-Saharan Africa ("the South"), and perhaps also white people from Europe and Asia ("the North"), as intellectually inferior. Even though Maimonides may elsewhere stress the equality of all humans, he does not count all human beings as within the category of "human," in line with the "scientific" views that were widespread among philosophers in the Middle East and Mediterranean regions (Melamed 2003: 139–48).

MAIMONIDES ON ORDINARY ETHICS VS. KNOWING GOD

Even those people whom Maimonides views without these prejudices, however, are also depicted as very distant from God. In his Parable of the Palace, Maimonides describes many groups of Jews who are in some ways inferior to the aforementioned groups, such as people with "incorrect opinions," who may deserve death, in certain circumstances, lest they lead others astray; those who frequently think about God but do so without knowledge are also very far from the palace. Most Jews who are fully obedient to halakhah are also unable to even see the palace. Those Torah scholars whose ideas are shaped by "traditional authority" rather than philosophical inquiry are able to wander around the palace grounds but cannot find the entrance. Only a small number of people are able to enter the palace, let alone enter the king's chambers, let alone catch a glimpse of the king (*GP* 3:51).

The allegory of the Garden of Eden also makes it clear that humanity has by and large lost its intellectual capacity—the power to distinguish truth from falsehood and follow truth rather than following mere human conventions. In the allegory, the first human beings lose their focus on truth and falsehood as they seek to "know good and evil" (Bible, Genesis 3:5), which Maimonides understands as referring to matters of subjective opinion and convention rather than objective truth. The "fall" of human beings comes when humans turn towards that which is merely conventional and "generally accepted" (*GP* 1:2; Weiss 2021).

One might wonder whether Maimonides is denigrating the value of all human affairs, including ethics and politics, that deal with issues of subjective opinion and convention rather than with the purely intellectual realm. Indeed, insofar as ethics and politics are matters of mere subjectivity, Maimonides does view them as inferior pursuits. But at the conclusion of the *Guide of the Perplexed*, he describes an ideal of human intellectual perfection that does seem to culminate in ethics.

Maimonides bases his conclusion on a Biblical passage in which God is said to declare:

> Let not the wise man glory in his wisdom, neither let the mighty man glory in his might, let not the rich man glory in his riches; but only in this should one glory: that he understands and knows Me, that I am the Lord who exercises lovingkindness, judgment and righteousness on earth, for in these things I delight.
>
> (Bible, Jeremiah 9:22–23)

Maimonides explains that human perfection does not occur through "riches" (wealth) or through "might" (physical strength) or through any ordinary "wisdom" (which Maimonides identifies with that which is "generally accepted"—i.e. ordinary ethics). Rather, human perfection requires intellectual knowledge of God—and the greatest form of intellectual apprehension seems to culminate with human beings, causing God's attributes of lovingkindness, righteousness, and judgment to be exercised on earth. "The way of life of such an individual, after he has achieved this apprehension," Maimonides concludes, "will always have in view lovingkindness, righteousness, and judgment" (GP 3:54). Ordinary ethics are a sign of the human fall from their original state in the Garden of Eden; but intellectual apprehension of God can be regained through an understanding of God that results in acts of lovingkindness, righteousness, and justice (Weiss 2021: 58–9).

MAIMONIDES ON THE TORAH OF MOSES

Maimonides contends that Moses was the greatest of prophets because he had perfected all of the intellectual virtues and all of the ethical virtues that are possible for a human being to perfect. On Mount Sinai, he was thus able to perceive God as clearly as is possible (CM Avot, Introduction, ch. 7). While Moses discovered that he could not see God's "face" (Bible, Exodus 33:20), meaning that he could not see God's essence, all of God's "goodness" passed before him (Bible, Exodus 33:19), meaning that he could behold all that exists in the world, in all of its goodness:

> "All my goodness" alludes to the display to him of all existing things of which it is said: "And God saw every thing that He had made, and, behold, it was very good" (Bible, Genesis 1:31). By their display, I mean that he will apprehend their nature and the way they are mutually

connected so that he will know how He governs them in general and in detail ... Accordingly, the apprehension of these actions is an apprehension of His attributes ... : "compassionate and gracious, slow to anger ..." (Bible, Exodus 34:6–7).

(GP 1:54)

Moses, it seems, perceives all that exists and how the world works, and what he beholds are divine attributes (or "actions") of graciousness, mercy, and lovingkindness. Crucially, Maimonides explains, Moses' goal is not to satisfy his curiosity but to emulate these divine attributes in governing the people of Israel—"to perform actions in governing them that I must seek to make similar to Your actions," Maimonides imagines Moses saying to God (*GP* 1:54). The divine attributes provide not only a model for the people in developing their own virtues but a model that Moses can use in governing the people of Israel and guiding them towards goodness (Kreisel 1999: 14–6, 80–1).

Maimonides views the Torah of Moses, which properly governs the people of Israel, as entirely rational: each of its hundreds of commandments must aim at one of three rational purposes: conveying truths about the universe (or preventing incorrect ideas); ensuring social justice (or preventing injustice); and instilling moral virtue within human beings (or preventing vice) (*GP* 3:31). The Torah cannot simply demand high levels of thought, politics, and virtue, however, but must work with people as they are—with their culturally-conditioned traditions and their resistance to quick change. Indeed, it is a general principle for Maimonides that "man, according to his nature, is not capable of abandoning suddenly all to which he was accustomed" (*GP* 3:31). Hence the exodus from Egypt was a slow and roundabout process, since a good deal of time in the desert was required for the people of Israel to cultivate courage and cast off their slavishness; and hence the commandments that were given to the people of Israel at Sinai included only what the people of Israel were capable of taking on. They were commanded to worship God by sacrificing animals, for example, because this was one of "practices to which they were accustomed" (*GP* 3:32). Though elsewhere Maimonides speaks of the Torah's perfection, he here recognizes that it is filled with concessions and imperfections. What makes it divine, however, is that it aims at human perfection (Halbertal 2021: 250–62).

Maimonides understands the commandments of the Torah in terms of law—a system that can be codified (as Maimonides does himself in the *Mishneh Torah*) without the disagreements found in Rabbinic literature. And he sees the Torah's laws as supporting rational purposes, including the ethical purposes of ensuring social justice or cultivating moral character. Laws related to compensation for injury, for example, serve to combat injustice. Laws mandating punishment more generally deter aggression, ensure order, and show mercy for the vulnerable (*GP* 3.35). The Mishnah's ruling to protect a woman's life over that of a fetus that is threatening her life (before its head emerges from her vagina) is reformulated in terms of justice by describing the fetus as a life-threatening "pursuer" to whom no pity should be shown (*MT Murderer and the Preservation of Life* 1:9). All of the commandments of the Torah relating to interpersonal ethics ultimately contribute to "the bestowal of lovingkindness" (*CM Peah* 1:1).

Maimonides views many of the commandments of the Torah as explicitly aiming at cultivating moral character. For example, the commandment prohibiting causing unnecessary suffering to non-human animals, which includes a prohibition on killing for sport,

> is set down with a view to perfecting us so that we should not acquire moral habits of cruelty and should not inflict pain needlessly without any utility, but that we should intend to be kind and merciful even with a chance animal individual, except in case of need ... for we must not kill out of cruelty or for sport.
>
> (*GP* 3:17)

The Torah's prohibitions on eating meat unless it is slaughtered in the most painless manner, or on slaughtering a mother and her young on the same day, or on taking a mother bird's eggs or chicks before her eyes, are also linked with the prohibition on causing suffering, and so to the concern with building habits of cruelty. In these contexts, Maimonides points to the importance of sensitivity to the suffering of non-human animals, as "animals feel very great pain, there being no difference regarding the pain between man and the other animals." Also, "the reason for the prohibition against eating a limb [cut off] a living animal is because this would make one acquire the habit of cruelty" (*GP* 3:48). Maimonides sees human consumption of animals as justified by health concerns, but he sees the Torah's regulations as ensuring compassion and reducing cruelty (Weiss 1989). Maimonides' concerns for non-human animals may be linked with his conviction that, according to the Torah, all species "have been intended for their own sakes," not to serve human beings (GP 3:13; Goodman 2002: 243–5).

Among the Torah's other laws that aim at shaping moral character are laws regulating sexual relations, which include the prohibitions in Rabbinic literature on incest, bestiality, adultery (a man having sex with a married woman, as polygamy is permitted), sex during menstruation, sex between Jews and Gentiles, male homosexual intercourse, and male ejaculation outside of permitted heterosexual intercourse. Rabbinic literature also includes a prohibition against lesbian marriage, noted in Chapter Two, and Maimonides built on this to explicitly prohibit lesbian sex as one of the forbidden "practices of the land of Egypt" (MT Forbidden Intercourse 21:8; Greenberg 2004: 88–90). The goal of all such laws regulating sex is to promote virtues of self-control and decrease desire—"to bring about a decrease of sexual intercourse and to diminish the desire for mating as far as possible" (GP 3:35). The requirement for Jewish men to be circumcised also serves to weaken their sexual excitement and decrease the vice of lust (GP 3:49; Stern 2013: 338–9).

In addition to such commandments that diminish vice and build character, Maimonides also sees an overarching commandment to cultivate virtue: one must "continually appraise one's character traits and evaluate them and direct them in the middle way so that one becomes perfect." One should "habituate oneself" to actions that build good character traits:

> Time after time, he shall perform actions in accordance with the character traits that are in the mean. He shall repeat them continually until performing them is easy for him and they are not burdensome and these character traits are firmly established in his soul.
>
> (MT Dispositions 1:7)

Maimonides invokes the Biblical injunction to "walk in God's ways" (Bible, Deuteronomy 28:9) as well as the Rabbinic tradition of emulating divine virtues that we saw in Chapter Two, while also invoking Aristotle's understanding of habituation and

Aristotle's doctrine of the mean—that virtue is a "middle way" that avoids both vices of excess and vices of deficiency. For example, one should not be gluttonous, but neither should one be overly ascetic and deprive one's body of what it needs: the middle way is that one should "only desire the things which the body needs and without which it is impossible to live" (*MT Dispositions* 1:4–6). To avoid arrogance, however, one should seek not "moderation" but extreme humility, perhaps given the natural human inclination towards haughtiness (MT *Dispositions* 2:3), and one should accept insults and humiliation while never insulting, humiliating, or oppressing others (MT *Dispositions* 5:13).

Maimonides characterizes those with bad character traits—vices—as possessing sick souls, and he teaches that "those with sick souls need to seek out the wise men, who are the physicians of the soul" (*CM Avot*, Introduction, ch. 3). Such physicians can prescribe habituating oneself to actions that counteract vices and bring the soul to health. People are not naturally inclined towards vice, in Maimonides' view, and even those who grew up habituated to evil actions can achieve significant moral virtue. Still, Maimonides does imply that achieving virtue is particularly difficult for those who do not follow the Torah, including those who are not Jewish. At one point, he quotes the Rabbinic text (cited in Chapter Two) claiming that the serpent's "filth" remains among Gentiles but was removed for the people of Israel at Sinai. For Maimonides, this text suggests that Gentiles, lacking access to the Torah, are generally unable to attain significant moral virtue. While in theory any human being can attain full virtue, those without the Torah are likely to be at a low moral level (*GP* 2:30; Kellner 1990: 28–9).

This assumption may undergird Maimonides' acceptance of Rabbinic laws that discriminate between Jews and Gentiles. In justifying one such case of discrimination, Maimonides teaches:

> Do not be troubled by this matter and do not be shocked by it, just as you aren't shocked by the slaughter of animals, even though they did nothing wrong. For one whose human characteristics are not perfected is not truly a human being.
>
> (*CM Bava Kamma* 4:3; Kasher 2019: 63)

Viewing the path of Torah as the best path to perfection, Maimonides therefore recommends joining the people of Israel—conversion—as the ideal for those not born Jewish. In contrast to Rabbinic literature, as discussed in Chapter Two, Maimonides speaks of the obligation to love the convert without any concerns about the convert's negative inclinations (*MT Dispositions* 6:4) and rather than viewing converts with suspicion views them as exemplary for their commitment to walking in God's ways (Diamond 2007: 16–8).

MAIMONIDES ON ETHICS IN A REDEEMED WORLD

Maimonides describes the Days of the Messiah as an ideal era not only for the people of Israel but for all of the nations of the world, who "will all return to the true law," such that "the occupation of the entire world will be to know God" (*MT Kings and Wars* 12:1, 12:5). With this phrasing, Maimonides seems to indicate that it would be ideal for all the people of the world to convert to the path of Torah established by Moses, realizing the ideal nature of its "true law." He does not, however, envision that all people in the world would be *forced* to observe the Torah, and indicates that it would be sufficient for all people to observe the seven laws first given in the Garden of Eden and to Noah—the "Noahide commandments" (Kreisel 2015: 19–39). Maimonides understands all human beings as obligated to follow the seven commandments named by Rabbi Yoḥanan in the Talmud: to establish courts of law and to refrain from murder, robbery, forbidden sexual relations, blasphemy, and eating the limbs of living animals. In his *Mishneh Torah*, Maimonides presents these as laws for all humanity and codifies most of the Talmud's discriminatory standards vis-à-vis Jews and Gentiles—for example, judging a Gentile as guilty of murder for killing a fetus, though this is permitted for Jews (*MT Kings and Wars* 9:1–14).

While Maimonides does not envision forcing the inhabitants of the world to convert to the path of the Torah (though Jews should be forced to observe the Torah, Gentiles should not), he does write that all Gentiles should be forced to accept the seven Noahide laws: "Moses was commanded by God to force all in the world to accept the commandments enjoined upon the descendants of Noah. Anyone who does not accept them is put to death" (*MT Kings and*

Wars 8:10). This is in line with his vision that a Jewish king should refrain from war with nations that submit to the Noahide commandments and accept a condition of inferior status and servitude (to the extent required by the king); war should proceed, however, against any nations that refuse these conditions, and all of their adult males should be put to death (or women and children as well when fighting Canaanites and Amalekites, the latter of whom Maimonides sees as continuing to exist in his day) (*MT Kings and Wars* 5:1, 6:1, 6:4; Horowitz 2006: 129–34). Maimonides' vision is grounded in Biblical and Rabbinic sources, though it departs from Rabbinic literature in its focus on compelling fulfillment of the Noahide commandments, perhaps influenced in part by certain Islamic conceptions of war (Blidstein 2001; Stroumsa 2009: 78).

Maimonides, notably, presents the figure of the Messiah—not God—as the one who will institute justice and "fight the wars of God" (*MT Kings and Wars* 11:4). He does not describe God as "sending" the Messiah, as Rabbinic literature often does, but instead implies, as scholars Menachem Kellner and David Gillis (2020: 283) have put it, that "it is up to humans to bring the messiah." It appears that what Maimonides describes as characterizing the Days of the Messiah—the wars of God, the end of subjugation to other nations, the ingathering of Jews to the Messiah's kingdom in the land of Israel, the rebuilding of the Jerusalem Temple and the reestablishment of animal sacrifices there, and eventually an era of peace and prosperity that allows for philosophical contemplation—are all things that human beings can bring about.

The redeemed world that Maimonides envisions is not radically different from the present world. Maimonides quotes the Rabbinic dictum suggesting that aside from the end of subjugation things will not be different in the Days of the Messiah, and he indicates that poverty will still exist (Kraemer 2008: 355). He clearly accepts Rabbinic teachings that imagine other nations kowtowing to the people of Israel, but he cautions that dominating other nations is not a worthy goal:

> The sages and prophets did not long for the Days of the Messiah so that they might exercise dominion over the whole world, or rule over the nations, or be exalted by the peoples, or to eat, drink, and celebrate, but rather so that they would be free to be devoted to Torah and its wisdom, with no one to oppress or disturb them.
>
> (*MT Kings and Wars* 12:4)

It appears that human beings have a duty to work to bring about this redeemed world, and occasionally Maimonides suggests that they should do so, as when he writes of how giving charity to those in need is necessary for redemption (*MT Gifts to the Poor* 10:1). He also does not codify the Rabbinic tradition that it is forbidden to move to the land of Israel before the time of redemption. Unlike some other interpreters of Rabbinic tradition, however, Maimonides does not include conquering the land of Israel or settling in the land in his list of commandments of the Torah; and, citing the people of Israel's oath not to settle the land of Israel, he cautions the Jews of Yemen to endure suffering and refrain from messianic fervor (Hartman 1985b: 167–8). It may also be significant that Maimonides argues that there is nothing inherently holy about the land of Israel. He depicts the land of Israel as sanctified by the people of Israel, and he expresses deep love of the land, but he does not appear to have the commitment to settling the land held by those who view it as inherently holy (Kellner 2006: 107–15; Firestone 2012: 125–33).

II THE *ZOHAR*

THE *ZOHAR* ON GOD, ISRAEL, AND BEING FULLY HUMAN

The *Zohar* provides counterpoints to a number of Maimonides' ethical ideas. While its authors share some of Maimonides' assumptions, including his assumption that Rabbinic literature is authoritative and that Biblical and Rabbinic texts must be decoded to reveal deeper truths, the *Zohar* offers some very different understandings of how to live, shaped by different ideas about creation, revelation, and redemption.

The *Zohar* was not published as a book until the sixteenth century, but most of it appears to have been composed by a group of anonymous authors in thirteenth- and fourteenth-century Spain, especially in Castile, under Christian rule, incorporating Rabbinic traditions as well as Christian, Gnostic, and Neoplatonic ideas. The *Zohar* presents itself, however, as having been composed in the land of Israel in the second century CE, and it narrates the experiences and insights of Rabbis from that place and time. Seen by its adherents as an ancient text—and as recording secrets first revealed to Adam at the dawn of creation and to Moses at Mount Sinai—the *Zohar* became foundational to an esoteric approach to Jewish tradition that came to be called "Kabbalah," meaning "received tradition," and whose adherents are known as "Kabbalists."

One of the secrets that the *Zohar* purports to reveal is that God should be identified with ten divine powers or personae (*sefirot*; Berman 2018: 8–10), each of which is associated with various words used to describe God in Biblical and Rabbinic literature, as well as different parts of the divine body. The upper powers include Keter (Crown), Ḥokhmah (Wisdom) and Binah (Understanding). Below these is a central group of powers gendered as male and described as the "Holy Blessed One," which include Ḥesed (Lovingkindness), Gevurah or Din (Might or Judgment), Tiferet (Beauty), Netzaḥ (Endurance), Hod (Majesty), and Yesod (Foundation, identified with the circumcised, divine phallus). At the bottom of the ten powers, and cut off from the rest of them, is God's female aspect, Malkhut (Kingdom), also known as the "daughter," "bride," "queen," or "divine presence" (Shekhinah), and identified with the land and people of Israel.

Whereas Maimonides emphasized that God is indivisible—the perfection that is beyond all division—the Zoharic authors imagined God divided into these various powers. Whereas Maimonides rejected the idea that God has a body or a gender, the Zoharic authors see God as embodied and imagined God as, for the most part, male (though including female powers). Notably, the Zoharic authors also imagine the people of Israel as the feminine part of God's body, while imagining the central part of God's body as looking just like the body of a circumcised, Jewish man, who seeks marriage, sexual union and mastery over his bride. The male body of God should be dominant over the female aspect of the divine, Malkhut, which should be absorbed within the male (Wolfson 1994). When in proper relation to the male body of God, Malkhut calls out: "I care only to be lying under You, with You ruling over Me" (*Zohar Ḥadash* 65c).

The human being was created as a replica of this "image of God," containing both male and female—but with the female in the subordinate position, "contained within the male" (*Zohar* 3:19a; Wolfson 1994: 175). The image of God is only reflected in a proper union of an Israelite man and Israelite woman; without such a union, a man "is not in the category of 'human'" (*Zohar* 3:5b). Adam and Eve—imagined as the founders of the people of Israel when they were first created—constituted "the complete image" in their sexual union (*Zohar* 1:19b), prior to Eve's illicit intercourse with the serpent in the garden of Eden that brought corruption and filth to the world. But proper, procreative heterosexual intercourse among Adam and Eve's Israelite descendants can restore blessing and joy to the world: "when a male unites with a female everything is one body, and all the worlds are joyous, for everything is blessed from the complete body" (*Zohar* 3:296a). Such sex, within marriage and guided by the commandments of the Torah, is in fact able to bring about the union of the male and female aspects of God and to weaken the demonic forces that threaten that divine union (Koren 2011: 70).

Male circumcision is also required to reflect the "image of God," as the *Zohar* builds on the idea first found in Rabbinic literature that Adam was created circumcised (*Tikkunei Ha-Zohar* 69, 116b). Adam, however, sought to undo his circumcision, stretching the skin on his penis to create a new foreskin, such that "he abandoned the holy covenant, cleaved to the foreskin, was seduced by the word of the serpent" (*Zohar* 1:35b). Adam's refusal of circumcision damages the "conduit through which blessings flow and gush to the world," the power of Yesod, the divine phallus which makes creation possible, and his sin empowered the demonic realm (*Zohar* 1:56a). But Adam's descendants, when they properly circumcise their sons, have the power to restore the flow of blessings, restoring the connection between Yesod and Malkhut and keeping demonic forces at bay (Wolfson 1987).

In Chapter Two, we saw that Rabbinic literature had framed the importance of both heterosexual marriage and circumcision by linking them with narratives about creation. The *Zohar* reworks these traditions with its vision of how proper behaviors directly influence the divine realm. Human behaviors such as these are not merely means to social, moral, and intellectual ends, as they are for Maimonides; instead, they have the power to restore the connection between the masculine and feminine parts of God that have—ever since the sins in the Garden of Eden—been separated from each other. Indeed, each righteous act that a Jew performs can help restore this connection, empowering the divine and bringing the cosmos closer to redemption. Conversely, each sin that a Jew commits, including a failure to marry properly or a failure to perform the commandment of male circumcision, strengthens the realm of the demonic.

Whereas Maimonides rejects beliefs in demonic forces, the Zoharic authors see the demonic realm as very real and very powerful. This realm is commonly described as "the other side," a realm that exists in parallel to the realm of the divine. Whereas the divine body described above is holy, good, and pure, the other side is an impure, evil, and "profane shadow," sometimes described as containing its own set of ten powers that parallel the ten powers of the divine body. Just as the divine body has a powerful male aspect and a female bride who may receive his flow, so too the demonic body has a powerful male aspect—Samael or Satan—and his female bride, Lilith. Since Malkhut, the bride on the side of holiness, is separated from her groom, she is easily captured by the demonic, and indeed the *Zohar* (3:282a) describes her in Samael's prison. The Zoharic authors' concern about the susceptibility of the divine feminine corresponds to their concerns that women are susceptible to evil, especially when menstruating, as menstruation is closely linked with demonic evil and impurity (Koren 2011).

Gentile nations are linked even more strongly with evil and impurity: the *Zohar* consistently describes these nations as part of the demonic "other side." We see this, for example, in one explanation of Genesis 1:24, "Let the earth bring forth: living beings, according to their kind; [and] cattle, creeping things, and wild beasts of every kind." "Living beings" refers to Israel, "who are souls of the supernal, holy living being." "Cattle, creeping things, and wild beasts" refers to "the other nations, who are not souls of the living being, but rather 'foreskin'"—that is, the demonic (*Zohar* 1:46b–47a). The people of Israel, who are a part of the divine (Malkhut), possess holy souls; the other nations have no such souls but are fundamentally impure and less than fully human (Wolfson 2006: 88–9).

We saw that some Rabbinic sources depicted Gentiles as created in God's image and called by the term "human" (*adam*), while other Rabbinic sources indicate that only the people of Israel were created in God's image and called "human." The *Zohar* consistently takes the latter perspective, as it is Israelites—and above all, married, circumcised male Israelites—who share the image of the divine and to whom God says: "You are human; the other nations are not." By contrast, "the spirit spreading through the other nations emerges from the side of impurity. It is not human, and so does not attain this name" (*Zohar* 1:20b). In this understanding, Gentiles are not created in God's image and are not called "human" (Wolfson 2006: 53–4). The dehumanization of Gentiles here seems to parallel efforts by Christians, under whose rule the Zoharic authors lived, to demonize Jews (Wolfson 2006: 45–6).

These ideas seem to encourage the Zoharic authors to embrace the discriminatory Rabbinic standards differentiating between Jews and Gentiles (Wolfson 2006: 80–1). They also lead to rulings that Jews should not mix with Gentiles, building on Rabbinic warnings about contact with Gentiles (Chapter Two). The Zoharic authors find sex between Jews and Gentiles to be especially noxious, as it is not only prohibited (as agreed in Rabbinic literature) but contaminates the purity of the people of Israel and the divine realm of which they are a part: "a person must not mingle his image with the image of a Gentile, since one is holy and the other impure" (*Zohar* 3:104b; Wolfson 2006: 81).

THE *ZOHAR* ON THE TORAH OF MOSES

The *Zohar* refers at many points to the Talmudic narrative that when they received God's Torah at Mount Sinai the people of Israel were freed from the filth that has otherwise afflicted all human beings since Eve had sex with the serpent in the Garden of Eden. Building on the Rabbinic idea that women are exempt from some commandments of the Torah (e.g. time-sensitive practices that they would not be able to perform, for lack of control over their own time), one Zoharic passage concludes that God only addressed male Israelites at Mount Sinai: "Torah was given only to males, as it is written: 'This is the Torah that Moses set before the *sons* of Israel' (Bible, Deuteronomy 4:44), for women are exempt from commandments of Torah" (*Zohar* 1:126b). Women, there-fore—like Gentiles—remain infected with filth and inclined towards demonic evil of all sorts. One passage claims that "were they not prevented by Heaven, women would be murdering and killing the whole world continually, at every moment" (*Zohar Ḥadash* 81c). The authority of men, who received the Torah and were freed from the filth at Mount Sinai, is also key to preventing such outcomes.

The revelation at Sinai was only so powerful, though, even for men; in the *Zohar*'s narration, the male Israelites' sinful worship of a golden calf shortly after the revelation at Sinai restored tremendous power to the Other Side: "after they sinned they all slipped back into their filth as before." Israelite men, however, can again free themselves from the grip of the Other Side through obedience to the Torah. Women are less able to do so: "it is harder to eliminate filth from a woman than from a man" (*Zohar* 1:126b).

For the Zoharic authors, each of the specific commandments revealed at Mount Sinai is a mechanism by which Israelites can be freed from the grip of the Other Side. Properly performing each of the commandments helps to purify the feminine aspect of God of which Israel is a part and unite that feminine aspect with God's masculine aspects, while disobeying commandments deepens the separation of God's masculine and feminine aspects and strengthens the power of the Other Side. We saw this above with commandments prescribing circumcision and regulating sex, which are linked to the very nature of creation but are also included in the Torah revealed at Sinai. Notably, for the *Zohar*, such commandments are not linked with diminishing sexual desire and shaping moral character as they are for Maimonides; rather, their purpose is to directly strengthen the divine. Because the *Zohar* sees menstrual blood as demonic, it gives special emphasis to the evils of sex during menstruation (Koren 2011). It also views the ejaculation of semen outside of proper heterosexual intercourse as the most heinous sexual crime, describing wasting semen as murdering one's children and the one sin "for which one cannot repent" (*Zohar* 1:219b). Engaging in proper sexual behavior, however, weakens the Other Side and furthers redemption.

The same is true with other commandments. For example, whereas Maimonides viewed animal sacrifices as concessions that would serve as means to certain ends, the *Zohar* describes animal sacrifice as uniting God's masculine and feminine parts (Tishby 1989: 883). Whereas Maimonides framed a number of the Torah's laws pertaining to the use and slaughter of animals as decreasing cruelty, the *Zohar* refers to cosmic ramifications. Notably, it understands one of these laws as in fact encouraging cruelty towards animals in ways that benefit the people of Israel: one passage describes how shooing away a mother bird before taking her eggs or chicks will hopefully cause distress to the mother and to the guardian angel for birds, which will in turn cause God to reason that the people of Israel are far more deserving of compassion, and to do nothing for the bird but instead to show compassion towards Israel (*Tikkunei Ha-Zohar* 23a). This passage suggests that deliberately acting with cruelty towards an animal can help one's people (Slifkin 2021: 443–4).

Though the *Zohar* does not see the Torah's commandments aiming at the improvement of character as Maimonides does, it does see the development of moral character as important. Scholar Eitan Fishbane (2023) has argued that the central virtues that the *Zohar* encourages include: loving friendship, as can be cultivated by the men joined together in a common quest for divine wisdom; giving the benefit of the doubt to one's fellow Jews, who may turn out to be sources of wisdom, as are many of the strangers encountered by the Rabbis in the *Zohar*'s narrative; compassion and care towards those who are poor and vulnerable; unconditional forgiveness; and avoiding and controlling anger. The *Zohar* also presents Moses as a model of seeking mercy, admiring Moses for his willingness to sacrifice his life for the sake of his people as he demanded that God forgive them after the sin of the golden calf (*Zohar* 1:106a).

THE *ZOHAR* ON REDEMPTION

The *Zohar* also provides models for enmity towards those who are linked with the Other Side, as can be seen in its discussions of liberation from slavery in Egypt and the evils of the non-Israelite "mixed multitude" that accompanied the people of Israel as they were redeemed. The Zoharic authors describe the mixed multitude as the children of Lilith, representing the worst elements within the demonic realm, who were responsible for the sin of worshipping the golden calf. The *Zohar* further indicates that the mixed multitude continues to hide among the people of Israel and that their sinfulness continues to threaten Israel's purity. In each generation, it seems, one can find those who may seem to be Israelites but who are in fact part of the non-Israelite Other Side, ensnaring the people of Israel in sin (Tishby 1989: 1432–8).

And so while in some contexts the *Zohar* sees it as a virtue to give the benefit of the doubt to strangers, who may turn out to be hidden sages, in other contexts it sees it as a virtue to suspect strangers, who may turn out to be from the mixed multitude. One passage in the *Zohar* focused on the mixed multitude begins with a story whereby two Rabbinic companions, Rabbi Yitzḥak and Rabbi Yehudah, discover their fellow traveler, Yose, having sex with a Gentile woman. They realize that they should not have befriended Yose, and discover that he is in fact not Jewish and that his ancestry is suspect in multiple ways. They warn against becoming "friends and companions" with such evildoers, learning from the example of the misguided welcome given to the mixed multitude, who caused endless sin, suffering, death, and the loss of God's presence (*Zohar* 2:45b). Notably, in contrast to the teachings of Maimonides, the *Zohar* casts suspicion on anyone whose origins are with other nations, even converts who join the people of Israel, because "it is difficult to remove filth from them, even up to three generations" (*Zohar* 3:14b).

The pure people of Israel, however, even when they were enslaved in the place of greatest impurity—Egypt—were able to resist that impurity to a significant degree. With its characteristic focus on male sexual purity, the *Zohar* emphasizes how Israelite men were able to procreate, refraining from abortion or infanticide, while avoiding forbidden forms of sexual intercourse (with Gentile women or with menstruating Israelite women):

> Even though they were exiled in Egypt, they guarded themselves against all these three: a menstruant, a Gentile woman—and they persevered in procreation. For even though it had been decreed "Every son that is born you shall throw into the Nile" (Exodus 1:22), not a single one of them killed a fetus in a woman's belly—all the more so, afterward. By virtue of this, they came out of exile.

> (*Zohar* 2:4a)

Continuing to guard against such sins appears to be key to redemption from the current exile as well, as the authors of the *Zohar* hope that, like the people described in the Torah, the present-day people of Israel will be restored to the land of Israel.

The land of Israel has a particular prominence in the *Zohar*'s vision of future redemption. Unlike Maimonides, who described the land of Israel as sanctified by the people of Israel, the Zoharic authors depict the land as inherently holy. The land is the dwelling place for Malkhut, God's feminine presence, which "does not dwell outside the Land" (*Zohar* 2:5a). Only the people of Israel are worthy to live in the land, and only if they follow the commandments, but if Israel sins, then the Other Side is empowered to dominate Malkhut, "obtaining dominion over the Holy Land" and sending the people of Israel into exile (*Zohar* 1:210b). Returning to the land is essential for restoring Malkhut to relationship with the masculine realm, and so the Zoharic authors see living in the land as an urgent need. But, drawing on the model of redemption throughout Rabbinic literature, the *Zohar* does not imply that the people of Israel themselves could take political or military action to return to the land. While obedience to the commandments helps to bring about redemption, the full restoration of the people to the land is carried out by God.

In contrast to Maimonides' portrait of how the world will be redeemed by human action and without vengeance, resulting in a world not radically different from the present world, the *Zohar* emphasizes that messianic redemption will happen through supernatural means and through vengeance, bringing about a very different world. Its descriptions of redemption include descriptions of vengeance on those who persecuted Israel, including the mixed multitude (Tishby 1989: 1437–8). One passage emphasizes how only the true people of Israel—and only the sexually pure among them—will "remain and be inscribed for eternal life," whereas others will be "smashed" by God's fury, just as Pharaoh's army was smashed at the time of the exodus from Egypt (*Zohar* 2:57b). In addition to drawing on the narrative of the exodus from Egypt, the *Zohar* also draws on narratives of creation as it imagines how a redeemed world will restore the state of perfection before Adam and Eve's sin in the Garden of Eden (Scholem 1971: 40).

CONSIDERING MEDIEVAL JEWISH APPROACHES TO ETHICS

The *Zohar* offers a distinctive read on Rabbinic traditions, with its focus on the supernatural power of proper behavior, emphasis on sexual purity, and sharp distinctions between men and women and

Israelites and Gentiles. By comparison, Maimonides offers an ethics that, compared with the *Zohar*, is distinguished by its naturalism, its stress on the cultivation of intellectual and moral virtue, and its theoretical openness to women and Gentiles attaining virtue.

Considering Maimonides' writings and the *Zohar* with reference to their ideas of creation, revelation, and redemption allows us to see how they could develop different approaches to Jewish ethics despite their common commitment to the authority of Rabbinic literature. Other medieval Jews who also accepted this literature took different approaches. Still other medieval Jews, such as members of the group known as Karaites, rejected the authority of Rabbinic literature altogether and adopted rather different perspectives.

The ideas found in this chapter represent ideas that attained influence among significant numbers of Jews, but neither the approach of Maimonides nor the approach of the *Zohar* are representative of "Jewish ethics." While the ideas of Maimonides and the Zoharic authors are often referenced by contemporary Jews who make claims about Jewish ethics, many contemporary Jews reject the ideas found in this chapter, especially ideas that seem ethnocentric, misogynistic, homophobic, or racist, and they would deny that such ideas should have anything to do with "Jewish ethics." Still, the ideas found in this chapter have played an important role in modern Jewish discourse, whether in arguments about why such ideas should be accepted or in arguments about why such ideas should be rejected. In Chapter Five of this book, we will see examples of how modern Jews have both accepted and rejected ideas found in this chapter.

In Chapter Four, however, we will focus on modern Jewish thinkers who rejected the theological focus that has been central to these past two chapters, whose ethical judgments and ideas about Jewish ethics have been developed without reference to God at all.

FURTHER READING

For an introduction to Maimonides' ethics, see Raymond L. Weiss, *Maimonides' Ethics: The Encounter of Philosophic and Religious Morality* (1991).

On Maimonides' code of law, see Menachem Marc Kellner and David Gillis, *Maimonides the Universalist: The Ethical Horizons of the Mishneh Torah* (2020).

On Maimonides' political thought, see Howard T. Kreisel, *Maimonides' Political Thought: Studies in Ethics, Law, and the Human Ideal* (1999).

On Maimonides' view of women and Gentiles, see Hannah Kasher, "Maimonides on the Intellects of Women and Gentiles" (2019).

On Maimonides' understanding of Biblical narratives including the Garden of Eden story, see Sarah Klein-Braslavy, *Maimonides as a Biblical Interpreter* (2011).

For a contrast of Maimonides' approach with Kabbalistic (and proto-Kabbalistic) approaches, see Menachem Marc Kellner, *Maimonides' Confrontation with Mysticism* (2006).

For an introduction to the *Zohar*, see Arthur Green, *A Guide to the Zohar* (2004).

For a literary study of the *Zohar* that considers ethical issues, see Eitan P. Fishbane, *The Art of Mystical Narrative: A Poetics of the Zohar* (2018). On conceptions of virtue in the *Zohar*, see Eitan P. Fishbane, "The Zohar" (2023).

On the *Zohar*'s view of women, see Sharon Faye Koren, *Forsaken: The Menstruant in Medieval Jewish Mysticism* (2011); and Elliot R. Wolfson, "Woman—The Feminine as Other in Theosophic Kabbalah: Some Philosophical Observations on the Divine Androgyne" (1994).

On the *Zohar*'s view of Gentiles, see Elliot R. Wolfson, *Venturing Beyond: Law and Morality in Kabbalistic Mysticism* (2006).

On medieval Kabbalistic approaches that draw on the *Zohar*, see Joseph Dan, *Jewish Mysticism and Jewish Ethics* (1986); and Patrick B. Koch, *Human Self-Perfection: A Re-Assessment of Kabbalistic Musar-Literature of Sixteenth-Century Safed* (2015).

On other medieval Jewish approaches to ethics, see Hava Tirosh-Samuelson, *Happiness in Premodern Judaism: Virtue, Knowledge, and Well-Being* (2003); Steven M. Nadler and Tamar Rudavsky, eds., *The Cambridge History of Jewish Philosophy: From Antiquity Through the Seventeenth Century* (2009), part 6; Geoffrey D. Claussen, Alexander Green, and Alan L. Mittleman, eds., *Jewish Virtue Ethics* (2023), chapters 5–15.

MODERN JEWISH ETHICS
WITHOUT GOD

There are some contemporary Jews who claim that "Jewish ethics" consists almost entirely of the sorts of views described in the previous two chapters: the ethical claims found in Rabbinic literature, supplemented by the claims of prominent medieval thinkers who uphold that literature such as Maimonides and the authors of the *Zohar*. But modern Jews—Jews living in the late eighteenth, nineteenth, twentieth, and twenty-first centuries—have commonly disagreed with those ancient and medieval claims, and many have presented Jewish ethics in very different terms. These distinctly modern forms of Jewish ethics are the subject of this chapter and the following chapter.

This book defines modern Jewish ethics as ideas developed by Jews from the late eighteenth century to the present about how humans should live (especially in relation to others), shaped by Jewish tradition, experience, history, or identity. I contend that one of the most basic things to know about modern Jewish ethics is just how contested it has been. While I focused the previous two chapters on a small number of premodern texts that have been particularly influential—and "canonical" for many Jews, who view such texts as essential to Jewish ethics—there is no clear canon for modern Jewish ethics. Amidst massive social changes throughout the world, modern Jews have produced many disparate claims about how to live, and they have often been at odds with each other. Crucially, thanks to modern technologies, we have records of just how wide-ranging the perspectives of modern Jews have been. This chapter and the following chapter will seek to illustrate some of the diversity of these perspectives—focusing on many of

DOI: 10.4324/9781003271338-4

the same issues that we saw discussed in Chapters Two and Three, while seeking to show how these issues have been treated in very different ways by diverse modern Jews.

While the next chapter will focus on theological—that is, God-focused—accounts of Jewish ethics, this chapter will focus on secular forms of modern Jewish ethics. The word "secular" here describes non-theological forms of Jewish ethics: ideas that do not focus on God and that do not involve God-centered concepts of creation, revelation, and redemption. Instead, this chapter will be organized around a series of modern secular ethical ideas that have engaged many modern Jews. (The following chapter will show how some of these ideas have also been understood in theological terms.)

These include: ideas about the equality of all people (egalitarianism), including with regards to gender (feminism); ideas about the obligations that one has to all people (universalism or cosmopolitanism); ideas about how nations should have political autonomy or sovereignty (nationalism), including the idea that Jews should have such power in the land of Israel (Zionism); and ideas about human obligations to the non-human environment (environmentalism).

The notion that ideas might constitute "Jewish ethics" without referencing God remains contentious for reasons discussed in Chapter One. In particular, some people have felt very strongly that authentic Jewish ethics must be theological or "religious," or that at least it must engage with theologically-oriented traditions found in Biblical or Rabbinic literature. But many Jews have claimed otherwise, and this chapter seeks to recognize those claims, in keeping with my commitment to introducing readers to the diversity of how Jewish ethics has been constructed.

THE EMERGENCE OF DIVERSE MODERN JEWISH ETHICS

How have modern Jews come to hold such a wide variety of perspectives? For one thing, Jews in the modern era have lived in every part of the world, influenced by a wide variety of ideas in a variety of political, social, and cultural contexts. Many Jews have viewed their interest in these ideas as shaped by their Jewish identities and experiences and have felt empowered to view these ideas as part of Jewish tradition.

In many respects, there is nothing new about Jews viewing new ideas stemming from various cultures as part of their own tradition. The editors of the Bible felt empowered to present a wide variety of ideas—including some that can be viewed as Canaanite, Babylonian, and Persian—as part of their Israelite tradition. We saw in Chapter Two that the Rabbis employed a wide variety of ideas—including Greek, Roman, and Zoroastrian ideas—in their literature. In Chapter Three, we noted that Maimonides and the *Zohar* introduced other new ideas to Jewish tradition that seem to stem from other traditions. Modern Jews have pointed to such precedents as they have adopted ideas stemming from various modern cultural contexts—such as egalitarianism, nationalism, or environmentalism—and presented those ideas as Jewish.

Many modern Jews, however, have been far more open about adopting new ideas and have not claimed deference to received traditions in the way that the Rabbis, Maimonides, or the authors of the *Zohar* did. Beginning in the late eighteenth century, as social and political structures that kept premodern Jews in more insular environments were weakened, many modern Jews have openly rejected established Jewish traditions. In countries such as the United States and France, government recognition of Jews as citizens possessing individual liberties—rather than as members of a Jewish community bound to the authority structures of that community—provided the freedom for Jews to challenge rabbinic authorities and other communal norms. Enlightenment-era ideals of rationalism, skepticism about tradition, empiricism, and individualism were deeply appealing to some Jewish intellectuals. The seventeenth-century philosopher Benedict (Baruch) Spinoza, who was excommunicated from the Jewish community of Amsterdam for his "horrible heresies" (his rejection of the authority of the Bible and the Rabbis, supernaturalism, and conventional ideas of God), was one source of inspiration for new Jewish traditions. While Spinoza did not frame his teachings as Jewish teachings, Jews beginning in the nineteenth century depicted him as a Jewish hero and a source for the development of non-Rabbinic and naturalistic Jewish teachings (Schwartz 2012).

Spinoza was an early example of a Jewish thinker who rejected the idea that the Bible was God's word. In later centuries, an understanding that the Bible was written by human beings whose perspectives need not be authoritative for shaping Jewish tradition became common among Jews. It has been even more common for Jews to question the authority of Rabbinic literature, a view that gained particular traction with the rise of the Reform movement in the nineteenth century. Challenges to the authority of these texts went hand in hand with looking to other authorities, which might include not only those identified as Jewish leaders (e.g. rabbis or communal leaders) but philosophers, historians, and political leaders. Beginning in the late eighteenth century, an emphasis on the authority of the State also emerged among Jewish intellectuals, who appreciated the government recognition and rights extended to Jews in the United States and parts of Europe. Other Jewish intellectuals of this era often stressed how moral ideals could be grounded in reason alone. Salomon Maimon, for example, was a prominent European Jewish philosopher who drew on Spinoza and the philosopher Immanuel Kant as he argued for reliance on reason and skepticism towards claims of divine revelation (Rosenstock 2014).

Other Jews appealed to history in crafting their ethical arguments. Historical methods were of particular interest to nineteenth-century European Jewish intellectuals, who sought to show that Jewish tradition was historically shaped rather than divinely ordained; some of these intellectuals also valued Jewish history because of the way that it provided models for the development of Jewish tradition in the present. The Bohemian historian Peter Beer, for example, challenged the authority of Rabbinic Judaism by pointing to the diverse array of ancient Judaisms; he also pointed to historical precedents in Jewish history for assimilating into other cultures in the way that he thought Jews should do in the present day (Meyer 1988b; Hecht 2005). The German intellectual Isaac Euchel argued that through the study of history, "one strengthens his ability to distinguish between truth and falsehood as well as to improve his moral qualities" (Meyer 1988b). In growing numbers, Jews began to point to diverse ethical lessons that could be learned from historical study, contributing to the diversification of Jewish ethics.

Another value that some Jewish thinkers began to champion in the late eighteenth century was individual autonomy. Individualism was hardly a value in premodern Rabbinic literature, which generally presupposed that God revealed a Torah at Sinai addressed to the people of Israel as a community rather than as individuals. But

European Enlightenment ideas about individual conscience and autonomy were of interest to a growing number of modern Jews beginning in the late eighteenth century, especially those who celebrated the recognition of Jews as individual citizens with individual liberties. For some Jews, Spinoza's defense of individual autonomy served as an inspiration (Schwartz 2012). The idea that individualism was an important Jewish value gained popularity over time, such that by the twentieth century the scientist Albert Einstein (1935) could identify "personal independence" as a key feature of Jewish tradition, and Jews sometimes appealed to individual conscience as they developed new and diverse approaches to ethics.

Many of the thinkers (including Maimon, Euchel, and Beer) who championed rationalism, historical inquiry, and individualism were associated with the eighteenth- and nineteenth- century "Haskalah," a Jewish European intellectual movement often referred to as the "Jewish Enlightenment," since it drew on the ideas of the broader European Enlightenment. As historian Olga Litvak (2012) has argued, the Haskalah is better understood as a Jewish Romantic movement, connected to the European Romantic movement. Its adherents sometimes championed rationalism and individualism, but many also appreciated emotion, imagination, and community. The Haskalah supported Jewish integration into non-Jewish societies while also seeking to strengthen Jewish identity. It often promoted values including moral universalism and egalitarianism; liberal politics; loyalty to the State; the idea of Judaism as a "religion" (rather than a national identity); and a commitment to general (not specifically Jewish) education. While Haskalah intellectuals were, for the most part, deeply committed to ideas of God and the theological categories of creation, revelation, and redemption (as discussed in Chapter Five), they also developed ideas that shaped secular Jewish discourse throughout the remainder of the modern era. We can see this influence as we consider the rise of a belief in human equality among modern Jewish thinkers.

THE RISE OF EGALITARIANISM AND UNIVERSALISM (1770s–1930s)

Haskalah thinkers called for equal rights for all men, especially as they advocated for Jews to receive equal rights as citizens of modern states. In late eighteenth-century Germany, the philosopher Moses

Mendelssohn critiqued the ways in which Christians had, for centuries, denied Jews "the dignity associated with the universal rights of humankind," and he called for a future in which all citizens, "whatever their opinions on religious matters may be," would "enjoy the equal rights of humanity" (Gottlieb 2011b: 45, 61).

Mendelssohn further argued that all people had moral duties to act with benevolence to others, duties which could be grounded in our "common sense" and rational understanding of human nature. Critiquing Maimonides' views of the Noahide laws, Mendelssohn presented a universalistic, cosmopolitan view of human morality, understanding that all human beings are equally part of a single community who owe benevolence to one another. Although Mendelssohn believed that some theological beliefs are necessary for morality, especially to ensure that people are motivated to act morally, his universal, rational ethics does not require the revelation of Torah and is grounded in reasoning about human nature (Gottlieb 2011a: 47–8).

Some Jews associated with the Haskalah stressed how, as Jews valued their own recognition, they must recognize the equal rights of other oppressed persons. The Polish-born French scholar Zalkind Hourwitz, for example, argued not only for the equal rights of Jews but also for the equal rights of foreigners, who did not have the privilege of being born in France, and for the rights of non-Jewish Black people (Malino 1996; Israel 2021: 203–32). Other light-skinned European Haskalah adherents, however, argued for the rights of "civilized" Jews like themselves, while viewing darker skinned and non-European peoples as inferior and less deserving (Idelson-Shein 2014). In Surinam, David de Isaac Cohen Nassy, inspired by the equal recognition of Jews in the United States and France, argued that "all men must have equal rights," but also justified colonization and the enslavement of Black people (Davis 2010; Israel 2021: 276–84).

Haskalah authors were almost entirely men, and they often depicted women as inferior and issued no calls for gender equality (Litvak 2012: 43–4). Through much of the nineteenth century, secular Jewish women who argued for gender or racial equality tended not to frame their arguments with reference to their Jewishness, though historians have argued that the Jewish feminist and atheist Ernestine Rose was shaped by her Jewish identity as she argued for women's rights and the abolition of slavery (Dubois

2007; Anderson 2017). In Vilna in 1879, author Taube Segal addressed Haskalah intellectuals as she declared a "woman's war" against those who spoke of freedom and equality while denying rights to women (Feiner 1999). In subsequent decades, as increasing numbers of Jews throughout Europe joined, developed, and were shaped by political movements with strong egalitarian commitments, one can find more widespread arguments for equality grounded in secular Jewish identities.

We find such arguments in Jewish socialist movements such as the General Jewish Labor Bund (Alliance) in Russia and Poland, which sought to unite Jewish workers throughout the Russian Empire. Bundists—those committed to the Bund—sought to end the oppression of impoverished workers, dismantle capitalist practices and institutions, and secure the civic rights and the national–cultural autonomy of all minority groups. Bundists favored democratic models of authority that would include the voices of all oppressed people, including women, and protect minorities. As Esther Frumkin wrote in 1906, the Bund demanded solidarity among the working class people of all nations, ensuring that "civil, political and national rights will be obtained by all oppressed nations and among them too the Jewish people" (Faigan 2018: 32). Rejecting God, religion, and the authority of rabbis was ethically essential; whereas past generations "were stupefied by the opium that is religion," new generations of Jews were "learning the truth of Marxism" (Faigan 2018: 234).

Secular, socialist approaches to ethics became widespread among Jews in the United States in the early twentieth century and were often framed with reference to Jewish identity, experience, and history. Yankev Levin, for example, developed models for character education that focused on virtues of cooperation, civility, and humanity towards all people—in Yiddish, *mentshlekhkeyt*—that he contrasted with American ideals of "minding your own business" (Michels 2005: 215). Anna Strunsky spoke out against anti-Black violence in the United States, comparing it with the anti-Jewish violence she witnessed in Eastern Europe (Zipperstein 2018: 198–203). Anarchist approaches opposed to all forms of state power and social domination represented another current of secular Jewish ethics on the Left, including approaches that, referencing Jewish experiences of statelessness, centered others who were stateless, non-citizens, or refugees (Torres 2024).

Jewish thinkers in the Middle East also advanced egalitarian and universalist approaches to ethics in the late nineteenth and early twentieth centuries. In Egypt, for example, feminist thinker Esther Moyal argued for the equal rights of women (Levy 2012: 140–5); the Karaite scholar Murād Farag argued for liberal democracy and for an ethics grounded in principles of equality (Behar and Ben-Dor Benite 2013: 48–61); and the Marxist activist Marsil Shirizi argued for democratic, communist social structures that would benefit Jews and all other peoples (Behar and Ben-Dor Benite 2013: 164–73).

The thinkers named in this section often disagreed with each other, even if all of them embraced secular frameworks and universalist and egalitarian ideas of one sort or another. All of their ideas were also opposed by many contemporary Jewish thinkers, whether on account of their secularism, their universalism or egalitarianism, or for other reasons. Needless to say, all of their approaches were also radically different from the approaches that we saw in Chapters Two and Three of this book.

THE RISE OF NON-ZIONIST NATIONALISMS (1850s–1930s)

Beginning in the nineteenth century, Jewish ethics were also shaped by the rise of modern nationalism, the belief that "nations" defined by ethnicity, race, culture, or territory are entitled to state sovereignty or some other form of political autonomy.

As various nationalisms emerged in the areas in which Jews lived, some Jews adopted these nationalisms and justified them with reference to Jewishness. Murād Farag, for example, argued for an Egyptian nationalism grounded in liberal principles that would unite Egyptian Jews, Christians, and Muslims. In Germany, some Jewish thinkers heralded the rise of the German nation-state into which Jews could be integrated, depicting Judaism as a "religion" fit for German citizens rather than as a national identity that would compete with German nationalism (Batnitzky 2011: 37). In the United States, some Jews depicted themselves as advancing the American nationalist cause by settling and colonizing land and bringing capitalism and "civilization" to Native Americans (Koffman 2019). During World War I, Jews living in various nations pledged their allegiance to their countries' nationalist causes and argued that their identity as Jews positioned them to defend these causes; the German scholar Heinrich Loewe, for example, argued that Jews would carry on the legacy of ancient Jewish warriors such as the Maccabees in defending their German "fatherland" (Presner 2007: 195).

Other Jews developed forms of Jewish nationalism, viewing the Jews as a nation entitled to political autonomy or sovereignty. In the late nineteenth and early twentieth centuries, the historian and political theorist Simon Dubnov (Dubnow) argued for the moral necessity of "Jewish autonomism," arguing that Jews in the Russian Empire (the world's largest Jewish population) were entitled not to political sovereignty but to certain national rights (such as rights to control their own educational, cultural, and communal institutions). Dubnov's ethical arguments were grounded above all in his understanding of history and his concerns about the consequences of political systems that granted individual rights to Jews but failed to recognize them as a national group. While Dubnov argued for liberal political structures that recognized national minority groups, a number of Bundist and other socialist thinkers similarly argued for Jewish national autonomy within socialist frameworks. Bundists such as Vladimir Medem stressed the ideal of doikayt, "hereness," arguing that Jews should focus on improving life where they lived rather than seeking power within new territories (Rabinovitch 2014).

By contrast, "territorialist" Jewish thinkers of the same period engaged in their own readings of Jewish history, arguing that Jews would be better protected if they were provided sovereignty within some territory granted to them by a foreign power (perhaps somewhere in Africa, Australia, or the Americas). The British author Israel Zangwill, for example, stressed humanitarian concerns for the survival of the Jewish people amidst antisemitic violence in Europe and argued that morality required the immediate provision of another territory in which Jews could be safe and sovereign; in working with imperial powers to secure such a territory, he also embraced European models of colonialism and imperialism (Rovner 2014; Alroey 2016; Almagor 2022).

THE RISE OF ZIONISM (1880s–1940s)

The most successful Jewish nationalist movement was the Zionist movement, a movement born in late nineteenth-century Europe that called for Jewish political autonomy and/or sovereignty in

Palestine, also known as the land of Israel or "Zion," a land primarily inhabited by non-Jewish Palestinian Arabs. Early secular Zionist thinkers such as Leon Pinsker were (like Zangwill) driven in large part by humanitarian concerns for Jews in the Russian Empire amidst rising antisemitic violence. Writing from within the Russian Empire, Pinsker argued that Jews needed to take matters into their own hands to establish a Jewish polity, and he came to view Palestine as a pragmatic location, rejecting the Rabbinic idea that Jews needed to wait for divine redemption before establishing a polity in that land (Avineri 2017).

Similarly, Theodor Herzl, the Austro-Hungarian founder of the political Zionist movement at the end of the nineteenth century, argued pragmatically for an autonomous or sovereign Jewish polity in Palestine that would offer Jews security in the face of antisemitism. Herzl envisioned a polity that would in many respects embrace civic equality for its Jewish and non-Jewish populations, though it would also clearly be "the Jews' state." Herzl's ethics are also marked by racism and colonialism, including in his depictions of European Jews as superior to Palestinian Arabs and his vision for how a polity for European Jews would be a "rampart of Europe against Asia, an outpost of civilization as opposed to barbarism" (Penslar 2005; 2020). Herzl sometimes pointed towards ideals of gender equality, but he also embraced patriarchal European ideals of masculine honor and power, which were even more pronounced in the thought of his close ally, Zionist leader Max Nordau (Presner 2007).

The contemporary secular Zionist thinker who most forcefully critiqued Herzl and Nordau's views was the Ukrainian-born author Ahad Ha-Am. Ahad Ha-Am saw Herzl and Nordau as peddling non-Jewish European ideas that undermined authentic Judaism; authentic Judaism, in his view, was grounded not in the sort of statecraft favored by Herzl, nor in religion, but in "national morals." Though Ahad Ha-Am himself was clearly shaped by the thinking of non-Jewish European philosophers, he contended that national morality was found within the history of Jewish culture (including parts of Biblical and Rabbinic literature). This morality, in his view, included a disdain for power and violence, a love of peace, and a concern for justice towards all peoples, including non-Jewish Palestinians—though Ahad Ha-Am joined Herzl in viewing

Palestinians as morally inferior (Dowty 2000). He also drew on European theorists of nationalism as he developed ideas about how national morality required doing what was in the national interest. Among his ethical claims was that marriage between Jews and non-Jews was morally problematic because it was harmful to the Jewish nation (Shapira 1990).

Ahad Ha-Am, however, was criticized by other secular Zionists, who saw him as insufficiently focused on Jewish national interests and power. Micha Yosef Berdichevsky, also a Ukrainian-born author in the late nineteenth and early twentieth centuries, relentlessly critiqued the Rabbinic ideals of bookishness, spirituality and quietism that appealed to Ahad Ha-Am. He called for Jews to reject the "culture of the book" and return to the "culture of the sword" that was prominent in earlier periods of Jewish history—among Biblical warriors, the Maccabees, who rebelled against Greek rule, and the Zealots at Masada, who refused to submit to Rome. Drawing inspiration from the philosopher Friedrich Nietzsche, Berdichevsky argued that Jews must overcome conventional moral restraints and recover their national will to power, acting like other nations that courageously fought for sovereignty in their land (Luz 1987: 54–6; Shapira 1992: 21–5).

Another militant form of Zionism was the influential "Revisionist Zionism" developed by Vladimir (Ze'ev) Jabotinsky, also a Ukrainian-born thinker. Jabotinsky drew inspiration from European ethnic nationalists and proto-fascists, arguing that Jews must embrace ethnic nationalism and devotion to the nation and its leaders (Heller 2017). "There is no value in the world higher than the nation and the fatherland," he wrote, and "there is no deity in the universe to which one should sacrifice these two most valuable jewels" (Luz 1987: 64; Avineri 2017: 174–82). Like other Zionist thinkers discussed above, Jabotinsky's views also reflect a belief in the inferiority of Middle Eastern cultures (including the cultures of Middle Eastern Jews) and that Zionism would not only restore Jewish honor but also create a colonial outpost for European civilization (Kaplan 2005: 140–1; Avineri 2017: 187–94). Like many other Jewish nationalists, he often argued that actions were justified if they led to good consequences (a philosophical position known as "consequentialism")—for example, arguing for the use of crushing violence against Palestinians so that they would acquiesce to Jewish rule in a Jewish-majority state in Palestine and Transjordan (Shlaim 2012: 58–9; Heller 2017: 85).

Jabotinsky's political opponent David Ben-Gurion, the first prime minister of the State of Israel and the leader of the socialist Labor Zionist movement for many decades, also shaped the tenor of secular Zionist ethics. The Polish-born Ben-Gurion was more moderate than Jabotinsky in his attitude towards nationalism, militarism, and Jewish territorial expansion, and unlike Jabotinsky he was a socialist; but, like Jabotinsky, he believed in ethnic nationalism, the use of military force, the inferiority of Middle Eastern cultures (Shohat 1988), and Jewish national unity in the land of Israel. Ben-Gurion argued that Jews should learn from history that disunity among Jews was always disastrous, and that Jews in the present day have a responsibility to move to the land of Israel and join together in supporting the Zionist state-building project (Yanai 1989; Hacohen 2003). While in some respects he advocated for cooperation between Jews and non-Jewish Palestinians in the land of Israel, he also advocated the policy of "Hebrew labor," whereby Jewish employers would only hire other Jews, an approach that he saw as necessary for the success of the Zionist program. While he advocated for Palestinian civil rights within the State of Israel, he demanded that the State have a Jewish demographic majority, and his support of military operations that displaced Palestinians was another sign of Ben-Gurion's consequentialist thinking (Segev 2019).

Pinsker, Herzl, Nordau, Ahad Ha-Am, Berdichevsky, Jabotinsky, and Ben-Gurion were men who especially influenced the development of Zionism. Some less well-known women took very different approaches. For example, the United States-born thinker Jessie Sampter, a queer, disabled socialist and pacifist, immigrated to Palestine in 1919 and joined a kibbutz, an agricultural and industrial commune. Although committed to Zionism's cele-bration of bodily strength, she advocated for a Zionism that included those with disabilities, and she wrote about the validity and value of her experience as a physically disabled woman (Imhoff 2022: 68–105). She also argued for a Zionism with "far less gender differentiation, far more personal freedom in terms of sexuality and religion, and a new structure of kinship once the nuclear model of man-woman-children would no longer be dominant" (Imhoff 2022: 120). While Sampter's views were sometimes orientalist and colonialist, she advocated for a shared Palestinian–Jewish binational state. And while she supported limited self-defense measures, she identified as a pacifist who opposed war, appealing to history to show the injustice of war and nearly all violence. "To believe that justice can grow out of killing," she argued, is "superstitious," "what the perpetrators of the Inquisition believed" (Chazan 2015: 91; Imhoff 2022: 144–92).

The various nineteenth- and early twentieth-century thinkers discussed in this section and the previous section were all nationalists, but they drew on Jewish experience, identity, and history in a wide range of ways as they made their ethical claims, all of them very different from the sorts of claims discussed in earlier chapters of this book. Even the smaller set of thinkers discussed in this section, all of them Zionists, passionately disagreed with one another and offered widely divergent perspectives. Many of their ideas continued to be controversial—among other Zionists, and certainly among non-Zionists or anti-Zionists—as Zionism became more widespread among Jews in the wake of the Holocaust and with the establishment of the modern State of Israel.

THE HOLOCAUST, THE STATE OF ISRAEL, AND PALESTINIANS (1940s–2020s)

Jewish ethics was reshaped by the Holocaust—also known as the Shoah (Hebrew for "catastrophe"), the systematic murder of two-thirds of Europe's Jewish population by the Nazi German regime and its collaborators between 1941 and 1945. As Adolf Hitler's Nazi party rose to power, and through the subsequent years of persecution and genocide, Zionist leaders in Palestine developed their arguments for the moral necessity of a Jewish polity that would protect Jews, whom the world was failing to protect, and they increasingly advocated for a Jewish-controlled sovereign state. Most argued for any measures that would save the lives of those fleeing Nazi-occupied Europe, though figures such as Ben-Gurion argued that refugees must be brought to Palestine and warned against efforts to bring them elsewhere, and the Zionist leader Yitzhak Gruenbaum argued for prioritizing the lives of those who would contribute to the Zionist cause, in line with his view that "Zionism is above everything" (Segev 1993: 15–110).

Elsewhere, other Jewish thinkers argued for rescuing European Jews and protecting refugees in very different terms. As the war raged, the political theorist Hannah Arendt—a refugee from Nazi Germany who eventually immigrated to the United States— argued that Jews needed to take responsibility for their political fate, in part by creating an independent Jewish army that would cooperate with Allied forces to battle the Nazis and rescue Jews. Arendt was a Zionist, but she opposed Zionists like Ben-Gurion who saw Palestine as the only refuge for Jews and who championed ethnic nationalism—and, all the more so, the disciples of Vladimir Jabotinsky, whose approaches Arendt identified as a Jewish equivalent of Nazism. Arendt's concern for refugees and stateless people was bound up with her critique of ethnic nationalism, which she saw as inevitably leading to the mistreatment of ethnic minorities and refugees, whether in the extreme case of Nazi Germany or in the State of Israel. While the State of Israel, founded in May 1948, would provide a home for Jewish refugees, Arendt criticized it for bringing about new injustices, as its founding created hundreds of thousands of Palestinian refugees who were prevented by the State from returning to their homes (Bernstein 1996; Beiner 2000).

Anti-Zionists also drew on Jewish historical experience in their ethical critiques of Israel's policy towards Palestinian refugees. For example, the World Coordinating Committee of Bundist and Affiliated Jewish Socialist Organizations argued that displaced Palestinian refugees must be allowed to return to their homes, as Jews who had been displaced from their homes by the Nazis—and by many others, over two millennia—should recognize the injustice of displacement. Refusing to allow Palestinian refugees to return to their homes, the committee contended, shows that "2000 years of suffering and of untold hardships caused by the misery of numerous deportations were entirely forgotten as soon as circumstances caused a fraction of the Jewish population to be placed in a position of self-government" (Arab Refugees 1948; Levin 2023: 65).

Some Israeli public figures also raised ethical concerns about the treatment of Palestinians amidst the war in Palestine in 1947–1948, appealing to the lessons of the Holocaust. "Jews too have committed Nazi acts," the politician Aharon Zisling asserted (Morris 2004: 488). Others, however, appealed to the Holocaust in justifying expulsions of Palestinians or in rejecting rights of return for refugees. The Israeli military and political leader Moshe Dayan, for example, argued that "there can be no doubt that only this country and only this people can protect the Jews against a second Holocaust. And hence every inch of Israeli soil is intended only for Jews" (Zertal 2005: 109).

In the decades that followed the establishment of the State, prominent Israeli Jews routinely appealed to the Holocaust to justify military operations, often invoking the myth that Jews had been passive victims of the Nazis and that exercising military strength was required thereafter. As Israel invaded Egypt in 1956 (primarily to reopen the Straits of Tiran and the Gulf of Aqaba), politician Yitzhak-Meir Levin appealed to the slaughter of children by the Nazis and insisted that now Jews "refuse to go to the slaughter, but defend themselves courageously" (Segev 1993: 297). Future Prime Minister Golda Meir proclaimed that the 1967 Six-Day War showed that Jews would stand up to threats, as "those that perished in Hitler's gas chambers were the last Jews to die without standing up to defend themselves." When Israeli Jewish intellectuals critiqued the ensuing military occupation of the Palestinian West Bank and Gaza Strip, invoking the Holocaust to express their moral concerns, Meir appealed to the threat of annihilation of the Jewish people, retorting that "for me, the greatest morality consists of the Jewish people's right to exist" (Klagsbrun 2017: 493, 513; Segev 1993: 393). In 1982, prime minister Menachem Begin justified Israel's invasion of Lebanon as "a national moral imperative resulting from the Holocaust," as historian Tom Segev (1993: 403) put it; meanwhile, philosopher Yeshayahu Leibowitz condemned Israeli Jewish soldiers for acting like "Judeo-Nazis" in Lebanon and in the occupied Palestinian territories (Segev 1993: 409). When prime minister Yitzhak Rabin signed a peace plan enabling Palestinian self-governance in the occupied territories, his right-wing opponents described him as a Nazi or Nazi collaborator, and Rabin's assassin suggested that his murder of Rabin in 1995 was justified just as it would have been justified to have assassinated Hitler to prevent the Holocaust (Naor 2003).

Outside of Israel, meanwhile, some Jewish thinkers critiqued Israel as a racist, settler-colonial state, such as the French Marxist scholar Maxime Rodinson (Linfield 2019: 113–39). As a Jew, Rodinson (1983: 10) saw himself as having a particular duty towards Palestinians, given the way that other Jews mistreated Palestinians. Other Jewish Marxists, such as the Polish scholar Isaac Deutscher, who described himself as "a Jew by force of my unconditional solidarity with the persecuted and exterminated" (1968: 51), saw the necessity of providing a refuge for Jews in the face of the Holocaust but condemned Israel for its "ferocious aggressiveness" (Linfield 2019: 162). The American scholar Sara Roy (1995; 2002) critiqued Israeli colonialism and described how her moral concern was shaped by her family's experience of surviving the Holocaust. Other thinkers, however, defended Israel as itself anti-colonialist: notably, the Tunisian scholar Albert Memmi, an influential critic of colonial regimes, defended Israel as a moral necessity, a State that liberated Jews who were colonized, persecuted, and oppressed both by European Christians and by Arab Muslims. An opponent of Israel's military occupation of the Palestinian territories captured in 1967, Memmi argued for the creation of a Palestinian state alongside the Jewish state of Israel as the only way to achieve political justice (Linfield 2019: 165–96).

Jewish debates about the ethics of war in Israel/Palestine have continued to rage in the twenty-first century. Jewish Israeli political and military leaders have continued to appeal to the Holocaust in justifying military action against Palestinians and opposing the formation of a Palestinian state. Efforts to describe Palestinians as Nazis were widespread, for example, during the Israel–Hamas war that began in October 2023, when the Palestinian terrorist group Hamas killed hundreds of Israeli civilians and the Israeli military responded by killing thousands of civilians in the Palestinian Gaza Strip. Israeli Prime Minister Benjamin Netanyahu (2024) justified the war by describing Hamas as "the new Nazis," "who came to perpetrate another Holocaust against the Jews"; meanwhile, he defended Israel against the accusation that it was itself guilty of genocide, arguing that it was "a moral low point in the history of nations" to make such an accusation of "the state of the Jews that arose from the ashes of the Holocaust." Israeli diplomat Tzipi Hotovely argued that Israel's military response was justified by positively comparing it to the Allied bombing of Dresden, Germany, in which thousands of German civilians were killed in an attempt to defeat the Nazis (Samudzi 2024). Some Jewish critics of Israel's use of force in Gaza, on the other hand, drew on Jewish experiences as they accused Israel of acting like Nazis. The Russian-American journalist Masha Gessen (2023) described Gaza as "like a Jewish ghetto in an Eastern European country occupied by

Nazi Germany"; in both cases, "an occupying authority can choose to isolate, immiserate—and, now, mortally endanger—an entire population of people in the name of protecting its own." The Israeli historian Raz Segal (2023), pointing to the history of Jews seeking "to protect a powerless group from powerful states" when fighting antisemitism, called on Jews to end what he described as a genocidal war perpetrated by Israel, a powerful state victimizing powerless Palestinians.

Twenty-first-century Jewish thinkers have also drawn on other histories of Jews being persecuted as they have made ethical judgments about Israel's treatment of Palestinians. For example, the British Mizrahi author Lyn Julius (2018) argued against the right of Palestinian refugees to return to their homes in Israel on the grounds that, just as Jewish refugees from Arab-majority countries were absorbed by Israel, so too other Arab countries should absorb Palestinian refugees. The Israeli Mizrahi scholar Yehouda Shenhav (2012) argued that such comparisons are baseless and immoral, especially because (in contrast to many Jewish refugees from Arab countries) Palestinian refugees were expelled or fled against their will and have sought to return to their homes. Meanwhile, Jewish thinkers arguing for Palestinian refugees' right of return have sometimes pointed to the history of Jews seeking a right to return to their ancestral homeland; American author Peter Beinart (2021) argued that if Zionists think it morally praiseworthy to support Jews seeking to return to their ancient home in Palestine, then it should also be praiseworthy to support Palestinians seeking to return to the homes in Palestine from which they fled or were expelled much more recently.

Contemporary Jewish critics of the State of Israel have drawn on history in various other ways in making ethical judgments regarding Israeli political and social ethics. For example, the Iraqi-born Israeli-American scholar Ella Shohat (2017) draws on the history of Arab (Mizrahi) Jews in arguing that Zionism has not only oppressed Palestinians but also Arab Jews, whom the State of Israel has seen as inferior or uncivilized. The Puerto Rican scholar Aurora Levins Morales (2017) looks to her family's experiences with colonialism, occupation, and oppression in Latin America and Ukraine and concludes that none of her varied ancestors would have supported Israeli colonialism, occupation, and oppression.

The Argentinian writer Juan Gelman draws on experiences of Jews being persecuted in Russia and Argentina and criticizes Israel for acting like these persecutors (Slabodsky 2014: 208–9). The American philosopher Judith Butler rejects Israeli violence, racism, colonialism, and exclusivist nationalism and has developed a "diasporic" Jewish ethics: "a political ethics that belongs to the diaspora, where Jews are scattered among non-Jews," informed by histories of diaspora Jewish critiques of Zionism as well as Palestinian critiques. Engaging Palestinian perspectives is crucial for Butler, who argues that Jewish ethics requires not only Jewish but also non-Jewish perspectives: "to be ethical, one must depart from Jewishness as an exclusive frame for ethics" (2012: 99).

Such debates among Jewish thinkers about the State of Israel and Palestinian rights have often been highly divisive, drawing on very different understandings of Jewish history, identity, and experience. Many of the perspectives here rely on passionate claims about what Jewish history must teach or what Jewish ethics must support. We can see how disparate claims about Jewish ethics are constructed by different thinkers pursuing different agendas.

UNIVERSAL CONCERN FOR ALL PEOPLE (1950s–2020s)

As the previous section demonstrated, many twentieth- and twenty-first-century Jewish thinkers have responded to the persecution of Jews by emphasizing obligations to protect Jews, including through the establishment of the State of Israel, and others have emphasized how Jews must not persecute others, including through their power in the State of Israel. But many of the thinkers discussed above also emphasized how the lessons of Jewish history and experience should create moral concern for all who are persecuted around the world, whatever their connection to Jews. They expressed egalitarianism and universalism—a commitment to human equality and concern for all people.

To take one example, Aurora Levins Morales (2012; 2017) describes how her commitment to justice for Palestinians is part of her larger commitment, shaped by her Jewish experience and ancestry, to be an ally to others who are oppressed. In her writing and activism, Levins Morales has given particular attention to injustices in Latin America and to oppression caused by racism, classism, sexism, nationalism, imperialism, colonialism, capitalism, ableism, and environmental injustice (Lober 2019; Wyse 2021).

Hannah Arendt also emphasized the universal dimensions of her ethical concerns. Her book *The Origins of Totalitarianism*, which begins with an analysis of the rise of antisemitism in Europe, features a broad critique of racism, colonialist imperialism, and the nation-state system that leaves millions of people stateless and unprotected. Arendt's concerns for Jewish and Palestinian refugees, noted above, were part of her broader concern for stateless people, who lack even "the right to have rights," a right that she insisted must be "guaranteed by humanity itself" (1951: 298).

Jewish thinkers who have built on Arendt's work in critiquing nationalism and calling for protections for stateless people and refugees include the Turkish-born American philosopher Seyla Benhabib. Benhabib has advanced a notion of cosmopolitanism understood as "the recognition that human beings are moral persons equally entitled to legal protection in virtue of rights that accrue to them not as nationals, or members of an ethnic group, but as human beings as such." As Benhabib has explained, her skepticism regarding nationalism and her embrace of cosmopolitanism were shaped by her family's experience of living as Jews in the cosmopolitan environment of Istanbul (Herrera 2021).

Others arguing in favor of accepting refugees have drawn on Jewish historical experiences of being refugees. Israeli Prime Minister Menachem Begin, for example, proclaimed in 1977 that Israel would offer asylum to a group of non-Jewish Vietnamese refugees, recalling how other countries tragically refused to accept European Jewish refugees in the 1930s. Israeli politician Tamar Eshel was among those who drew on Jewish experience in arguing for accepting additional Vietnamese refugees: "especially us, because we have also been refugees—some of us in our own lifetime, while others carry the memory of their ancestors—we must be especially sensitive to the suffering of all refugees" (Havkin 2021: 192). Israeli activist Ziva Mekonen-Degu argued on behalf of Israel accepting non-Jewish Sudanese refugees, drawing on her experience of receiving care in Sudan as an Ethiopian Jewish refugee in the 1980s (Eglash 2012). Scholar Shira Havkin is among those who have criticized Israel's refusal to grant asylum to non-Jewish refugees except in exceptional, symbolic cases—and, even then, for refusing to grant them refugee status and recognize what Hannah Arendt described as their "right to have rights" (Havkin 2021: 205).

Jewish thinkers have also framed commitments to preventing mass atrocities elsewhere in the world with appeals to the Holocaust. The American activist Ruth Messinger, for example, was among those who publicly spoke out during the genocide in Darfur in the early twenty-first century, framing her advocacy with reference to the Holocaust and Jewish history in insisting that genocide must "never again" occur and that Jews must not be "bystanders to genocide" (Leder 2021: 122). The Romanian-born American writer Elie Wiesel spoke as a Holocaust survivor in calling for action to prevent genocides around the globe, in calling for perpetrators to be put to justice, and also in his opposition to capital punishment for perpetrators in nearly all cases (Cotler 2017; Wiesel and Heffner 2001). Some Jewish calls to prevent atrocities elsewhere have implicated the State of Israel: for example, the Israeli historian Yair Auron (2017) excoriated the Israeli government for having "desecrated the memory of the Holocaust" by selling weapons to the Myanmar government while it was carrying out a genocide against the Rohingya people.

In the United States, a country built on white supremacy, Black slavery, and anti-Black racism, Jewish ethical discourse has also frequently engaged with questions of racial justice. White Jewish Americans have often expressed their concern for racial injustice by invoking Jewish experiences of persecution in Europe, a framing we saw with Anna Strunsky's advocacy for Black Americans in the early twentieth century. The German-American rabbi Joachim Prinz, at the 1963 March on Washington, similarly expressed Jews' "sense of complete identification and solidarity" with Black people, "born of our own painful historical experience" (Prinz 2007: 261). Other thinkers have critiqued depictions of white Jewish Americans as fellow victims alongside Black people, when white Jews have benefitted from or even supported structures of white supremacy in the United States. As the Romanian-born American scholar Marianne Hirsch argued, standing with Black people requires

> accepting the limits of our knowledge and resisting the urge to tell our own stories. It means eschewing identification and even empathy, in favor of accompaniment, solidarity and co-resistance in the political fight

for systemic change. Importantly, it means examining our own implication in the structural racism and injustice ... [and] refusing to participate in such a system for one day longer.

(Myers 2020)

Meanwhile, a number of African-American Jewish thinkers have challenged the Eurocentric frameworks that have dominated modern Jewish ethical discourse. Psychologist Buffie Longmire-Avital (2023) explores how "racial and ethnic Jewish socialization is rooted in shared storytelling" and encourages telling a "multi-racial Jewish story" that challenges Jews to recognize and disrupt racism. Scholar Lewis Gordon (2018: 222) has pointed out the ethical significance of accepting that "the Transatlantic and East Indian Ocean Slave Trades are part of Jewish history." Scientist Chanda Prescod-Weinstein (2017) questions whether American Jews' sympathy for "the American act of state-building relying on anti–Black and settler-colonialist domestic policies" deepened as "American Jews became enmeshed with the act of colonial state-building in Israel."

All of the disparate thinkers discussed in this section draw on Jewish experience, history, or identity as they argue for justice towards oppressed people, including those who are racialized, victims of atrocities, refugees, or stateless, whether they are Jewish or not. Their constructions of Jewish ethics reflect egalitarian and universalistic ideas that have been of great interest to many modern Jews. Other modern Jewish thinkers, however, have framed modern Jewish ethics in ways that reject many of these ideas. For example, some Jewish thinkers, in the wake of the Holocaust, cautioned Jews to focus less on issues of international justice and more on issues of "Jewish survival"—supporting Israel, fighting antisemitism, and combating assimilation and intermarriage (Woocher 1986; Barnett 2016). And others have argued that various ideas discussed here should not count as Jewish ethics, for any number of the reasons discussed in Chapter One of this book.

THE FLOURISHING OF JEWISH FEMINISM (1960s–2020s)

One other major form of egalitarianism that has shaped Jewish ethics in recent decades has been gender egalitarianism, also known as feminism. We saw, above, some early examples of secular Jewish feminism from the nineteenth and early twentieth century. By the 1960s, a "second wave" of feminism emerged in the United States, led in part by secular Jewish women who sought to dismantle pervasive systems of sexism. For many of these women, Jewish identity, history, and experience fueled their feminism. Activist Heather Booth traced her activism to an experience at Israel's Holocaust Museum, where she vowed that "in the face of injustice I would struggle for justice." Writer Andrea Dworkin saw Jewishness as at the heart of her values, asserting that "everything I know about human rights goes back in one way or another to what I learned about being a Jew." Writer Joan Ditzion articulated how her feminist collective, which produced *Our Bodies, Ourselves* and other work on women's health and sexuality, expressed what she saw as "Jewish family values" (Antler 2018: 20, 47, 185).

Other feminist thinkers in the United States more forcefully identified their work as part of a Jewish feminist movement. Aviva Cantor, for example, fostered self-consciously Jewish activism within the international women's liberation movement, including in her efforts to defend the State of Israel from anti-Zionist feminists (Antler 2018: 249–57). Donna Berman (2001) grounded her Jewish feminist ethics, which seeks to "redeem Jewish women—and men—from oppressive texts"—in the writings of the Jewish anarchist Emma Goldman as well as ethnographic interviews with contemporary Jewish women. Irena Klepfisz (1990: 162) located her class-conscious lesbian feminism within secular Yiddish culture and drew inspiration from the Bundist women who fought for justice in early twentieth-century Eastern Europe. Melanie Kaye/Kantrowitz (1992) called for Jewish feminists to identify as Jews as they joined with other groups in fighting sexism, homophobia, racism, antisemitism, militarism, and economic injustice. Her feminism was also rooted within diasporism, which she described as an alternative to Zionism, drawing on the Bundist idea of doikayt—that "Jews enter coalitions wherever we are, across lines that might divide us, to work together for universal equality and justice" (2007: 198–9).

Building on the work of Kaye/Kantrowitz, political philosopher Marla Brettschneider (2016) has critiqued frameworks used by Jewish feminists that fail to understand intersectionality—i.e., how gender and sex oppression takes different forms depending on race, class, sexuality, religion, ability, and other factors. Her work explores, for example, how race and class is always a factor in Jewish feminism, including in important struggles for reproductive justice. Brettschneider draws on Jewish thinkers who have often not been recognized as such, such as the Afro-Caribbean author Jamaica Kincaid and her writings on the experiences of immigrant domestic workers. Drawing on her experience in a Jewish, queer, multiracial, adoptive family, Brettschneider (2006) has also critiqued homophobia, ideals of monogamous marriage, and assumptions that biological connections should be the foundation of family.

Other feminist Jewish engagements with issues of reproductive justice have looked to Jewish history. The scholar Michal Raucher (2023a), for example, urges Jewish abortion rights activists to stop turning to ancient Rabbinic texts that do not support individuals making their own decisions about reproduction. Instead, she argues for drawing on the history of modern Jews arguing for reproductive rights: activists such as Emma Goldman, who advocated for sexual and reproductive freedom in the early twentieth century; Dr. Lena Levine, co-founder of the International Planned Parenthood Federation; and Heather Booth, the feminist activist mentioned above, who founded the underground Abortion Counseling Service of Women's Liberation. Furthermore, Raucher (2023b) calls for Jewish discussions about abortion to center the lived experiences of Jews who have had abortions.

In Israel, Jewish feminist advocacy for reproductive justice has often clashed with Israeli Jewish pronatalism—an ethical commitment and state policy that encourages Jewish women to have children. This pronatalism, advanced by leaders including David Ben-Gurion, is significantly shaped by non-theological factors including a desire to ensure a Jewish demographic majority in the State of Israel, and a sense that birthrates among Palestinians represent a "demographic threat." Other Israeli pronatalists have focused on the need to enlarge the size of the Jewish people worldwide, especially in the wake of the Holocaust and demographic losses attributed to assimilation and intermarriage. These ideas have shaped secular Israeli opposition to abortion rights (Yuval-Davis 1989; Yefet 2016). Israeli feminists including Yael Hashiloni-Dolev, Zahava Gal-On, Nurit Tsur, and Tal Tamir have protested that these attitudes and the policies they have generated maintain patriarchal control over women's bodies and rob women of their reproductive autonomy (Steinfeld 2015). The Israeli Mizrahi feminist scholar Karin Carmit Yefet (2022), also arguing for reproductive autonomy, has offered an intersectional analysis of Israeli legal regulations on reproduction and has shown how they have favored procreation for higher-class Ashkenazi Jewish women but not for Mizrahi women or women of Ethiopian descent.

Yefet focuses on the struggles of disempowered, lower-class Mizrahi women and critiques Ashkenazi Israeli feminism for centering struggles that benefit privileged, higher-class Ashkenazi women. Related critiques have been leveled by other Mizrahi (Arab-Jewish) feminists including Henriette Dahan Kalev, Vicki Shiran, Pnina Motzafi-Haller, and Ella Shohat, who have also pointed to ways in which the oppression of Mizrahi women has been intertwined with the oppression of non-Jewish Palestinian women (Motzafi-Haller 2014).

Other feminists have called for attention to the experiences of trans and non-binary people. For example, the Mizrahi, Kurdish trans female author A.S. Hakkâri (2024) has explored how her experiences of being marginalized or hated because of each of the pieces of her identity shapes her commitment to support those who are most marginalized. The Israeli scholar Ido Katri (2019) critiques efforts to separate sex from gender and establish a male–female sex binary, which causes harm to trans and gender nonconforming people, paralleling efforts by the Zionist movement to establish a binary between Jews and Arabs, which causes harm to Arab (Mizrahi) Jews. In the United States, the artist Micah Bazant has developed their vision for trans justice through engaging with family stories of surviving the Holocaust, the lives of nonbinary Jews such as the artist Claude Cahun, and experiences of transphobia within Jewish communities (Strassfeld 2022a: 196).

The Jewish feminist thinkers discussed in this section have drawn on many different understandings of Jewish tradition, history, identity, and experience, often in controversial ways. Challenging many of the forms of exclusion featured elsewhere in this book, Jewish thinkers have constructed a wide variety of approaches to Jewish feminism.

ENVIRONMENTALISM AND ANIMAL RIGHTS (1900s–2020s)

Jewish thinkers have also developed a wide variety of secular ethical claims regarding how human beings should relate to the non-human environment, including non-human animals. The Israeli scholar Yuval Jobani (2023) has described the Zionist thinker A.D. Gordon as the "first Jewish environmentalist." Writing in early twentieth-century Palestine, Gordon sought to develop a form of nationalism that rejected domination and aggression, including in relationship to the natural world. A vegetarian who adopted veganism later in life, Gordon condemned the exploitation of animals and called for human beings to ally themselves with nature rather than seeking to "conquer" it.

Amidst the deepening environmental crises of the late twentieth century, and the emergence of the Jewish environmental movement, one secular Jewish environmental ethic can be found in the writings of Aurora Levins Morales (1995). Levins Morales shares Gordon's concern about humans seeking to control nature, and she argues for the abolition of land ownership, as "ownership shatters ecology. For the land to survive, for us to survive, it must cease to be property." Unlike Gordon, however, Levins Morales does not frame her environmentalism as allied with Zionism; rather, she critiques Zionism and other forms of nationalism for seeking to control land and natural resources that cannot rightfully be claimed by any one nation.

The American philosopher Eric Katz (1997) developed a secular Jewish environmental ethic that sees connections between the destruction of the earth's biosphere and the Nazis' attempt to exterminate European Jews. In both the Holocaust and environmental destruction, Katz sees forms of domination at work and argues that "we must resist the practice of domination in all its forms. We must act so as to preserve the free and autonomous development of human individuals, communities, and natural systems."

Jewish thinkers have also drawn parallels between the Holocaust and cruelty towards animals. The Polish-American fiction writer I.B. Singer drew particular attention to these parallels through the statement in one of his stories that, "In relation to [animals], all people are

Nazis; for the animals, it is an eternal Treblinka" (Patterson 2002). The legal scholar Sherry Colb (2015), writing as the child of Holocaust survivors, has criticized "cheap comparisons" between the Holocaust and animal rights abuses, but argues that we should not close our eyes to important parallels between those who felt entitled to murder Jews and those who feel entitled to kill animals. Drawing on insights from Singer and from the Holocaust survivor and animal rights activist Alex Hershaft, Colb (2015: 281; 2019) advocates for Jewish veganism and concludes that "we serve justice when victims … identify with other victims and extend the compassion and justice that should rightly have been extended to them, to the rest of sentient creation."

Others advocating for animal rights have drawn on other aspects of Jewish literary and artistic history. The Israeli scholar Hadas Marcus (2019), for example, points to concerns for animal welfare in the writings of figures such as I.B. Singer, the nineteenth-century English thinker Lewis Gompertz, the Yiddish author Mendele Mocher Sforim, and the Bohemian Jewish writer Franz Kafka, and in the art of the Belarusian-French painters Chaim Soutine and Marc Chagall. Secular Jewish artists and writers such as these "conveyed their heartfelt pity for innocent chickens, sheep, goats, and cows with their paintbrushes and pens" and, in Marcus' view, promote compassion for non-human animals.

We can see, here, some of the various ways that secular Jewish environmental ethics and animal ethics have been constructed. Like other ideas discussed throughout this chapter, some of the ethical ideas discussed here have aroused controversy, especially among Jews who have viewed environmental degradation or animal cruelty as trivial concerns. Secular Jewish approaches to environmentalism and animal welfare have, however, had significant influence in shaping modern Jewish ethical discourse.

CONCLUSIONS

This chapter considers how modern Jews have used secular frameworks to answer ethical questions that we also saw addressed by the ancient Rabbis, in Chapter Two, and by Maimonides and the Zoharic authors, in Chapter Three. What is the relative moral status of Jews and non-Jews, of marginalized people such as "strangers" or refugees, and of people of different genders, races, and sexualities? What makes for good political governance? When is war justified, and how may Jews ethically settle in the land of Israel? What is an ethical approach to abortion? What is the moral status of non-human animals and the broader non-human environment? Who or what has the authority to determine what counts as Jewish ethics?

The modern Jews discussed in this chapter have answered these questions in very different ways than the Jews discussed in the previous two chapters. Their responses have not invoked God. They developed their ideas in very different contexts, drawing on modern concepts that were unfamiliar to premodern Rabbinic Jews, such as egalitarianism, feminism, universalism, nationalism, Zionism, and environmentalism. They have often rejected premodern Jewish traditions and the authority of rabbis, sometimes locating authority within the state, within various communities, or within individuals. They have often embraced rationalism, skepticism, historical inquiry, and individualism.

Those who feel that authentic Jewish ethics must be grounded in theology, or in Biblical or Rabbinic literature, may view the ideas found in this chapter as Jewishly inauthentic. Those who insist that Jewish ethics must uphold certain sorts of ideas may doubt that some of the ideas discussed in this chapter can count as Jewish ethics. Those who defer to hierarchies related to gender, sexuality, disability, race, ethnicity, and class may doubt the value of ideas from thinkers who are not male, straight, able-bodied, white, Ashkenazi, or upper-class. But this chapter has sought to introduce the diversity of modern secular Jewish ethics, and so I have sought to include a wide range of views shaped by Jewish tradition, experience, history, or identity. We can see from this chapter how secular Jewish ethics has been framed in very different ways by Jews of different identities in different contexts, including by those who have often been marginalized in histories of Jewish ethics.

The ideas discussed in this chapter have been "secular" in the sense that they do not invoke God or God-centered concepts of creation, revelation, and redemption. The lines separating secular thinkers from religious thinkers, however, are not always clear. Some of the thinkers whose secular arguments are featured in this chapter have, elsewhere, engaged with theology, and so their ideas will also appear in the next chapter, which focuses on theological concepts. Secular ideas have been an important part of modern Jewish ethics. But, as we will see in the next chapter, theology has also continued to be an important part of modern Jewish ethical discourse. The next chapter will explore how Jewish ethics has continued to be shaped by ideas about God's creation of the world, the revelation of Torah, and the redemption of the people of Israel.

FURTHER READING

On early modern Jewish ideas of universalism and equal rights, see Jonathan Israel, *Revolutionary Jews from Spinoza to Marx: The Fight for a Secular World of Universal and Equal Rights* (2021).

On the development of liberal, secular, and nationalist approaches to politics in the first part of the twentieth century, see Ezra Mendelsohn, *On Modern Jewish Politics* (1993); and Moshe Behar and Zvi Ben-Dor Benite, eds., *Modern Middle Eastern Jewish Thought: Writings on Identity, Politics, and Culture, 1893–1958* (2013).

On Zionism, see Shlomo Avineri, *The Making of Modern Zionism: The Intellectual Origins of the Jewish State*, 2nd ed. (2017); Ehud Luz, *Wrestling with an Angel: Power, Morality, and Jewish Identity* (2003); and Derek J. Penslar, *Zionism: An Emotional State* (2023).

On the role of the Holocaust in shaping Israeli Jewish ethics, see Tom Segev, *The Seventh Million: The Israelis and the Holocaust* (1993); and Idith Zertal, *Israel's Holocaust and the Politics of Nationhood* (2005).

On criticism of Zionism, see Judith Butler, *Parting Ways: Jewishness and the Critique of Zionism* (2012); Santiago Slabodsky, *Decolonial Judaism: Triumphal Failures of Barbaric Thinking* (2014); and Geoffrey Levin, *Our Palestine Question: Israel and American Jewish Dissent, 1948–1978* (2023).

On secular Jewish feminism, see Esther Fuchs, *Israeli Feminist Scholarship: Gender, Zionism, and Difference* (2014); Marla Brettschneider, *Jewish Feminism and Intersectionality* (2016); and Joyce Antler, *Jewish Radical Feminism: Voices from the Women's Liberation Movement* (2018).

MODERN JEWISH THEOLOGICAL ETHICS

As we have seen, modern Jewish ethics has been shaped by a wide range of ideas, including universalism, feminism and other forms of egalitarianism, Zionism and other forms of nationalism, and environmentalism. Modern Jewish thinkers have also challenged models of authority that were widespread in premodern Rabbinic sources. But these ideas and new ways of thinking about authority have not only shaped the secular Jewish discourse that we saw in the previous chapter of this book; they have also shaped Jewish discourse about God's creation, revelation, and redemption.

Like the thinkers we explored in Chapters Two and Three, Jews in the modern era have often made claims about how to live by referencing God and theological narratives about the creation of the world, the revelation of Torah, and the redemption of Israel. Just as Chapters Two and Three were structured around how narratives of creation, revelation, and redemption shaped Jewish ethics, this chapter will also be structured around those narratives. This structure allows us to see the diverse ways that modern Jewish thinkers have engaged in ethical discourse, and how they have often come to conclusions very different from those of the Rabbis, Maimonides, or the Zoharic authors. I will begin by discussing modern Jewish concepts of revelation, and then discuss creation and redemption, considering how these concepts have shaped ethical claims. To facilitate easy comparison with other chapters, I continue to focus on the issues discussed in previous chapters: issues regarding authority, Jews and Gentiles, gender, race, disability, sexuality, abortion, animals and the environment, violence and war, settling the land of Israel, political governance, the rights of

DOI: 10.4324/9781003271338-5

refugees, strangers, and others in need, and the development of moral virtues including love, compassion, justice, and humility.

I THE REVELATION OF TORAH

FOUR NINETEENTH-CENTURY APPROACHES TO REVELATION AND ETHICS

Many modern Jewish thinkers have developed ethical stances that rely on ideas about God revealing Torah to the people of Israel. Some influential ideas have been associated with Jewish movements that first began to emerge in nineteenth-century Europe: the Reform movement, which encouraged ideas of Judaism as a religion and challenged many widespread Rabbinic and Kabbalistic teachings and practices; the Conservative movement, whose forerunners sympathized with some Reform movement ideas but sought to conserve tradition as they saw it; and the Orthodox movement, whose leaders rejected the possibility of changing tradition, insisting that what they saw as normative Jewish practice reflects divine revelation. Those who shaped these movements as they emerged in Western and Central Europe accepted (in varying degrees) key ideas associated with the Haskalah (the Jewish Enlightenment), discussed in Chapter Four, including ideas of universalism, egalitarianism, liberalism, the idea of Judaism as a religion, and a commitment to general, secular education. Especially in Eastern Europe, however, many Orthodox Jews rejected these Haskalah values and developed traditionalist Orthodox approaches that have come to be described as "Haredi" or "ultra-Orthodox."

The rabbis who developed the Reform movement in nineteenth-century Germany often taught that God's revelation to the people of Israel at Mount Sinai consisted of a core, universal message of ethics and morality, and not the halakhah (understood as "law") that the ancient Rabbis saw as so central to God's revelation. Such thinkers were shaped by the Haskalah (the Jewish Enlightenment), secular philosophical thought, and the same social forces discussed in Chapter Four that gave rise to universalistic and egalitarian approaches to secular Jewish ethics. The Reform rabbi Samuel Holdheim, for example, taught that God's primary revelation, the eternal core of Judaism, was an egalitarian and universalist ethical message. For Holdheim, some of these core teachings became a part of the Bible, "the human reflection of divine illumination." But much of the Bible's ethics are anachronistic, reflecting not divine values but the political and cultural needs of bygone eras, as Maimonides recognized with regards to the Bible's system of animal sacrifices. Similarly, for Holdheim, the Biblical commandment of male circumcision had its place at one time but was not part of God's core revelation and can be recognized as exclusivist and unnecessary. Holdheim was all the more concerned about later Rabbinic traditions that he saw as distorting God's ethical message. Rabbinic restrictions on marriage between Jews and Christians, for example, struck Holdheim as out of line with the universal values that were at the core of God's revelation (Philipson 1919: 63–97; Meyer 1988a: 81; Kohler 2012: 196).

Some more conservative thinkers who sympathized with the Reform movement's general moral concerns nonetheless viewed such claims about divine revelation as far too radical. For example, the nineteenth-century German scholar Zacharias Frankel, often viewed as a forerunner of Conservative Judaism, valued universalist and ega-litarian ideas and many other ideas favored by the Reform move-ment, but he was appalled by figures like Holdheim, who rejected so many Biblical and Rabbinic teachings. Frankel saw the Biblical "Written Torah" as divinely revealed at Sinai, while he described the Rabbinic "Oral Torah" as "the independent and creative unfolding of Sinaitic revelation"—developed over time to reflect God's will, in accordance with the sacred will of the Jewish people. In Frankel's view, ancient scholars recognized that "the letter of the law is not decisive, but rather that the spirit must animate the law and raise it to a divine status worthy to become a norm to man," as they reinter-preted Biblical texts about corporal punishment ("an eye for an eye") as in fact referring to monetary compensation. Frankel understood this sort of "humanitarian" reinterpretation as in line with the spirit of divine revelation and the will of the Jewish people. But the more radical changes favored by Holdheim (for example, regarding cir-cumcision or intermarriage) seemed to Frankel to be quite contrary to the popular will and the spirit of revelation (Brämer 2007: 219–21; Dorff 2005: 45–57).

In contrast to both Holdheim's Reform view and Frankel's proto-Conservative view, those who developed Orthodox Judaism were distinguished by their assertion that God's Torah does not change over time; authentic Torah, in this view, can be found in the writings of the ancient Rabbis and, above all, in the Babylonian Talmud. The nineteenth-century German rabbi Samson Raphael Hirsch, the forerunner of "Modern Orthodox Judaism," insisted that the rabbis quoted in the Talmud presented the Torah as it had been revealed by God to Moses at Sinai. Ethical objections to the Torah such as those made by Holdheim were abominable, and Frankel's conviction that law could change over time was misguided. Despite these claims, Hirsch himself was attracted to modern universalism and egalitarianism and was uncomfortable with the Rabbinic traditions that rejected those values. He developed novel interpretations that allowed him to support non-egalitarian Rabbinic teachings while also claiming a commitment to egalitarian values. For example, he explained that the commandment for male circumcision did not in fact privilege men over women, as Rabbinic literature suggested; rather, women were naturally more devoted to God and did not need the sort of reminder that circumcision provided to men (Harris 1995: 223–8; Baader 2006: 89).

Other nineteenth-century Orthodox rabbis, while sharing Hirsch's view that the Talmud reflects divine revelation and that Torah does not change over time, fiercely rejected universalistic and egalitarian ideas and saw them as contrary to God's Torah. These "traditionalist" thinkers, indebted to the *Zohar* and subsequent Kabbalistic traditions, were the forerunners of ultra-Orthodox or Haredi Judaism. A sub-group of them were members of the Hasidic movement, a movement distinguished by its acceptance of the authority of charismatic rabbis viewed as linking the people of Israel with higher divine realms. Rabbi Naḥman of Bratslav, Ukraine was one such rabbi whose teachings emphasized not only the need to submit to God's revelation as captured within the Written Torah and rabbinic literature, but also the need to submit to the truly exceptional rabbi, the *tzaddik* ("the righteous one"). Just as the ancient Israelites learned to devote themselves entirely to Moses, God's prophet, the present-day Jew must "connect oneself to the *tzaddik* of the generation, and accept his words, whatever he says, whether important or unimportant, and not deviating (God forbid) from his words to the right or left." Doing so requires distancing oneself from any non-Jewish wisdom, the study of philosophy (including Maimonides' *Guide*), or indeed any independent thinking whatsoever: "purge your mind so that it is as if one had no intellect other than what one receives from the *tzaddik*, the rabbi of one's generation" (Naḥman of Bratslav 2010: 1:123). For a thinker like Naḥman, the kind of ideas advocated by Holdheim were demonic perversions of Torah. Notably, in stark contrast to Holdheim, Naḥman saw the Torah as demanding separation from non-Jews, whom Kabbalistic tradition linked with metaphysical impurity and evil, and he saw male circumcision as essential for receiving God's Torah (Wolfson 2002).

Considering these four nineteenth-century approaches allows us to see how different views of divine revelation have shaped different approaches to ethics. While we have focused here on different attitudes towards male circumcision and the Rabbinic prohibition on intermarriage, these thinkers held similar attitudes towards other issues. Naḥman's Hasidism stressed the authority of Rabbinic and Kabbalistic ideas as understood by charismatic Hasidic rabbis, emphasizing submission to those rabbis and separation from non-Jewish ideas. Hirsch's Modern Orthodox perspective depicted Rabbinic teachings as eternal but also sought to appreciate the modern values of universalism and egalitarianism. Frankel's proto-Conservative perspective saw Rabbinic tradition as encouraging gradual efforts to reinterpret tradition, in line with the spirit of revelation and popular will. Holdheim's Reform perspective rejected Rabbinic traditions that did not conform to the egalitarian and universalist values that he saw at the core of God's revelation.

THE RELATIONSHIP BETWEEN REVELATION AND ETHICS

Over the course of the twentieth century, many other Jewish thinkers developed the non-Orthodox idea that at least some Biblical and Rabbinic ideas were not ethical and therefore could not reflect divine revelation. Such thinkers developed new concepts of what the revelation of God's Torah might mean.

Writing in early twentieth-century Germany, for example, the philosopher Hermann Cohen described revelation in rational and ethical terms, building on Maimonides' ideas about God as well as the insights of philosopher Immanuel Kant. God, for Cohen, is not a being with a personality, but the archetype of moral goodness, an ideal towards which human beings must strive. God's revelation was not a historic event that took place on a certain mountaintop, but rather is the ongoing discovery of ethics through reason (something which is clearly accessible to all people, not just the Jewish people). The core content of God's revelation is the universal moral law: that all people must be treated as possessing equal dignity (as "ends in themselves"). To count as a part of divine revelation, other laws must flesh out or support this fundamental moral law. The divine ideal also calls for the cultivation of virtues such as humility, courage, humanity, and truthfulness (Seeskin 1997; Billet 2023).

Other early twentieth-century German-Jewish thinkers, often described as "existentialists," challenged rationalist approaches such as Cohen's and described revelation as far more open-ended. The philosopher Martin Buber, for example, rejected the idea that law could be a part of divine revelation. For Buber, each moment requires its own ethical response which cannot be determined by law and can only be determined by the individuals who are present. Where divine revelation may be encountered is in "I-You" moments, in which individuals actualize their potential and show respect and responsiveness for one another, loving their fellows as themselves. In Buber's model, divine revelation is thus accessible to all people, and is in no way something exclusive to the Jewish people (Crane 2013; Plevan 2023).

Building on ideas such as these, the French philosopher Emmanuel Levinas described revelation of Torah as the revelation of responsibility for other persons. For Levinas, there is no way that God is revealed in the world other than through ethical responsibility for "the Other":

> Ethics is not the corollary of the vision of God, it is that very vision. Ethics is an optic, such that everything I know of God and everything I can hear of His word and reasonably say to Him must find an ethical expression.
>
> (Levinas 1990: 17)

There is no such thing as "Torah," for Levinas, outside of ethics. Torah is certainly not confined to what the Rabbis described as Written and Oral Torah, though those teachings do constitute Torah insofar as they point the way to ethical responsibility. Revelation is, for Levinas, clearly accessible to all human beings, insofar as they respond ethically towards the other (Morgan 2011).

Cohen, Buber, and Levinas each rejected ancient Rabbinic ideas about the content of the Torah, and they each rejected the Rabbinic idea that divine revelation was only given to the people of Israel. Other non-Orthodox thinkers even more emphatically rejected the ancient Rabbis' exclusivism. The Lithuanian-born American rabbi Mordecai Kaplan, founder of the Reconstructionist movement and a major influence on the larger branches of organized non-Orthodox Judaism (Conservative and Reform) in the United States, argued that the doctrine that Jews are the chosen people necessarily implies their superiority and so must be rejected. Embracing scholarship showing the human authorship of Biblical texts, Kaplan also firmly opposed the Rabbinic idea that the Written Torah was revealed by God at Sinai, as well as the idea that Rabbinic literature constituted divinely-revealed Oral Torah. Kaplan understood God in naturalistic terms, as the process that allows for goodness in the world, and so he rejected any notion that God was a supernatural being or transcendent presence who revealed anything. He did think, however, that the human discovery of moral truth should be described as "revelation." That which fosters love and justice among human beings must be included as part of "Torah" (Scult 2013; Kaplan 1956: xiii, 154–5, 204–6).

Rabbi Abraham Joshua Heschel, a Poland-born theologian who escaped Nazi Germany for the United States and also had significant influence in shaping non-Orthodox (especially Conservative) Judaism there, took a very different approach. For Heschel, revelation is not the discovery of rational truths by human beings but an event initiated by God out of God's concern for human beings. God, for Heschel, is a living, supernatural being with a will that God revealed to the people of Israel at Sinai. Such a revelation is captured in part by the Written Torah, but Heschel contends that God's revelation is something "which human language will never be able to portray" (Heschel 1955: 184–5). Since moral authority is found only in God's will, but God's will has not yet been fully written down, human beings must seek to attune themselves to God's revelation and draw forth new understandings of Torah. The ancient Rabbis did this in developing the Oral Torah, and Heschel indicates that later generations must continue to develop the Oral Torah, guided by values such as justice and righteousness, which stand at the core of God's revelation (Heschel 1955: 257–76; Held 2013: 94–134; LaGrone 2013).

A number of these views of how new understandings of ethics may be revealed draw on the ancient Rabbis' own conceptions of how understandings of Torah may change over time, discussed in Chapter Two. Orthodox thinkers in the twentieth century, by contrast, reacted to these claims by arguing that Torah was revealed clearly by God to the people of Israel and that it will not change over time. God "willed that man abide by His commandments and that that will was communicated in discrete words and letters," the American Modern Orthodox rabbi Norman Lamm (1966: 124–5) wrote. Moreover, the Torah is in no way separate from God but is "an aspect of God Himself." As such, for Lamm, "all of the Torah is binding on the Jew," and judging parts of it as irrational or unethical is a rejection of God.

While Haredi rabbis accepted such thinking, they also constructed additional ideas about Rabbinic authority not shared by Modern Orthodox thinkers. Notably, a number of Haredi thinkers developed the idea that authoritative rabbis possess clear insight into divine revelation, such that their views about all matters should be described as "Torah understanding" (da'at Torah) and granted complete authority. While these thinkers believed that people were becoming more corrupt over time and intellectual capacity was declining as the revelation at Sinai receded further into the distant past ("the decline of the generations"), they believed that God continued to reveal God's Torah to select, righteous rabbis. Such rabbis, uncorrupted by modern secular ideas such as universalism and egalitarianism, were aided by God's holy spirit (the source of prophecy) to teach "pure" Torah (Kaplan 2000: 305). The Haredi thinker Eliyahu Eliezer Dessler, based in England and then Israel, argued that one should submit unquestioningly to such leaders, understanding that one's own vision "is null and void and utterly valueless compared with the clarity of their intellect and the divine aid they receive" (Brown 2014: 281). In sharp contrast to the non-Orthodox thinkers who depicted God revealing a universal ethics accessible to all people and shaped by many perspectives, Haredi thinkers such as Dessler depicted God as revealing God's non-universalistic and non-egalitarian vision only to a small group of elite rabbis. The very different views of revelation, here, correlate with very different approaches to ethics.

REVELATION AND FEMINIST ETHICS

In the United States in the 1960s and 1970s, Jewish feminist thinkers began to re-envision Jewish theology and ethics, developing concepts of divine revelation and new ideas about the content of Torah.

The American theologian Judith Plaskow is particularly well-known for such work. Plaskow's book *Standing Again at Sinai* (1990: 3) critiques how Biblical and Rabbinic sources construct God as male, the people of Israel as a male collectivity, and Torah as "a revelation as men perceived it." Plaskow insists that, to the contrary, Torah must reflect the experiences of people of all genders, as well as an expansive and non-hierarchical understanding of the people of Israel and ideas about God that do not imagine God as male. Reconstructing Torah requires reconstructing the perspectives of Jewish women who struggled against patriarchy but whose perspectives were erased from Jewish memory. For Plaskow, much of divine revelation has been hidden, and

> insofar as we can begin to recover women's experience of God, insofar as we can restore a part of their history and vision, we have more of the primordial Torah, the divine fullness, of which the present Torah of Israel is only a fragment and sign.
>
> (1990: 34)

So too, recovering the experiences of others who have been marginalized contributes to the recovery of the hidden Torah. Plaskow rejects all forms of hierarchy, including the idea of Israel as God's chosen people, as well as hierarchical and patriarchal conceptions of God, and she points to the ethical harms caused by such ideas. Plaskow also rejects all models of sexuality that require domination and control, and she develops a Jewish ethic that celebrates sexual energy and pleasure, LGBTQ identities, and non-hierarchical sexual relationships (Tirosh-Samuelson 2014).

The American theologian Rabbi Rachel Adler has given particular attention to ways in which human claims about what Torah teaches, especially when expressed as law (halakhah), can perpetuate injustice. Rejecting liberal efforts to improve established systems of halakhah, she points to the systemic injustices of those halakhic systems and argues for reimagining halakhah altogether. Adler (1998: 21) stresses the potential ethical value of such halakhah, conceived not as "a closed system of obsolete and unjust rules, but as a way for communities of Jews to generate and embody their Jewish moral visions." Like Plaskow, Adler articulates a Jewish sexual ethic that rejects all forms of domination, drawing especially on Biblical texts—such as the Song of Songs and the Book of Ruth—that value "both sensuous delight and the recognition of the other's subjectivity" (1998: 111). Adler also rejects the Rabbinic model for consecrating marriage, which inexorably positions men in a dominant position over women; she instead develops a new model for fully egalitarian marriage (between people of any genders) using models from a different part of Rabbinic law (the laws of business partnership). While Adler challenges the Rabbis' ideas of sexuality and marriage, she builds new norms on the basis of Rabbinic traditions, and she sees her work as in line with the Rabbinic idea that God depends on human beings to develop ethical norms governing human behavior (1998: 212).

Adler, eventually ordained as a rabbi within the Reform movement, previously identified as an Orthodox Jew before coming to reject the Orthodox assumption that norms accepted in Orthodox communities reflect God's will. Some other feminists, while critiquing Orthodox gender norms, have nonetheless sought to remain within Modern Orthodox communities and have developed new Orthodox approaches to revelation that can accommodate feminist critique. The Israeli philosopher Tamar Ross, for example, argued against the Orthodox doctrine of "the decline of the generations" and has claimed that divine revelation is ongoing and includes the insights of feminism. The established Written and Oral Torah are divine, in Ross' understanding, and reflect the reality that patriarchy was "necessary for its time"; but today, when patriarchy is no longer necessary, we may "consider the emergence of feminism as a new revelation of the divine will." Just as Orthodox Jews can consider Maimonides' Aristotelian ideas or the *Zohar*'s Gnostic and Neoplatonic ideas as part of Torah, they should consider feminist ideas in the same light (Ross 2004: 210). Ross opposes radical revisions to Orthodox halakhah but does allow for halakhic innovation that is "made in the context of the community, with appeal to established authorities, and finally, with reference to divine revelation" (Sufrin 2011: 243).

American feminist thinkers have developed a variety of other ideas about the revelation of Torah. Orthodox scholar Blu Greenberg (1981) has argued that revelation empowers rabbis to develop halakhah in line with ethical values, following the historic precedent that "where there was a rabbinic will, there was a halakhic way." Conservative rabbi Benay Lappe (2009), who specializes in queer theory and the study of Talmud, has developed an understanding of Torah grounded in the Talmudic Rabbis' understanding of "their informed internal ethical impulse as an authentic source of God's will." Reconstructionist rabbi Rebecca Alpert (1997), focusing on the experience of Jewish lesbians, has argued for expanding what is understood as "Torah" to include a wide range of literature including contemporary Jewish lesbian fiction. Rabbi Jill Hammer (2015), whose work has focused on developing earth-based and Goddess-centered Hebrew Priestess traditions, explores how prophetic revelation may be found in intuition, dreams, visions, and nature. Scholar Laurie Zoloth (1999), building on the approach of Emmanuel Levinas, argues that God's commanding voice is revealed in the voice of the disempowered other, as can be seen in narratives of disempowered women in the biblical book of Ruth. Scholar Mara Benjamin (2018) has explored how the meaning of Torah and obligation may be found through the experiences of caring for children. Scholar Michal Raucher (2020) has shown how, when making decisions about reproduction, contemporary Haredi women in Israel challenge conventional structures of rabbinic authority and instead rely on their own lived experiences and discernment of God's will.

On questions of reproductive justice, however, many other Jewish thinkers—whether Reform, Conservative, Orthodox, or otherwise affiliated, and including feminist thinkers—have focused less on women's autonomy and more on halakhic texts in the Mishnah and Talmud. Conservative rabbi Susan Grossman (2003), for example, argues that abortion is permissible according to Jewish law on the basis of the Mishnah's ruling (quoted in Chapter Two) giving precedence to a woman's life over that of a fetus, Rabbinic texts that see "the fetus as part of its mother's body," and a wide range of halakhic precedents that build on these and related Rabbinic traditions. Like many Jewish scholars who discuss abortion as a matter of halakhah, Grossman rules that abortion is required to directly save the life of a person giving birth and also permitted to protect her mental and physical health and well-being. But Grossman indicates that abortion is prohibited if it cannot be justified in such terms. Raucher (2022; 2023a; 2023b) has critiqued approaches such as this that are shaped by a "justification framework," which assumes abortion to be wrong unless it meets certain criteria; she argues that, rather than looking to halakhah developed by men who do not support bodily autonomy, contemporary halakhic discourse about abortion should center the value of bodily autonomy and the experiences of those who have had abortions. The different approaches to abortion taken by Grossman and Raucher reflect two different feminist approaches to understanding Torah, one of which centers Rabbinic halakhah and one of which centers voices that have been historically marginalized in the history of Jewish ethics.

SAVING LIVES AS A PRINCIPLE OF TORAH

Critics of feminism, by contrast, have more stridently opposed abortion except in very narrow circumstances. Canadian-American rabbi David Novak (2007), who left the Conservative movement in opposition to its ordination of women as rabbis in the 1980s, has argued against abortion unless a fetus or embryo poses a direct threat to the life of a pregnant woman. Building on Maimonides' understanding that a woman's life should be protected as a matter of self-defense against a life-threatening "pursuer," Novak sees warrant for abortion only when it is required to save a woman's life.

Not only with regards to abortion but with regards to a wide range of other issues, Jewish thinkers have developed the ancient Rabbinic principle that "saving a life" (*pikuah nefesh*) overrides most other commandments and considerations. Many thinkers, shaped by egalitarianism and universalism, have stressed that the principle demands going to great lengths to save anyone's life, regardless of whether they are Jewish and regardless of their gender, sexuality, disability, race, ethnicity, or class. Examples abound of calls to prioritize saving human lives through appeals to this principle: for example, in advocating for the LGBTQ people around the globe who are most marginalized and whose lives are most threatened (Eli 2020); in pointing to the need to donate money to organizations that can use those funds to save the lives of those endangered by treatable diseases (Teutsch 2009: 38); in calls for systems that protect the lives of all people, including those who are disabled, amidst global pandemics (Epstein-Levi 2020); in claims that it is obligatory to donate organs after death to save others' lives (Prouser 1995); in opposition to capital punishment (Zoosman 2022); in support of creating systems to protect refugees, asylum seekers, and migrants whose lives may be threatened (Goldstein 2023); and in calls to end wars—or in justifications for wars seen as saving lives (Dorff 2002). Some have suggested that the principle might also extend to protecting the lives of non-human animals (Croland 2019).

Among Orthodox thinkers, some have understood the priority of "saving a life" in less universalistic ways. Some have upheld the value of the Mishnah's rule that "the man takes priority over the woman with reference to saving a life," in a situation in which limited medical resources are available and all other considerations are equal (Zohar 1997: 116). Some have also defended the ancient Rabbinic ruling that a Jew is obligated to desecrate the Sabbath to save the life of someone who is Jewish but prohibited from saving the life of a Gentile; and some have extended the prohibition to also include a Jew who does not observe the Sabbath (on the grounds that the intent of the ruling is that one may desecrate the Sabbath to save a life only if it will enable the person being saved to observe future Sabbaths). Other Orthodox thinkers who believe that the ancient Rabbinic ruling reflects divine revelation, but are uncomfortable with its reasoning, have found ways to rule that a Jew should desecrate the Sabbath to save the lives of non-Jews as well as Jews. The Polish-Mexican Orthodox rabbi Jacob Avigdor, for example, taught that while Torah's halakhic rule does not require saving a non-Jew's life on the Sabbath, the virtue of compassion—also part of the Torah—does require it (Sagi 2021: 301–4).

On questions of war and peace, while many Orthodox thinkers have understood "saving a life" to refer to the lives of Jews above all, they have reached different conclusions based on their different understandings of the consequences of war and peace. The Israeli rabbi Ovadia Yosef supported the State of Israel giving up control of land for the sake of peace on the grounds that saving Jewish lives through a peace settlement with Palestinians would override the commandment for Jews to settle the land of Israel (Yuchtman-Yaar and Hermann 2000: 35). The Israeli rabbi Avraham Shapira, by contrast, argued that peace settlements would endanger Jewish lives—and that, in any case, the commandment to settle the land of Israel overrides the commandment to save lives (Heilman 1997: 347–9).

Seeing disagreements such as these allows us to see how one ethical principle, while depicted by some as central to the Torah, has been applied in very different ways by different modern Jewish thinkers.

LOVE, COMPASSION, JUSTICE, AND HUMILITY

Modern Jewish thinkers have also commonly depicted virtues such as love, compassion, justice, and humility as central to the Torah, while often understanding these virtues in strikingly different ways. Drawing on a longer discussion (Claussen 2022) of the genre of musar—Jewish discourse regarding virtue and character—this section presents some diverse approaches to these virtues.

Modern Jewish discourse about love often cites the central Biblical command to "love your fellow as yourself," that verse's Aramaic rephrasing in the Talmud, "Do not do anything to your fellow that is hateful to you," or the related Biblical commandment to "love the stranger as yourself." In the eighteenth century, German Haskalah leader Naphtali Herz Wessely stressed that the commandment to love one's fellow required seeing the equality of all human beings—seeing others as "like yourself." For Wessely, the virtue of love requires respecting the interests and feelings of all others and avoiding causing them pain. Other thinkers, such as Simhah Zissel Ziv—a leader of the nineteenth-century Musar movement, a Lithuanian Orthodox movement focused on the development of moral character—stressed the lengths to which one must go in cultivating love and compassion for others, understanding "as yourself" to mean that one's concern for others should be as strong as one's natural love for oneself or one's family. Emmanuel Levinas stressed that love required the life of one's fellow to take precedence over one's own, recognizing one's infinite responsibility for the other. American Renewal rabbi Lynn Gottlieb stressed how the obligation to love must include one's enemies, opposition to war, and a commitment to nonviolence;

she also pointed to the importance of love and compassion for oneself. The contemporary American Modern Orthodox rabbi Shmuly Yanklowitz is among those who have stressed the obligation to cultivate love and compassion not only for human beings but also for non-human animals (Claussen 2022: 235–71).

For Yanklowitz, the Torah's commandment to have compassion for non-human creatures is reflected in its prohibition on causing unnecessary suffering to animals. We saw in Chapter Three that Maimonides viewed a number of the Torah's commandments as linked with this commandment, preventing habits of cruelty and cultivating compassion, and Yanklowitz builds on this tradition. While he argues that compassion for animals should encourage a vegan lifestyle, he sees the commandments of the Torah as seeking to cultivate compassion towards animals even as they condone the use of animal products. Thus, for example, the commandment to shoo away a mother bird before taking her eggs or chicks teaches us "to be mindful of the pain we cause [animals] and to do everything we can to prevent their unnecessary suffering" (Yanklowitz 2020: 34–5).

We may contrast Yanklowitz's understanding of this particular commandment with modern Jewish approaches that see the commandment regarding the mother bird as an antiquated text, lacking compassion, that should not be valued at all. On the other hand, we may draw a contrast with modern Jewish approaches that follow the *Zohar*'s interpretation of this commandment, discussed in Chapter Three. In line with that interpretation, some modern Jewish thinkers have argued that one should intentionally cause distress to mother birds on the grounds that acting with cruelty towards them will bring divine compassion to the people of Israel (Slifkin 2021: 453).

Some modern Jewish thinkers have also pushed back against tendencies to see the Torah as commanding love for all human beings or as requiring a recognition of human equality. For example, the eighteenth-century founder of the Chabad Hasidic movement, Rabbi Shneur Zalman of Liadi (Belarus), stressed that the command to love one's fellow as oneself requires Jews to cultivate love for other Jews because of the divine soul that links nearly all Jews, but which is not possessed by non-Jews or unrepentant Jewish sinners. Similar teachings were taken up by later Chabad thinkers such as the Israeli rabbi Yitzchak Ginsburgh, who combined Shneur Zalman's approach to love with an embrace of militant Zionism and efforts to establish a Jewish theocracy in Israel and beyond. Notably, Ginsburgh—in stark contrast to figures such as Gottlieb who link love with nonviolence—sees the virtue of love as properly guiding Jews to support the violence necessary for building such a theocracy (Claussen 2022: 240–4, 255–8).

We can see similar tensions among modern Jewish thinkers who have seen justice as a virtue at the heart of God's Torah. In the United States in the early twentieth century, for example, the Reform rabbi Kaufmann Kohler depicted the core of the Torah as an ideal of impartial, rational justice and a commitment to defending not law but the rights of any oppressed human being. Notably, he depicted the Torah's commitment to reasoned justice as "masculine," contrasted with the virtue of love, which he associated with Christianity and femininity.

Contemporary American Reconstructionist rabbi Rebecca Alpert is among those who have criticized such efforts to associate gender with justice or to place love and justice in opposition to one another, highlighting ways in which a commitment to justice requires loving respect for all people, nonviolence, and addressing structural injustices. The contemporary American theologian Marc Ellis rejects Kohler's ideal of impartial justice and rationality, instead embracing a "prophetic" commitment to justice centered on the needs of the oppressed and marginalized, especially Palestinians facing injustices committed by the State of Israel. The contemporary African-American scholar Amanda Mbuvi articulates a vision of the Torah's sense of justice that is informed by diverse perspectives from a variety of peoples and cultures, in line with what she describes as "the Torah's vision of blessed interdependence."

Other modern Jewish thinkers have viewed the Torah's approach to justice rather differently. For example, a conception of justice developed by nineteenth-century Lithuanian Orthodox rabbi Israel Salanter, founder of the Musar movement, emphasizes the divine character of Rabbinic tradition for determining justice and insists on deference to present-day rabbinic authorities. The contemporary Orthodox rabbi Steven Pruzansky has articulated a vision of justice that similarly stresses the divinity of Rabbinic tradition, that refuses to be swayed by modern conceptions of justice that are merely the "clamoring" of human beings, and that understands Zionism as the will of God. Pruzansky recommends that Zionism be animated by God's sense of justice as reflected in the Bible, which sometimes demands violence and collective punishment carried out against "enemies" of the Jewish people (for Pruzansky, in the modern context, Palestinians) (Claussen 2022: 317–54).

Modern Jewish debates about how humility may be a core value of the Torah reflect many related disagreements regarding universalism, egalitarianism, feminism, and Zionism. While the late eighteenth-century Lithuanian Orthodox rabbi Pinḥas of Polotsk emphasized that elite scholars of Torah must show proper humility by holding themselves above the "ignorant masses," the contemporary American Conservative rabbi Ira Stone stresses that a humble person must learn from all human beings. While the twentieth-century Israeli Orthodox rabbi Shalom Noah Berezovsky developed a conception of humility as "taking up no space"—which he saw as a feminine quality—the contemporary American Reform rabbi Ruth Abusch-Magder teaches that humility requires taking up sufficient space, and that in a patriarchal world humility requires that women take up significant space and show significant pride. While Hasidic rabbi Naḥman of Bratslav links illicit pride with illicit forms of sexuality, including homosexuality, Reconstructionist rabbi Rebecca Alpert develops an idea of humility that involves accepting one's sexuality and seeing the holiness of gay and lesbian attraction. While the twentieth- century militant Israeli Orthodox rabbi Meir Kahane saw humility as encouraging a militant form of Zionism, the pacifist Eastern European Orthodox rabbi Aharon Shmuel Tamaret saw humility as demanding the rejection of war and nationalism. While thinkers such as Pinḥas, Berezovsky, Naḥman, and Kahane saw humility as compatible with the idea that the people of Israel are God's chosen people, thinkers such as Mordecai Kaplan viewed doctrines of chosenness as a sign of arrogance. In these and many other ways, what the Torah teaches about humility has been the subject of debate among modern Jewish thinkers (Claussen 2022: 55–88).

How is Torah revealed, and what is its ethical message? Modern Jewish thinkers have answered these questions in an astoundingly wide variety of ways. They have often emphasized virtues, principles, and laws that are named in classical Rabbinic texts, but they have understood these virtues, principles, and laws quite differently from the ancient Rabbis and quite differently from one another. These differences often reflect not only their varying ideas about God but also their very different positions on universalism, feminism and other forms of egalitarianism, Zionism and other forms of nationalism, and the relationship between human beings and non-human animals.

II THE CREATION OF THE WORLD

THE PLACE OF HUMAN BEINGS IN CREATION

Modern Jewish thinkers have also made diverse ethical claims with reference to ideas about God's creation of the world. These include claims about the role of human beings in relation to non-human animals and the broader non-human environment.

In the nineteenth century, Samson Raphael Hirsch developed the Rabbinic prohibition on "unnecessary destruction" by linking it directly to the Biblical commandment for humans to "master" the earth at the dawn of creation (Genesis 1:28). For Hirsch, the dominion over creation that God granted human beings must be limited by God's prohibition on wanton human destruction (Yoreh 2019: 123). As global environmental crises grew in the twentieth century, others applied that same Rabbinic prohibition to contemporary environmental concerns. The Israeli environmentalist Jeremy Benstein (2006: 100–1), for example, suggests that ensuring "the ongoing well-being of Creation" may require prohibiting environmentally destructive practices. In Benstein's model, human beings must also recognize their creation in God's image and so take responsibility to protect creation from destruction, in line with the commandment given in the Garden of Eden to "protect" God's creation (Bible, Genesis 2:15).

Modern Jewish thinkers have understood the link between creation and environmental ethics in a range of other ways. American environmentalist Ellen Bernstein (2009) highlights how the concept of creation may be understood in non-fundamentalist, feminist terms that can help Jews to recognize the goodness of the world, human interdependence with other creations, and the imperatives of living sustainably. Judith Plaskow (1990: 155, 231) points to the importance of affirming "that the earth is holy and that all parts of creation have intrinsic value" as a corrective "to the view that human beings are the measure of all things," and she has called for a feminism that entails "an active awareness of, and responsibility to, the complex web of life." Scholar Hava Tirosh-Samuelson (2023) emphasizes how virtues such as humility, modesty, temperance, and simplicity must be cultivated to care for God's creation. American rabbi David Seidenberg (2015) advances the idea that the entire created world reflects God's image, an idea that should lead humans to take a less anthropocentric view of creation and see its intrinsic value.

Jewish thinkers have also drawn on creation narratives in addressing the treatment of non-human animals. The American modern Orthodox rabbi Joseph Soloveitchik (2005: 34) pointed to the Torah's ideal of vegetarianism and the subsequent "concession … made to an evil drive" when God agreed to permit the "murder" of animals. Ben Ammi, the leader of the African Hebrew Israelites of Jerusalem, advocated for veganism as the diet of the Garden of Eden, "in harmony with the will of the creator" (Miller 2021: 422). The American scholar Aaron Gross (2014: 156) explores ways in which "divine concern for the sanctity of all life" is upheld in Biblical creation narratives as well as in later Jewish literature. Gross (176) also points to the agency of animals themselves in challenging human understandings of creation, as with the calf who responds with gestures and tears to Rabbi Judah's assertion that "for this you were created" (see Chapter Two of this book).

Other Jewish thinkers have advanced a "dominionist ethic," claiming that animals were created to benefit human beings (Gross 2014: 180). Some have also minimized many of the environmental concerns discussed above, often claiming that Jewish ethics privileges human economic interests above such concerns (Schwartz 1997). As with all issues, Jewish thinkers pursuing different agendas have constructed a wide range of claims about Jewish ethics.

THE NOAHIDE COMMANDMENTS

Modern Jewish thinkers have also engaged with the Rabbinic idea that God's commandments for all humanity—the "Noahide" commandments—were revealed at the dawn of creation or shortly thereafter. Hermann Cohen, for example, understood the seven central Noahide commandments discussed in Rabbinic sources as the core of a universal, rational ethic that could be derived through reason by any human being. Whereas the Talmud understood these commandments in a discriminatory fashion, Cohen understood them as treating all people equally and as revealing the rational, universalistic foundations of Jewish ethics (Novak 1981).

Are these seven commandments truly rational and universal, as Cohen claimed? While many modern Jewish thinkers have viewed the obligation to establish courts of law and the prohibitions on murder and robbery and some forms of sexual relations in such terms, others have questioned the universality and rationality of some of the other commandments, such as prohibitions on idolatry, blasphemy, eating a limb from a living animal, or the prohibition on male homosexual intercourse understood as part of the prohibition on illicit sexual relations.

David Novak has argued for the rationality of such commandments, arguing that the Noahide commandments can be understood as an expression of the rational "natural law" built into the fabric of creation. Like many thinkers, he suggests that the prohibition of "eating a limb" may be generalized into the prohibition on causing unnecessary suffering to animals. He further suggests that the prohibition on blasphemy "can be generalized into a rationally cogent prohibition of 'hate speech' against anyone's religion/god" and that the prohibition of idolatry "can be generalized into a rationally cogent prohibition of a type of modern pagan ideology, like Nazism, that advocates murder, robbery, and rape" (Novak 2005: 233). In defending a prohibition on homosexuality, Novak cites the Biblical narrative of creation, with its stress on heterosexuality and procreation, as he argues that "in Jewish tradition, homosexuality has been considered to be inconsistent with human nature and, therefore, to be avoided as humanly inappropriate behavior" (Novak 2000: 172). He also argues for the rationality of the Rabbinic understanding that the Noahide prohibition of murder includes a prohibition of abortion (Novak 1974).

Such arguments have been widely criticized. With regards to homosexuality, for example, the scholar Louis Newman (1998a: 49) has critiqued Novak's claim that "nature" shows procreation to be the primary purpose of sexuality, when other purposes (e.g. "pleasure and personal communion") seem no less "natural." And though many queer Jews have eschewed claims about what is natural and unnatural, some have used this language to affirm queer sexuality. In the language of the Su Kasha lesbian and gay Jewish community in New York: "We affirm that each human being must be taught that the awakening of sexual feeling and the desire for sexual activity are natural and good" (Plaskow 2005: 176).

Other Jewish thinkers have built on other approaches to the Noahide commandments. The contemporary scholar and rabbi Mira Wasserman, for example, has explored how the alternative Rabbinic framing of these commandments (discussed in Chapter Two) that prohibits animal castration and cross-breeding teaches "how to act in harmony with God and creation" and "align humans with other species." While Wasserman raises moral concerns with this tradition, she sees it as providing encouragement for developing "a Jewish ethics that honors human entanglements with other species, that cultivates our attachments and fellow-feeling, and that honors our own animal selves" (Wasserman 2019: 63–4).

CREATION IN THE IMAGE OF GOD

Modern Jewish discourse about creation and ethics has more often highlighted ways in which human beings are distinct from other creatures, uniquely created "in the image of God."

The idea that all humans are equally created in God's image has been central to modern Jewish theological frameworks for egalitarian and universalistic ethics. In the eighteenth century, for example, Naphtali Herz Wessely drew on the statement of Rabbi Akiva discussed in Chapter Two—"Beloved is the human being, who was created in the image"—to argue that the commandment to love all human beings requires seeing any other human being as "equal to you, similar to you, for he was also created in the image of God" (Claussen 2022: 240).

In the nineteenth century, such ideas played an important role for Jewish advocates of the abolition of slavery. The German-American Reform rabbi David Einhorn described the Biblical idea of creation in God's image as the "proclamation of the innate equality of all rational beings" and as teaching that slavery was a wicked institution. Yes, Biblical law permitted slavery, he acknowledged, but the true spirit of the Bible was contained in its teaching regarding creation:

"Can that Book hallow the enslavement of any race, which sets out with the principles, that Adam was created in the image of God (Gen. 1:27), and that all men have descended from one human pair?" For Einhorn, "to enslave beings created in His image" was "rebellion against God" (Wiese 2007: 352; Saperstein 2008: 211–2).

During the twentieth century, Jewish thinkers developed various understandings of what it means for all human beings to be created in God's image. Hermann Cohen (1995 [1919]: 85–93), for example, pointed to the rational/ethical capacities that link human beings with the idea of God. Martin Buber (1948: 73) wrote of the possibility of each individual perfecting their likeness to God through nurturing their unique potential. Emmanuel Levinas explored how the idea of human creation in God's image is a way of describing how other human beings show themselves as requiring our responsibility, generosity, and care (Morgan 2011: 145). American Modern Orthodox theologian Irving Greenberg anchored his thinking in the Mishnah's teaching that "whoever destroys a single soul is deemed by Scripture as if he had destroyed a whole world," which he interpreted to mean that all humans are unique, equal, and of "infinite value" (Greenberg and Freedman 1998: 31).

The Israeli rabbi David Hartman (2000: 143), advocating for a liberal form of Orthodox Zionism, argued that a Judaism respecting human rights could build on precedents in Rabbinic literature and the writings of Maimonides for recognizing all human beings as created in God's image, even as he acknowledged that these premodern sources did not readily embrace such egalitarian ideas. Hartman (2009) particularly criticized contemporary Israelis who "forget that Palestinians are human beings created in the image of God." Anti-Zionists have invoked similar rhetoric in defending Palestinian rights, as when American Reconstructionist rabbi Brant Rosen finds support from "the great sage Rabbi Ben Azzai, who famously taught that the concept of humanity being created in the divine image is the most central value of Torah" (Omer 2019: 170). Jessica Montell (2013), director of the Israeli human rights organization named after the concept of creation in the divine image—"B'tselem," "In [God's] Image"—frames the concept as "the religious source for the statement in the Universal Declaration of Human Rights that we are all created equal in dignity and rights."

Early twentieth-century pacifists such as Aharon Shmuel Tamaret and Natan Hofshi (Polner and Goodman 1994: 89, 93), as well as contemporary pacifists such as Lynn Gottlieb (2013: 92), have pointed to the imperative of seeing all people as created in God's image and so to refrain from war. Others, such as the contemporary Israeli philosopher Noam Zohar (2007: 177), have argued that war can be justified if "in fighting we take the utmost care to protect non-combatants, remembering that all humans are created in the divine image."

Ideas of creation in God's image have also played a notable role in modern Jewish advocacy against anti-Black racism. Abraham Joshua Heschel (1966: 95), for example, denounced racial injustice by arguing that every human being "must be treated with the honor due to a likeness representing the King of kings." Responding to ongoing racial injustices in the United States more than fifty years later, African-American Reconstructionist rabbi Sandra Lawson (2021) argued that "if we truly believe that all are created in God's image, it is time for us to live up to our values of freedom and justice for all and see each other's humanity." Scholar Amanda Mbuvi (2016: 151) has explored how the Biblical book of Genesis does not engage categories of race but instead connects diverse peoples and the rest of creation to a common family tree.

As American scholar and rabbi Julia Watts Belser (2023: 223–7) has pointed out, the idea of creation in God's image has also played an important role in modern Jewish affirmations of the rights and dignity of disabled people. But Belser points to the dangers of distinguishing between who has been created in God's image and who has not been, which often excludes those who are disabled. Maimonides' idea that the image of God refers to intellectual capacities suggests that those with intellectual disabilities are not in God's image. Those who have linked the image of God with capacity for speech indicate that nonspeaking people are not in God's image. Those who have linked upright posture with the image of God suggest that those without such posture are not in God's image. Belser also notes how the idea of creation in God's image is used to claim that "humans are more holy than other animals," ignoring the way that other species also mirror the divine. In Belser's own conception of the idea of God's image,

God reflects each one of us. Human beings, in all our radical particularity, offer a hundred thousand windows into holy possibility. God's gender is nonbinary, stone butch, faerie, and a thousand words we haven't named. God knows wheels and blindness from the inside. God has felt a runner's high and the exhilaration of the climb. God is Deaf. God is Black. God is Brown. God is queer. And it isn't only humankind. The dolphin's God has a dorsal fin. God is kin to us, to each of us, with all the paradox that this implies.

(Belser 2023: 227)

CREATION AND GENDER

Modern Jewish thinkers have also critiqued Rabbinic understandings that only men are created in God's image, often citing the egalitarian language of the Bible—"male and female he created them" (Genesis 1:27, 5:2)—as demanding gender equality. Blu Greenberg (1981), for example, grounded her Orthodox feminism in the idea of the equal dignity "of man and woman as created in the image of God" (11) while also rejecting "the notion that equality means androgyny. From the perspective of Judaism there can be separate, clear-cut roles in which men and women may function as equals without losing separate identities" (20). More liberal thinkers have argued for gender equality while rejecting such binary distinctions. The American Reform rabbi Margaret Moers Wenig (2009: 16), for example, looks to ancient Rabbinic traditions regarding the diversity of sex and gender, as well as literary devices used by biblical authors, in understanding Genesis 1:27 as pointing to the equality of "male and female and every combination in between."

American Reform rabbi Elliot Kukla (2008: 218–21), a trans and disabled activist, draws inspiration from Rabbinic traditions indicating that "not all of Creation can be understood within binary systems." These include the traditions discussed in Chapter Two that the first human being was created as an *androginos*, a gender non-binary person, and that the *androginos* is a "unique creation," or, as Kukla puts it, "he is a created being of her own." For Kukla, "the injunction to see one another as 'created beings of our own' is the basis of a liberation theology for men, women, transgender people, and everyone else."

Other thinkers have critiqued the emphasis on heterosexual marriage and procreation found in Rabbinic conceptions of creation. Judith Plaskow (1990: 210), for example, points to the ways in which all sexualities marked by respect and mutuality are paths to holiness reflecting the image of God. American Conservative rabbi Jessica Fisher (2023) has critiqued claims about procreation and parenthood, arguing that "if we truly believe that a person's value is derived from being created … in the image of the Divine," individuals must be celebrated "with no correlation to the number of children they raise, how they parent, or how those children connect to Judaism."

In contrast to Rabbinic traditions, modern Jewish interpreters have often viewed the Biblical character of Eve as an ethical exemplar. In a midrash written by the Israeli educator Miri Westreich (2022), for example, Eve "understands that Adam views her as merely a part of himself, and not as an independent entity with a mind and a will of her own." In exemplary fashion, she takes matters into her own hands and acts independently, eating from the Tree of Knowledge and thereby awakening Adam's ethical consciousness.

Many feminist thinkers have also reimagined the character of Lilith in positive terms. A midrash written by Judith Plaskow imagines that Adam—offended by Lilith's demand for equality—told stories to Eve about how Lilith was a demon. But Eve managed to meet Lilith and discovered that she was in fact a beautiful, brave, and kind woman. They shared stories, taught each other, "and the bond of sisterhood grew between them." Lilith is the heroine of the story in many respects, but Lilith is powerless on her own. Sisterhood, Plaskow writes, is "the real heroine of the story" (Plaskow 2005: 31–2).

NON-EGALITARIAN CREATION NARRATIVES

Other modern Jewish thinkers have constructed creation narratives that are not gender-egalitarian. Eliyahu Eliezer Dessler (1955: 4:116–7) described how the first woman was created for the sake of procreation—"just as a vessel for the man, with no free will of her own"—and how women in subsequent generations must continue to marry and focus on physical needs while their husbands focus on the realm of the spirit. The American Haredi rabbi Avigdor Miller (1980: 339–45) claimed that a wife's submissiveness is "natural" and railed against the "anti-natural" teachings of feminism and the "unrealistic dream of equal leadership in the family." The Israeli Orthodox rabbi Asher Meir (2005) claims that those not in heterosexual marriages do not fully reflect God's image, and he points to the importance of wives showing "deference to the husband." The Moroccan-born Israeli Bratslav Hasidic rabbi Shalom Arush (2010) describes a woman as created for the purpose of marrying and serving as a "helpmate" for her husband so that he may "grow in Torah" (379, 395); Arush also urges women to procreate and refrain from using birth control (except in rare circumstances, with a rabbi's permission), since "preventing the birth of children is the most contradictory thing there can be to all of creation" (191–2). The Ukraine-born American Chabad Hasidic rabbi Menachem Mendel Schneerson promulgated the Kabbalistic teaching that "the image of God" should be identified with the circumcised male Jewish form (Wolfson 2009: 154).

Schneerson's identification of the image of God with a form that is not only male but also distinctly Jewish is part of the history of modern Jewish thinkers whose thought is grounded in Rabbinic and Kabbalistic ideas of Jewish supremacy. The founder of Chabad Hasidism, Shneur Zalman of Liadi, described Gentile souls as coming from "impure shells which have no goodness in them whatsoever"—such that "all the good that the nations do is done for selfish motives." By contrast, Jews are created with two souls, one linked with impurity but able to be purified, and one that is "literally a part of God above" (Claussen 2022: 243). Elaborating on this scheme, Yitzhak Ginsburgh describes how Gentiles occupy the highest level of nature, but Jews are created superior to Gentiles, for they are linked with the realm above nature (Satherley 2013: 70–1). Non-Haredi Orthodox figures such as Meir Kahane (1998: 640–3) also constructed narratives of creation that privileged Jews, drawing on Rabbinic texts about how only Jews are called "human" and how only killing a Jew counts as having "destroyed a world." A core principle for Kahane (1998: 744) is that God's creation is marked by "separation ... to establish the inequality between one thing and another," including the inequality of Israel and other nations.

These are just a few of the approaches taken by modern Jewish thinkers who reject the idea that God created all people equally. Others have rejected ideas of racial equality (Goldstein 2006) or equality with regards to ability (Belser 2023). While universalistic and egalitarian understandings of creation have been widespread in modern Jewish ethics, non-universalistic and non-egalitarian approaches to creation have persisted throughout the modern era.

Looking more broadly over the range of views in this chapter's discussion of creation, we can see that Jewish thinkers have understood the ethical implications of creation in many different ways, reflecting very different views of God as well as different views of universalism, feminism and other forms of egalitarianism, and environmentalism.

III REDEMPTION FROM OPPRESSION

UNIVERSAL IMPLICATIONS OF THE EXODUS

Modern Jewish thinkers have also made diverse ethical claims drawing on narratives of redemption from slavery in Egypt as well as ideas about future messianic redemption. Whereas Rabbinic sources on redemption focused on the redemption of the people of Israel, modern Jewish thinkers have often focused on the universal implications of the exodus from Egypt and have also imagined messianic redemption in universalist terms.

The evils of Pharaoh's oppression of the Israelites in Egypt have often been imagined as evils that should not be inflicted upon any people. Some Jewish thinkers have engaged the exodus narrative while scorning its depiction of divine liberation, such as the members of the Jewish Labor Bund in Russia and Poland, who wrote in 1900 that "today we have over us thousands of Pharaohs who torment us" and saw the solution not in God's outstretched arm but in the workers of the world joining together to fight capitalism (Shuldiner 1999: 155–64). But others appealed directly to God, as when in the United States in the 1860s David Einhorn condemned defenders of slavery who acted like Pharaoh in claiming a historic right to enslave others (Saperstein 2008: 212). A century later, Abraham Joshua Heschel denounced the defenders of racial oppression who continued to act like Pharaohs (1966: 98).

Israeli philosopher Yeshayahu Leibowitz warned the Israeli government that its policies towards Palestinians were turning it into Pharaoh (Magid 2023a: 2). Looking at Pharaoh's decision to oppress the Israelites because they represented a "demographic threat," Brant Rosen (2016) accused the State of Israel of acting like Pharaoh in viewing Palestinians as a "demographic threat" to its identity as a Jewish state.

Whereas Rabbinic sources understood the Biblical commandments not to "oppress the stranger nor pressure him, for you were strangers in the land of Egypt" and to "love [the stranger] as yourself, for you were strangers in the land of Egypt" as referring to converts who join the people of Israel, many modern Jewish thinkers have understood these commandments as referring to marginalized groups among any people or nation. American Rabbi Morris Lazaron urged Jews to remember being strangers in Egypt and so to support Palestinian refugees' rights to return to their homes in the state of Israel (Levin 2023: 1–2). Ethiopian-Israeli politician Shlomo Molla insisted that Jews must remember their experience of slavery in Egypt and oppose racism and cruelty towards asylum seekers from Sudan and Eritrea (Eglash 2012). Judith Plaskow (1990: xviii) argues that "to have been a slave in the land of Egypt is the basis of a profound religious obligation to do justice"—to identify with those who suffer oppression, including women and including Palestinians under Israeli control. Drawing on the Bible's commandments and her experience of marginalization as a trans woman, the American scholar Joy Ladin (2019: 147) centers God's "demand that those who are seen as strangers be treated equally and included fully in communal life." The American Conservative rabbi Shai Held (2017: 156; 2024: 189–91) argues that "to take Jewish ethics seriously is to remember what it feels like to be a stranger and therefore to love the stranger," siding with "the weak and vulnerable against those who would harm them," and ensuring care for and protection of immigrants and foreigners.

For many modern interpreters, the Biblical heroes who defied Pharaoh were focused not just on liberating Israelites but on liberating others across lines of difference. For example, whereas Rabbinic sources viewed the midwives Shifra and Puah as Israelites concerned for their own people, modern thinkers often point to the uncertainty of their identities or imagine them as Egyptians whose concerns extended beyond their own group. The American liturgist Marcia Falk (2022: 83) describes Shifra and Puah as exemplars of compassion and courage, writing that "if they are indeed Egyptians, their defiance of their king in order to save children who are not of their own people is truly extraordinary." Conservative rabbi Sharon Brous (2021: 168) describes Shifra, Puah, and Pharaoh's daughter Batya as teaching contemporary Americans facing crises of rising white nationalism, climate change, and a global pandemic "to do whatever we can to stop the forward motion of an evil empire, protecting first and foremost the lives and humanity of those most vulnerable."

Amanda Mbuvi (2021) describes Pharaoh's misguided approach to ethics as distinguishing "between those humans who count and those who matter less, or not at all. It attributes authentic humanity only to a select group." By contrast, God calls for recognizing the interdependence of all creation and acting with solidarity and empathy. The story of the exodus presents characters whose identities are not easily sorted into Pharaoh's binary categories, including the midwives and Moses, and who are able to show solidarity with others—including with the diverse "mixed multitude" that joins the people of Israel in escaping from Egypt. For Mbuvi, the diversity within a political community that Pharaoh experienced as a threat can be recognized as "a source of strength," and "the alliance with the mixed multitude illustrates the potential for partnerships that transcend the covenantal particulars that constitute the people of Israel's distinctive identity" (Claussen 2022: 314).

Other thinkers have focused on Miriam as an ethical exemplar. In one midrash, Margaret Moers Wenig (2003) imagines Miriam refusing to believe that God would want all of the Egyptians to suffer. Challenging the plan to kill all Egyptian firstborns, Miriam helps to lead a coalition of Israelite and Egyptian women (including Shifra, Puah, Yocheved, and Batya) in a campaign of nonviolent resistance against Pharaoh. While Moses rejoices when the Egyptians drown in the sea, celebrating God as a "man of war," Miriam is saddened by the violence and death and is scarcely able to sing.

THE EXODUS AND JEWISH WELL-BEING

For other modern interpreters, the heroes of the exodus narrative are exemplary because of how they contribute to the well-being of their people—the people of Israel. Whereas the approaches discussed above were "universalistic"—focused on obligations to all people—these approaches can be described as "particularistic," focused on obligation to one's own particular people. The Israeli scholars Yedidia Stern and Karen Friedman-Stern (2017), for example, see the exodus narrative as teaching later generations of Jews that they must maintain high Jewish birthrates to maintain their nation: Shifra and Puah's legacy is appropriately taken up by the State of Israel as it advances policies that will promote Jewish fertility, ensuring that Israel has a majority Jewish population.

Meir Kahane (2014: 77–125) emphasized that the midwives were Jewish—indeed, that they were Miriam and Yocheved—and that they were exemplary in their love for the people of Israel, their willingness to sacrifice themselves for God and their people, and their understanding of the evils of abortion. Kahane (2014: 293–339) also points to the exemplary nature of Moses' behavior in Egypt, especially in his killing of the Egyptian taskmaster who had struck an Israelite, showing his sense of justice and his love for a fellow Israelite (Magid 2021a: 52–3). Moses also acts righteously when he leads the Israelites in song as the Egyptians drown, teaching later generations to rejoice in the downfall of their enemies (Kahane 2010: 119). And for Kahane, the "mixed multitude" was not a blessing but a curse, a source of foreign influences that contaminated the Jewish people. The mixed multitude is still found among those so-called Jews who propagate ideas contrary to the Torah, such as leftists who oppose the expulsion of Palestinians from Israeli territory; this mixed multitude must be fought through "an uncompromising battle" (Magid 2021a: 187).

The leading thinker of early twentieth-century Orthodox Zionism in Palestine, Rabbi Abraham Isaac Kook, also grounded his ideas in the story of the exodus from Egypt. Kook saw the Zionist settlement of the land of Israel as part of the redemptive process that began with the exodus from Egypt. He insisted that even secular Zionists, whom he viewed as evil and insolent in many ways, were contributing to the process of messianic redemption. Kook believed that Moses was right to accept even the "mixed multitude" that left Egypt along with Israel; similarly, Kook sought to accept secular Zionists as part of the ultimate redemption now taking place. Later Orthodox Zionists living after the formation of the State of Israel built on Kook's teachings to explain how humans were entitled to engage in the sort of violence that was reserved for God in the story of the exodus. The French-born Israeli rabbi Shlomo Aviner, for example, explained that at the time of the exodus "we were like babies for which everything was done." But "now, we are no longer babies," such that the Israel Defense Forces can emulate God directly rather than seeking God's supernatural intervention. For Aviner, the Biblical description of God as a "man of war" defeating the Egyptians at the time of the exodus is an attribute that Israelis can emulate: "Just as the Holy Blessed One is a 'man of war,' so we enlist in the Israel Defense Forces" (Claussen and Filler 2019).

For some anti-Zionist Orthodox Jews, by contrast, Zionism was an ideology created by Satan. It was an appalling heresy to claim that redemption could come by creating a Jewish state, clearly forbidden by the Torah prior to the coming of the Messiah. Kook's contemporary in Palestine, Rabbi Yeshaya Asher Zelig Margaliot, argued that Zionists were not truly a part of the people of Israel but part of the "mixed multitude," which Margaliot viewed as a demonic, non-Jewish group—"the offspring of Pharaoh"—that continually led the people astray with their foreign ideas. Whereas Kook saw Moses as accepting the mixed multitude, Margaliot saw Moses as wisely rejecting them from the community of Israel, and he insisted that present day rabbis follow Moses' example in hating and excluding present-day Zionist heretics. Later Orthodox anti-Zionists living after the formation of the State of Israel, such as the Satmar Hasidic rabbi Yoel Teitelbaum, similarly identified Zionists with the demonic mixed multitude and insisted that the well-being of the Jewish people would only be ensured if true, righteous Jews distanced themselves from such heretical Zionists (Inbari 2016: 182–98).

FUTURE REDEMPTION IN THE LAND OF ISRAEL

Anti-Zionist Orthodox Jews such as Margaliot and Teitelbaum (like the Zionist Orthodox Jews discussed above) fervently hoped for the Days of the Messiah when God would bring the people of Israel to the land of Israel. They believed, however, that Jews were forbidden from assuming political power in the land of Israel prior to that future redemption, a prohibition which the people had sworn not to violate (as per the tradition discussed in Chapter Two). "To go up [to the land of Israel] by force and to seize sovereignty and freedom by themselves, before the appointed time," Teitelbaum wrote, was "awful heresy, the like of which has not been seen since the world was created," "thousands of times worse than the golden calf," certainly a form of idolatry in which one should refuse to participate even if doing so would lead to one's death as a martyr. Teitelbaum argued that Zionism was the work of Satan, a demonic force that tested the Jewish people's resolve to trust in God, a false messiah whose power characterizes the period of great wickedness that precedes the time of the true messiah and true redemption (Ravitzky 1996: 65; Magid 2014).

Abraham Isaac Kook, by contrast, saw the Zionist movement of his day as bringing about the messianic age. In Kook's view, secular Zionists were unwittingly guided by "the divine spirit" and "repenting," making possible the eventual emergence of a state that would be guided by Orthodox understandings of Torah. Believing that the land of Israel was where God's presence dwelled, Kook argued that establishing Jewish sovereignty in the land would repair the broken cosmos. Kook's son, Rabbi Tzevi Yehuda Kook, built on his father's message after the establishment of the State of Israel, which he viewed as "divine." He stressed the need for the Jewish State to conquer and control every inch of the holy land, part of God's redemptive political agenda, which "no earthly politics can supersede." Relying on Kabbalistic ideas of how Jews were obligated to settle the land, his followers led efforts to settle the land conquered by Israel in 1967 and the opposition to returning any conquered land to Palestinians (Ravitzky 1996: 86–133). Even more radical figures such as Meir Kahane rejected the idea that the State of Israel was divine but pointed to its messianic potential if it supported violence against God's enemies (both the "mixed multitude" and Palestinians who refused to submit to the Noahide commandments) and liberated the land of Israel, including the site of the ancient Jerusalem Temple, for Jewish sovereignty (Magid 2021a: 187).

Liberal Orthodox Zionists challenged these models of messianism. David Hartman, for example, rejected the idea that there was something inherently holy in the land of Israel or the state of Israel but drew on the legacy of Maimonides in arguing that the land could become holy—and the state could potentially enable something "messianic"—if those living there acted with humanistic values. In line with Maimonides' depiction of a redeemed world, a messianic era would be possible in the land of Israel only without "triumphalist power-seeking nationalism" and only with the expansion of "knowledge, wisdom, and love" (Hartman 1985a: 291).

Prominent figures who identified with Israel's secular Jewish parties also drew on ideas about future messianic redemption. David Ben-Gurion depicted the State of Israel as "the beginning of the Redemption," gathering together Jews from the "four corners of the earth" as ancient prophets had foretold (Segev 2019: 407; Havrelock 2020: 101). As a "Messianic movement," Zionism would create a "model state" and transform life for people throughout the world, bringing about the end of human suffering (Ohana 2010: 15, 41; Luz 2003: 81). The Revisionist Zionist leader Uri Zvi Greenberg, by contrast, developed a messianic vision characterized by vengeance wrought by a warrior Messiah against other nations, and also requiring ongoing vigilance against enemies. In one of Greenberg's poems, his mother—who was murdered in the Holocaust—warns him that even "when the Redeemer comes and they beat their swords into plowshares" he should not do so, lest other nations again rise up against the Jewish people (Luz 2003: 183; Halevi 2023).

Jewish pacifists developed rather different visions of messianic futures, often eschewing the idea that there would be a single "messiah" but envisioning a peaceful messianic age towards which humanity could strive. Jessie Sampter envisioned humanity wisely beating its swords into plowshares and argued that the Jewish people would "become a beacon to mankind, a Messiah to the world," bringing redemption through its own suffering as it developed a peaceful socialist democracy in Palestine in peace with other peoples (Imhoff 2022: 151; Rock-Singer 2020: 434–42). Defining "messiah" as a term for "the expansion of ethical awareness" that would embrace nonviolence, Aharon Shmuel Tamaret imagined that Jews would eventually flourish in the land of Israel at the end of days—but only with the awareness, acquired through their experience in diaspora, of the foolishness of nationalism and its violent quest for territorial control (Gendler 2020: 135, 209).

FUTURE REDEMPTION BEYOND THE LAND OF ISRAEL

Many other modern Jewish thinkers, also disdaining the idea of an individual messiah, imagined the future messianic era in global terms without imagining Jews returning to the land of Israel. Early Reform movement leaders such as Kaufmann Kohler believed that in the messianic era Judaism would be adopted as the world's universal religion, or would at least be the major influence in shaping a worldwide commitment to monotheism and universalistic ethics. Such a future would be made possible by universal education and improvements to society and politics throughout the world. Jews had a duty to be involved in building such a future by spreading themselves throughout the world and spreading their universalistic message—certainly not by secluding themselves in the land of Israel and certainly not by supporting parochial political Zionism (Ariel 1991).

Other non-Orthodox Jewish thinkers developed similar concepts of the messianic mission of the Jewish people. Hermann Cohen, for example, emphasized how a messianic era would be characterized by socialism, a peaceful world ensured by an international confederation of states, and the ethical development of all human societies. Crucially, for Cohen, the messianic age is an ideal that will always remain out of reach—there is always more that can be done to improve the world—but humans are obligated to move closer towards the ideal. Jews, even as they may suffer, are tasked with living among diverse peoples and pointing towards universalistic, messianic ethical ideals (Schwarzschild 1956; Seeskin 1997).

As they have imagined future redemption in global terms, Jewish thinkers have often drawn different ethical conclusions. Some have justified their support of war by appealing to messianic ideals of peace but telling their audiences that such a messianic future could only come through war, as the early twentieth-century British-born American Reform rabbi J. Leonard Levy did in justifying his support of World War I (Saperstein 2008: 337). The German-born American rabbi Steven Schwarzschild, by contrast, insisted that messianic ideals of peace demand that Jews act in line with those ideals, opposing war, as "the road toward the messianic realization is hewn out of the rock of history by messianic actions" (Polner and Goodman 1994: 21). Along similar lines, some have viewed vegetarianism as an ideal for the messianic age but something not yet appropriate for the present time, as Abraham Isaac Kook argued. The American writer Roberta Kalechofsky (1998: 29), by contrast, argued that embracing the messianic ideal of vegetarianism in the present will bring the world towards the messianic future.

Jewish thinkers have also imagined that a messianic era would be characterized by gender justice and pointed to the imperative to work towards such an ideal. Rachel Adler employs a Yiddish folktale of Skotsl, a woman who seeks to climb to heaven to present God with evidence of gender injustice on earth; in Adler's interpretation, Skotsl is "the messiah" who seeks to correct God's misunderstandings. For Adler, the messianic work of correcting misguided conceptions of Torah must now take place on earth, where Jewish feminists have inherited Skotsl's messianic task "to engender a new world" (Adler 1998: 21–59). Drawing on Biblical texts, American Renewal rabbi Arthur Waskow (1978: 167–91) has explored how the messianic task of dismantling patriarchy is linked with other messianic tasks, including achieving ecological harmony, economic justice, security for all people, and the abolition of war. Julia Watts Belser (2015b; 2023) critiques visions of redemption in which bodies of people with disabilities must be "healed" to match able-bodied norms, and she draws on other Jewish texts as she dreams of a world in which people with bodies of all kinds will be safe and will thrive.

In recent decades, many modern Jewish thinkers have used the Hebrew phrase *tikkun olam*—"repairing the world," sometimes understood as "perfecting the world"—to refer to ethical action that would bring the world closer to redemption. *Tikkun olam* is often invoked to describe an obligation to pursue social justice (e.g. Blumenfeld 2012 on LGBTQ rights, Weisberg and Landsberg 2021 on climate justice, Lawson 2023 on racial justice, Barenblat 2024 on reproductive justice). Pointing to the ideal of a world that has been "repaired" or "perfected," it is sometimes directly linked with the language of messianism, as when the American rabbi Jill Jacobs (2015: 517) describes *tikkun olam* as improving law and policy "in order to help society to flourish, while also drawing inspiration from the possibility of summoning the divine presence and moving closer to the messianic era."

These aspirational visions give little attention to (or explicitly reject) the particularistic aspects of ancient Rabbinic messianism such as the return of the Jewish people to the land of Israel, and those who think authentic Jewish ethics must adopt such Rabbinic ideas sometimes view these modern visions as inauthentic. So too, those who think that authentic Jewish ethics must center the State of Israel claim that universalistic visions of "repairing the world" that show little interest in Israel are inauthentic (Barnett 2016; Neumann 2018).

Looking over the range of ethical claims made with reference to redemption in this chapter, we can see that Jewish thinkers have understood the ethical implications of redemption in many different ways, reflecting varying views of universalism, feminism and other forms of egalitarianism, Zionism and other forms of nationalism, and environmentalism. And Jews continue to argue about which of these ideas should be included in and which should be excluded from presentations of Jewish ethics.

CONCLUSIONS

Modern Jewish thinkers have often made ethical claims with reference to creation, revelation, and redemption. They have also drawn on other sorts of theological ideas and narratives not connected to these three categories, but creation, revelation, and redemption have played a significant role, and focusing on these categories allows us to see how modern Jewish thinkers have often arrived at very different conclusions even as they have drawn on these common motifs. We can further see how their ethical claims, shaped by uniquely modern contexts and ideas, are often quite different from the claims of the premodern thinkers discussed in Chapters Two and Three of this book. Many of their claims are also quite different from the claims discussed in Chapter Four that were made without reference to theological frameworks (though some modern Jewish thinkers have engaged both theological and non-theological frameworks, which may complement one another, and some of those thinkers have been mentioned both in the previous chapter and in this chapter).

As with ideas discussed throughout this book, some may view various ideas discussed in this chapter as outside the bounds of what should count as Jewish ethics. Those who believe that Jewish ethics is defined by egalitarianism and universalism may view the non-egalitarian and non-universalistic teachings in this chapter as beyond the bounds of Jewish ethics. Those who believe that authentic Jewish ethics must accept the non-universalistic and non-egalitarian ideas found in Biblical and Rabbinic sources may doubt the authenticity of the universalistic and egalitarian ideas in this chapter. Others may doubt the authenticity of perspectives in this chapter that do not defer to the authorities they think have the right to define the boundaries of Jewish ethics. Others may doubt the authenticity of perspectives from marginalized populations, perhaps because they associate authenticity with hierarchies of gender, sexuality, disability, race, ethnicity, and class. But this chapter has sought to introduce the diversity of modern theological Jewish ethics, and so I have sought to include a wide range of views, including those that have often been marginalized in histories of Jewish ethics.

The examples in this chapter, considered along with the examples cited throughout the rest of this book, enable us to see how Jews in different contexts have developed a wide range of ethical ideas shaped by Jewish tradition, experience, history, and identity.

This chapter supports the overall argument of this book: that the most basic thing to know about "Jewish ethics" is that it has been constructed in different ways by different people in different contexts and for different reasons. While this book does not explore the details of those contexts and reasons, it is intended as an introduction that opens the door to further study. I hope that it will inspire further inquiry and reflection on the ethical ideas developed by Jews and by others.

FURTHER READING

On the approaches of modern Jewish religious movements and influential modern Jewish thinkers, see Elliot N. Dorff and Jonathan K. Crane, eds., *The Oxford Handbook of Jewish Ethics and Morality* (2013).

On modern Jewish debates about virtue, see Geoffrey D. Claussen, *Modern Musar: Contested Virtues in Jewish Thought* (2002).

On the implications of the exodus narrative, see Geoffrey D. Claussen and Emily A. Filler, "The Exodus and Some Possibilities of Jewish Political Thought" (2019).

On messianism and Zionism, see Aviezer Ravitzky, *Messianism, Zionism, and Jewish Religious Radicalism* (1996); and David Ohana, *Political Theologies in the Holy Land: Israeli Messianism and Its Critics* (2010).

On gender and sexuality, see Elyse Goldstein, ed., *New Jewish Feminism: Probing the Past, Forging the Future* (2009); and Gregg Drinkwater, Joshua Lesser, and David Shneer, eds., *Torah Queeries: Weekly Commentaries on the Hebrew Bible* (2009).

On disability, see Julia Watts Belser, *Loving Our Own Bones: Disability Wisdom and the Spiritual Subversiveness of Knowing Ourselves Whole* (2023).

On race, see Jonathan K. Crane, ed., *Judaism, Race, and Ethics: Conversations and Questions* (2020).

On environmental ethics, see Martin D. Yaffe, ed., *Judaism and Environmental Ethics: A Reader* (2001); and Jeremy Benstein, *The Way into Judaism and the Environment* (2006).

On animal ethics, see Jacob Labendz and Shmuly Yanklowitz, eds., *Jewish Veganism and Vegetarianism: Studies and New Directions* (2019).

REFERENCES

PREMODERN SOURCES

Alphabet of Ben Sira. Translation from David Stern and Mark Mirsky, eds., *Rabbinic Fantasies: Imaginative Narratives from Classical Hebrew Literature* (Philadelphia: The Jewish Publication Society, 1990).

Avot de-Rabbi Natan. Translated from the Hebrew text at https://www.sefaria. org/Avot_DeRabbi_Natan.

Babylonian Talmud (BT). Translated from the Hebrew and Aramaic text, consulting the translation and commentary by Adin Even-Israel Steinsaltz, at https://www.sefaria.org/texts/Talmud/Bavli.

Bible. Translation generally follows *Tanakh: The Holy Scriptures* (Philadelphia: The Jewish Publication Society, 1985).

Ecclesiastes Rabbah. Translated from the Hebrew text at https://www.sefaria. org/Kohelet_Rabbah.

Genesis Rabbah. Translated from the Hebrew text at https://www.sefaria.org/ Bereshit_Rabbah.

Maimonides, *Commentary on the Mishnah* (CM). Translations from Raymond L. Weiss and Charles E. Butterworth, eds., *Ethical Writings of Maimonides* (New York: New York University Press, 1975); and Hannah Kasher, "Maimonides on the Intellects of Women and Gentiles," in *Interpreting Maimonides: Critical Essays*, ed. Charles H. Manekin and Daniel Davies (Cambridge: Cambridge University Press, 2019), 63.

Maimonides, *Guide of the Perplexed* (GP). Translation, with minor modifications, from *The Guide of the Perplexed*, trans. Shlomo Pines, 2 vols. (Chicago: University of Chicago Press, 1963).

Maimonides, *Mishneh Torah* (MT). Translated from the Hebrew text at https:// www.sefaria.org/texts/Halakhah/Mishneh%20Torah.

Mekhilta de-Rabbi Yishmael. Translated from the Hebrew text at https://www. sefaria.org/Mekhilta_DeRabbi_Yishmael.

Mishnah. Translated from the Hebrew text, consulting the translation by Joshua Kulp, at https://www.sefaria.org/texts/Mishnah.

Palestinian Talmud (PT). Translated from the Hebrew and Aramaic text at https://www.sefaria.org/texts/Talmud/Yerushalmi.

Sifra. Translated from the Hebrew text at https://www.sefaria.org/Sifra.

Tikkunei Ha-Zohar. Translated from the Aramaic text at https://www.sefaria.org/Tikkunei_Zohar.

Zohar. Translation from *The Zohar (Pritzker Edition)*, 12 vols., trans. Daniel Matt, Nathan Wolski, and Joel Hecker (Stanford: Stanford University Press, 2004–2017).

Zohar Ḥadash. Translated from the Aramaic text at https://www.sefaria.org/Zohar_Chadash.

MODERN SOURCES

Abrams, Judith Z. 1998. *Judaism and Disability: Portrayals in Ancient Texts from the Tanach Through the Bavli.* Washington: Gallaudet University Press.

Adler, Rachel. 1998. *Engendering Judaism: An Inclusive Theology and Ethics.* Philadelphia: The Jewish Publication Society.

Almagor, Laura. 2022. *Beyond Zion: The Jewish Territorialist Movement.* Oxford: The Littman Library of Jewish Civilization.

Alpert, Rebecca T. 1997. *Like Bread on the Seder Plate: Jewish Lesbians and the Transformation of Tradition.* New York: Columbia University Press.

Alroey, Gur. 2016. *Zionism Without Zion: The Jewish Territorial Organization and Its Conflict with the Zionist Organization.* Detroit: Wayne State University Press.

Anderson, Bonnie S. 2017. "How Jewish Was Ernestine Rose?" *Jewish Book Council.* January 25. https://www.jewishbookcouncil.org/pb-daily/how-jewish-was-ernestine-rose.

Antler, Joyce. 2018. *Jewish Radical Feminism: Voices from the Women's Liberation Movement.* New York: New York University Press.

"Arab Refugees." 1948. *Jewish Labor Bund Bulletin* 1 (8–9): 4.

Arendt, Hannah. 1951. *The Origins of Totalitarianism.* New York: Harcourt, Brace and Co.

Ariel, Yaakov. 1991. "Kaufmann Kohler and His Attitude Toward Zionism: A Reexamination." *American Jewish Archives* 43 (2): 207–223.

Arush, Shalom. 2010. *Women's Wisdom: The Garden of Peace for Women Only.* Translated by Lazer Brody. Jerusalem: Chut Shel Chessed Institutions.

Auron, Yair. 2017. "Israel, Partner in Genocides." *Haaretz.* October 2. https://www.haaretz.com/opinion/2017-10-02/ty-article/.premium/israel-partner-in-genocides/0000017f-e33b-d804-ad7f-f3fb30370000.

Avineri, Shlomo. 2017. *The Making of Modern Zionism: The Intellectual Origins of the Jewish State.* 2nd ed. New York: Basic Books.

Baader, Benjamin Maria. 2006. *Gender, Judaism, and Bourgeois Culture in Germany, 1800–1870*. Bloomington: Indiana University Press.

Baker, Cynthia M. 2017. *Jew*. New Brunswick: Rutgers University Press.

Barenblat, Rachel. 2024. "Bringing Repair: A D'var Torah for #reproshabbat." *Velveteen Rabbi*. February 8. https://velveteenrabbi.blogs.com/blog/2024/02/repair.html.

Barer, Deborah. 2023. "Rabbinic Literature." In *Jewish Virtue Ethics*, edited by Geoffrey D. Claussen, Alexander Green, and Alan L. Mittleman, 51–64. Albany: SUNY Press.

Barnett, Michael N. 2016. *The Star and the Stripes: A History of the Foreign Policies of American Jews*. Princeton: Princeton University Press.

Baskin, Judith R. 2002. *Midrashic Women: Formations of the Feminine in Rabbinic Literature*. Waltham: Brandeis University Press.

Batnitzky, Leora. 2011. *How Judaism Became a Religion: An Introduction to Modern Jewish Thought*. Princeton: Princeton University Press.

Behar, Moshe, and Zvi Ben-Dor Benite, eds. 2013. *Modern Middle Eastern Jewish Thought: Writings on Identity, Politics, and Culture, 1893–1958*. Waltham: Brandeis University Press.

Beinart, Peter. 2021. "Teshuvah: A Jewish Case for Palestinian Refugee Return." *Jewish Currents*. May 11. https://jewishcurrents.org/teshuvah-a-jewish-case-for-palestinian-refugee-return.

Beiner, Ronald. 2000. "Arendt and Nationalism." In *The Cambridge Companion to Hannah Arendt*, edited by Dana Villa, 44–62. Cambridge: Cambridge University Press.

Belser, Julia Watts. 2015a. "Disability, Animality, and Enslavement in Rabbinic Narratives of Bodily Restoration and Resurrection." *Journal of Late Antiquity* 8 (2): 288–305.

Belser, Julia Watts. 2015b. "Violence, Disability, and the Politics of Healing: The Inaugural Nancy Eiesland Endowment Lecture." *Journal of Disability and Religion* 19 (3): 177–197.

Belser, Julia Watts. 2016. "Judaism and Disability." In *Disability and World Religions: An Introduction*, edited by Darla Y. Schumm and Michael Stoltzfus, 93–113. Waco: Baylor University Press.

Belser, Julia Watts. 2018a. "Queering the Dissident Body: Race, Sex, and Disability in Rabbinic Blessings on Bodily Difference." In *Unsettling Science and Religion: Contributions and Questions from Queer Studies*, edited by Lisa Stenmark and Whitney Bauman, 161–181. Lanham: Lexington Books.

Belser, Julia Watts. 2018b. *Rabbinic Tales of Destruction: Gender, Sex, and Disability in the Ruins of Jerusalem*. New York: Oxford University Press.

Belser, Julia Watts. 2023. *Loving Our Own Bones: Disability Wisdom and the Spiritual Subversiveness of Knowing Ourselves Whole*. Boston: Beacon Press.

Belser, Julia Watts, and Lennart Lehmhaus. 2016. "Disability in Rabbinic Judaism." In *Disability in Antiquity*, edited by Christian Laes, 434–451. Abingdon: Routledge.

Benjamin, Mara H. 2018. *The Obligated Self: Maternal Subjectivity and Jewish Thought*. Bloomington: Indiana University Press.

Benstein, Jeremy. 2006. *The Way into Judaism and the Environment*. Woodstock: Jewish Lights.

Berkowitz, Beth A. 2012. *Defining Jewish Difference: From Antiquity to the Present*. New York: Cambridge University Press.

Berkowitz, Beth A. 2018. *Animals and Animality in the Babylonian Talmud*. Cambridge: Cambridge University Press.

Berman, Donna. 2001. "Nashiut Ethics: Articulating a Jewish Feminist Ethics of Safekeeping." Ph.D. Thesis, Drew University.

Berman, Nathaniel. 2018. *Divine and Demonic in the Poetic Mythology of the Zohar: The "Other Side" of Kabbalah*. Boston: Brill.

Bernstein, Ellen. 2009. "Creation Theology: Theology for the Rest of Us." In *New Jewish Feminism: Probing the Past, Forging the Future*, edited by Elyse Goldstein, 42–53. Woodstock: Jewish Lights.

Bernstein, Richard J. 1996. *Hannah Arendt and the Jewish Question*. Cambridge: MIT Press.

Billet, Shira. 2023. "Hermann Cohen." In *Jewish Virtue Ethics*, edited by Geoffrey D. Claussen, Alexander Green, and Alan L. Mittleman, 337–351. Albany: SUNY Press.

Blidstein, Gerald J. 2001. *Ekronot Mediniyim Be-Mishnat Ha-Rambam (Political Concepts in Maimonidean Halakhah)*. 2nd ed. Ramat Gan: Bar Ilan University Press.

Blidstein, Gerald J. 2008. "Prayer Rescue and Redemption in the Mekilta." *Journal for the Study of Judaism* 39 (1): 68–87.

Blumenfeld, Warren J. 2012. "LGBT Discrimination and the Promise of Tikkun Olam." *HuffPost*. January 14. https://www.huffpost.com/entry/the-promise-of-tikkun-ola_b_1183985.

Boyarin, Daniel. 1990. *Intertextuality and the Reading of Midrash*. Bloomington: Indiana University Press.

Boyarin, Daniel. 1993. *Carnal Israel: Reading Sex in Talmudic Culture*. Berkeley: University of California Press.

Boyarin, Daniel. 1997. *Unheroic Conduct: The Rise of Heterosexuality and the Invention of the Jewish Man*. Berkeley: University of California Press.

Boyarin, Daniel. 2019. *Judaism: The Genealogy of a Modern Notion*. New Brunswick: Rutgers University Press.

Boyarin, Daniel. 2023. *The No-State Solution: A Jewish Manifesto*. New Haven: Yale University Press.

Brämer, Andreas. 2007. "Samuel Holdheim and Zacharias Frankel: Comparative Perspectives." In *Redefining Judaism in an Age of Emancipation: Comparative*

Perspectives on Samuel Holdheim (1806–1860), edited by Christian Wiese, translated by William Templer, 209–227. Leiden: Brill.

Brettschneider, Marla. 1999. "Theorizing Diversity from a Jewish Perspective." *Race, Gender and Class* 6 (4): 13–23.

Brettschneider, Marla. 2006. *The Family Flamboyant: Race Politics, Queer Families, Jewish Lives*. Albany: SUNY Press.

Brettschneider, Marla. 2010. "Critical Attention to Race: Race Segregation and Jewish Feminism." *Bridges: A Jewish Feminist Journal* 15 (2): 20–33.

Brettschneider, Marla. 2016. *Jewish Feminism and Intersectionality*. Albany: SUNY Press.

Brous, Sharon. 2021. "Sometimes Love Is a Call to Action." In *No Time for Neutrality: American Rabbinic Voices from an Era of Upheaval*, edited by Michael Rose Knopf with Miriam Aniel, 163–176.

Brown, Benjamin. 2014. "Jewish Political Theology: The Doctrine of Daat Torah as a Case Study." *Harvard Theological Review* 107 (3): 255–289.

Buber, Martin. 1948. *Israel and the World: Essays in a Time of Crisis*. New York: Schocken Books.

Butler, Judith. 2012. *Parting Ways: Jewishness and the Critique of Zionism*. New York: Columbia University Press.

Chazan, Meir. 2015. "'The Wise Woman of Givat Brenner': Jessie Sampter on Kibbutz, War, and Peace, 1934–1938." In *The Individual in History: Essays in Honor of Jehuda Reinharz*, edited by ChaeRan Y. Freeze, Sylvia Fuks Fried, and Eugene R. Sheppard, 83–96. Waltham: Brandeis University Press.

Claussen, Geoffrey D. 2022. *Modern Musar: Contested Virtues in Jewish Thought*. Lincoln and Philadelphia: University of Nebraska Press and The Jewish Publication Society.

Claussen, Geoffrey D., and Emily A. Filler. 2019. "The Exodus and Some Possibilities of Jewish Political Thought." In *T&T Clark Handbook of Political Theology*, edited by Rubén Rosario Rodriguez, 301–316. London: T&T Clark.

Claussen, Geoffrey D., Alexander Green, and Alan L. Mittleman, eds. 2023. *Jewish Virtue Ethics*. Albany: SUNY Press.

Cohen, Hermann. 1995 [1919]. *Religion of Reason Out of the Sources of Judaism*. Translated by Simon Kaplan. Atlanta: Scholars Press.

Cohen, Shaye J.D. 2005. *Why Aren't Jewish Women Circumcised? Gender and Covenant in Judaism*. Berkeley: University of California Press.

Colb, Sherry F. 2015. "Decoding 'Never Again'." *Rutgers Journal of Law and Religion* 16: 254–281.

Colb, Sherry F. 2019. "Linking Judaism and Veganism in Darkness and in Light." In *Jewish Veganism and Vegetarianism: Studies and New Directions*, edited by Jacob Labendz and Shmuly Yanklowitz, 267–288. Albany: SUNY Press.

Cotler, Irwin. 2017. "Elie Wiesel: Conscience of Humanity." *Loyola of Los Angeles International and Comparative Law Review* 39: 307–318.

Crane, Jonathan K. 2013. "Ethical Theories of Hermann Cohen, Franz Rosenzweig, and Martin Buber." In *The Oxford Handbook of Jewish Ethics and Morality*, edited by Elliot N. Dorff and Jonathan K. Crane, 134–149. Oxford: Oxford University Press.

Crane, Jonathan K. ed. 2020. *Judaism, Race, and Ethics: Conversations and Questions*. University Park: The Pennsylvania State University Press.

Croland, Michael. 2019. "Vegetarianism and Veganism among Jewish Punks." In *Jewish Veganism and Vegetarianism: Studies and New Directions*, edited by Jacob Labendz and Shmuly Yanklowitz, 95–116. Albany: SUNY Press.

Dan, Joseph. 1986. *Jewish Mysticism and Jewish Ethics*. Seattle: University of Washington Press.

Davis, Dena S. 1991. "Beyond Rabbi Hiyya's Wife: Women's Voices in Jewish Bioethics." *Second Opinion* 16 (March): 10–30.

Davis, Natalie Zemon. 2010. "David Nassy's 'Furlough' and the Slave Mattheus." In *New Essays in American Jewish History: Commemorating the Sixtieth Anniversary of the Founding of the American Jewish Archives*, edited by Pamela S. Nadell, Lance J. Sussman, and Jonathan D. Sarna, 79–93. Cincinnati: American Jewish Archives.

Dessler, Elijah Eliezer. 1955. *Mikhtav Me-Eliyahu*. Edited by Aryeh Carmel and Alter Halpern. London.

Deutscher, Isaac. 1968. *The Non-Jewish Jew, and Other Essays*. London: Oxford University Press.

Diamond, James Arthur. 2007. *Converts, Heretics, and Lepers: Maimonides and the Outsider*. Notre Dame: University of Notre Dame Press.

Dorff, Elliot N. 2002. *To Do the Right and the Good: A Jewish Approach to Modern Social Ethics*. Philadelphia: Jewish Publication Society.

Dorff, Elliot N. ed. 2005. *The Unfolding Tradition: Jewish Law After Sinai*. New York: Aviv Press.

Dorff, Elliot N., and Jonathan K. Crane, eds. 2013. *The Oxford Handbook of Jewish Ethics and Morality*. Oxford: Oxford University Press.

Dowty, Alan. 2000. "Much Ado about Little: Ahad Ha'am's 'Truth from Eretz Yisrael,' Zionism, and the Arabs." *Israel Studies* 5 (2): 154–181.

Drinkwater, Gregg, Joshua Lesser, and David Shneer, eds. 2009. *Torah Queeries: Weekly Commentaries on the Hebrew Bible*. New York: New York University Press.

Dubois, Ellen Carol. 2007. "Ernestine Rose's Jewish Origins and the Varieties of Euro-American Emancipation in 1848." In *Women's Rights and Transatlantic Antislavery in the Era of Emancipation*, edited by Kathryn Kish Sklar and James Stewart, 279–296. Yale University Press.

Dzmura, Noach, ed. 2010. *Balancing on the Mechitza: Transgender in Jewish Community*. Berkeley: North Atlantic Books.

Eglash, Ruth. 2012. "Ethiopian Israelis Slam Attacks Against Migrants." *The Jerusalem Post*. May 6. http://www.jpost.com/LandedPages/PrintArticle.asp x?id=272700.

Eilberg-Schwartz, Howard. 1994. *God's Phallus and Other Problems for Men and Monotheism*. Boston: Beacon Press.

Einstein, Albert. 1935. *The World As I See It*. Translated by Alan Harris. London: John Lane The Bodley Head.

Eli, Adam. 2020. *The New Queer Conscience*. New York: Penguin Workshop.

Epstein-Levi, Rebecca J. 2020. "In the Time of COVID-19, Ventilators Are Scarce. How Do We Decide Who Gets Them?" *Berkley Forum*. April 13. https://berkleycenter.georgetown.edu/responses/in-the-time-of-covid-19-ve ntilators-are-scarce-how-do-we-decide-who-gets-them.

Epstein-Levi, Rebecca J. 2023. "Jewish Feminism." In *Jewish Virtue Ethics*, edited by Geoffrey D. Claussen, Alexander Green, and Alan L. Mittleman, 369–482. Albany: SUNY Press.

Faigan, Suzanne Sarah. 2018. "An Annotated Bibliography of Maria Yakovlevna Frumkina (Esther)." Ph.D. Thesis, The Australian National University.

Falk, Marcia. 2022. *Night of Beginnings: A Passover Haggadah*. Philadelphia and Lincoln: The Jewish Publication Society and University of Nebraska Press.

Faur, José. 1968. "Understanding the Covenant." *Tradition: A Journal of Orthodox Jewish Thought* 9 (4): 33–55.

Feiner, Shmuel. 1999. "Haskalah Attitudes Toward Women." *Jewish Women's Archive, Shalvi/Hyman Encyclopedia of Jewish Women*. https://jwa.org/ency clopedia/article/haskalah-attitudes-toward-women.

Filler, Emily. 2015. "Classical Rabbinic Literature and the Making of Jewish Ethics." *Journal of Jewish Ethics* 1 (1): 153–170.

Firestone, Reuven. 2012. *Holy War in Judaism: The Fall and Rise of a Controversial Idea*. New York: Oxford University Press.

Fishbane, Eitan P. 2018. *The Art of Mystical Narrative: A Poetics of the Zohar*. New York: Oxford University Press.

Fishbane, Eitan P. 2023. "The Zohar." In *Jewish Virtue Ethics*, edited by Geoffrey D. Claussen, Alexander Green, and Alan L. Mittleman, 137–148. Albany: SUNY Press.

Fisher, Jessica. 2023. "*I Am a Single Rabbi Without Children. I Shouldn't Be Made to Feel I Am Not 'Doing My Part'*." *Jewish Telegraphic Agency*. January 24. https:// www.jta.org/2023/01/24/ideas/i-am-a-single-rabbi-without-children-i-sho uldnt-be-made-to-feel-i-am-not-doing-my-part.

Fonrobert, Charlotte Elisheva. 2013. "Ethical Theories in Rabbinic Literature." In *The Oxford Handbook of Jewish Ethics and Morality*, edited by Elliot N. Dorff and Jonathan K. Crane, 51–70. Oxford: Oxford University Press.

Fuchs, Esther. 2014. *Israeli Feminist Scholarship: Gender, Zionism, and Difference*. Austin: University of Texas Press.

Fuchs, Esther. 2018. *Jewish Feminism: Framed and Reframed*. Lanham: Lexington Books.

Gendler, Everett, ed. 2020. *A Passionate Pacifist: Essential Writings of Aaron Samuel Tamares*. Teaneck: Ben Yehuda Press.

Gessen, Masha. 2023. "In the Shadow of the Holocaust." *The New Yorker*, December 9. https://www.newyorker.com/news/the-weekend-essay/in-the-shadow-of-the-holocaust.

Goldstein, Elyse, ed. 2009. *New Jewish Feminism: Probing the Past, Forging the Future*. Woodstock: Jewish Lights.

Goldstein, Eric L. 2006. *The Price of Whiteness: Jews, Race, and American Identity*. Princeton: Princeton University Press.

Goldstein, Lizz. 2023. "Shoftim: 'Thus Blood of the Innocent Will Not Be Shed' The Necessity of Sanctuary." *T'ruah*. August 15. https://truah.org/resources/lizz-goldstein-shoftim-moraltorah_2023_.

Goodman, Lenn E. 2002. "Respect for Nature in the Jewish Tradition." In *Judaism and Ecology: Created World and Revealed Word*, edited by Hava Tirosh-Samuelson, 227–259. Cambridge: Center for the Study of World Religions, Harvard Divinity School.

Gordon, Lewis R. 2018. "Afro-Jewish Ethics?" In *Jewish Religious and Philosophical Ethics*, edited by Halla Kim, Berel Dov Lerner, and Curtis Hutt, 213–227. New York: Routledge.

Gottlieb, Lynn. 2013. *Trail Guide to the Torah of Nonviolence*. Paris: Éditions Terre d'Espérance.

Gottlieb, Michah. 2011a. *Faith and Freedom: Moses Mendelssohn's Theological-Political Thought*. New York: Oxford University Press.

Gottlieb, Michah. ed. 2011b. *Moses Mendelssohn: Writings on Judaism, Christianity, and the Bible*. Translated by Curtis Bowman, Elias Sacks, and Allan Arkush. Waltham: Brandeis University Press.

Green, Arthur. 2004. *A Guide to the Zohar*. Stanford: Stanford University Press.

Greenberg, Blu. 1981. *On Women and Judaism: A View from Tradition*. Philadelphia: Jewish Publication Society of America.

Greenberg, Irving, and Shalom Freedman. 1998. *Living in the Image of God: Jewish Teachings to Perfect the World*. Northvale: Jason Aronson.

Greenberg, Steven. 2004. *Wrestling with God and Men: Homosexuality in the Jewish Tradition*. Madison: University of Wisconsin Press.

Gross, Aaron S. 2014. *The Question of the Animal and Religion: Theoretical Stakes, Practical Implications*. New York: Columbia University Press.

Grossman, Susan. 2003. "'Partial Birth Abortion' and the Question of When Human Life Begins." *Rabbinical Assembly*. https://www.rabbinicalassembly.

org/sites/default/files/public/halakhah/teshuvot/20052010/grossman_partial
_birth.pdf.

Hacohen, Dvora. 2003. *Immigrants in Turmoil: Mass Immigration to Israel and Its Repercussions in the 1950s and After.* Syracuse: Syracuse University Press.

Hakkâri, A.S. 2024. "Life on the Borderlands: Mizrahiut, Transfemininity, and Stateless Diasporas." In *Jewcy: Jewish Queer Lesbian Feminisms for the Twenty-First Century*, edited by Marla Brettschneider, 91–97. Albany: SUNY Press.

Halbertal, Moshe. 1997. *People of the Book: Canon, Meaning, and Authority.* Cambridge: Harvard University Press.

Halbertal, Moshe. 2021. "The Nature and Purpose of Divine Law." In *Maimonides' Guide of the Perplexed: A Critical Guide*, edited by Daniel Frank and Aaron Segal, 247–265. Cambridge: Cambridge University Press.

Halevi, Yossi Klein. 2023. "The Wounded Jewish Psyche and the Divided Israeli Soul." *The Times of Israel.* July 28. https://www.timesofisrael.com/ the-wounded-jewish-psyche-and-the-divided-israeli-soul.

Hammer, Jill. 2015. *The Hebrew Priestess: Ancient and New Visions of Jewish Women's Spiritual Leadership.* With Taya Shere. Teaneck: Ben Yehuda Press.

Harris, Jay Michael. 1995. *How Do We Know This?: Midrash and the Fragmentation of Modern Judaism.* Albany: SUNY Press.

Hartman, David. 1985a. *A Living Covenant: The Innovative Spirit in Traditional Judaism.* New York: Free Press.

Hartman, David. 1985b. "Discussion of the Epistle to Yemen." In *The Epistles of Maimonides: Crisis and Leadership*, edited by Abraham S. Halkin and David Hartman. Philadelphia: The Jewish Publication Society.

Hartman, David. 2000. *Israelis and the Jewish Tradition: An Ancient People Debating Its Future.* New Haven: Yale University Press.

Hartman, David. 2009. "Israeli and Palestinian Relations: Into the Future." *Shalom Hartman Institute.* February 2. https://www.hartman.org.il/israeli-a nd-palestinian-relations-into-the-future.

Havkin, Shira. 2021. "Israel: Asylum Without Refugee Status: Israel's Reception of Vietnamese Exiles." In *When Boat People Were Resettled, 1975–1983: A Comparative History of European and Israeli Responses to the South-East Asian Refugee Crisis*, edited by Becky Taylor, Karen Akoka, Marcel Berlinghoff, and Shira Havkin. Cham: Palgrave Macmillan.

Havrelock, Rachel S. 2020. *The Joshua Generation: Israeli Occupation and the Bible.* Princeton: Princeton University Press.

Hayes, Christine Elizabeth. 2015. *What's Divine About Divine Law?: Early Perspectives.* Princeton: Princeton University Press.

Hecht, Louise. 2005. "The Beginning of Modern Jewish Historiography: Prague: A Center on the Periphery." *Jewish History* 19 (3/4): 347–373.

Heilman, Samuel C. 1997. "Guides of the Faithful: Contemporary Religious Zionist Rabbis." In *Spokesmen for the Despised: Fundamentalist Leaders of the Middle East*, edited by R. Scott Appleby, 328–362. Chicago: University of Chicago Press.

Heinze, Andrew R. 2004. *Jews and the American Soul: Human Nature in the Twentieth Century*. Princeton: Princeton University Press.

Held, Shai. 2013. *Abraham Joshua Heschel: The Call of Transcendence*. Bloomington: Indiana University Press.

Held, Shai. 2017. *The Heart of Torah: Essays on the Weekly Torah Portion*. Vol. 2. Philadelphia and Lincoln: The Jewish Publication Society and University of Nebraska Press.

Held, Shai. 2024. *Judaism Is About Love: Recovering the Heart of Jewish Life*. New York: Farrar, Straus and Giroux.

Heller, Daniel Kupfert. 2017. *Jabotinsky's Children: Polish Jews and the Rise of Right-Wing Zionism*. Princeton: Princeton University Press.

Herberg, Will. 1955. *Protestant, Catholic, Jew: An Essay in American Religious Sociology*. Garden City: Doubleday.

Herrera, Linda. 2021. "Cosmopolitan Middle East?: An Interview with Seyla Benhabib." In *Global Middle East: Into the Twenty-First Century*, edited by Asef Bayat and Linda Herrera, 319–330. Oakland: University of California Press.

Heschel, Abraham Joshua. 1955. *God in Search of Man: A Philosophy of Judaism*. New York: Farrar, Straus & Cudahy.

Heschel, Abraham Joshua. 1966. *The Insecurity of Freedom: Essays on Human Existence*. New York: Farrar, Straus & Giroux.

Heschel, Susannah. 2002. "Preface." In *Best Jewish Writing, 2002*, edited by Michael Lerner, xiii–xviii. San Francisco: Jossey-Bass.

Hirsch, Samson Raphael. 1956. *Judaism Eternal*. Translated by Isadore Grunfeld. Vol. 2. London: Soncino Press.

Horowitz, Elliott S. 2006. *Reckless Rites: Purim and the Legacy of Jewish Violence*. Princeton: Princeton University Press.

Idelson-Shein, Iris. 2014. *Difference of a Different Kind: Jewish Constructions of Race During the Long Eighteenth Century*. Philadelphia: University of Pennsylvania Press.

Imhoff, Sarah. 2022. *The Lives of Jessie Sampter: Queer, Disabled, Zionist*. Durham: Duke University Press.

Inbari, Motti. 2016. *Jewish Radical Ultra-Orthodoxy Confronts Modernity, Zionism and Women's Equality*. Translated by Shaul Vardi. New York: Cambridge University Press.

Isaac, Walter. 2006. "Locating Afro-American Judaism: A Critique of White Normativity." In *A Companion to African-American Studies*, edited by Lewis R. Gordon and Jane Anna Gordon, 512–542. Malden: Blackwell.

Isack, Arielle. 2023. "What Comes Next for Jews of Color Activism?" *Jewish Currents*. March 23. https://jewishcurrents.org/what-comes-next-for-jews-of-color-activism.

Israel, Jonathan. 2021. *Revolutionary Jews from Spinoza to Marx: The Fight for a Secular World of Universal and Equal Rights*. Seattle: University of Washington Press.

Jacobs, Jill. 2015. "Tikkun Olam as an Antidote to Hashhatat Yishuvo Shel Olam (The Destruction of Society)." In *Tikkun Olam: Judaism, Humanism, and Transcendence*, edited by David Birnbaum and Martin S. Cohen, 517–529. New York: New Paradigm Matrix.

Jobani, Yuval. 2023. *The First Jewish Environmentalist: The Green Philosophy of A.D. Gordon*. New York: Oxford University Press.

Julius, Lyn. 2018. *Uprooted: How 3000 Years of Jewish Civilisation in the Arab World Vanished Overnight*. London: Vallentine Mitchell.

Kahane, Meir. 1990. *Israel: Revolution or Referendum?* Secaucus: Barricade Books.

Kahane, Meir. 1998. *The Jewish Idea*. Translated by Raphael Blumberg. Vol. 2. Jerusalem: Institute for Publication of the Writings of Rabbi Meir Kahane.

Kahane, Meir. 2010. *Beyond Words: Selected Writings of Rabbi Meir Kahane, 1960–1990*. Edited by David Fein. Vol. 7. Jerusalem: Institute for Publication of the Writings of Rabbi Meir Kahane.

Kahane, Meir. 2014. *Commentary on Exodus: Perush HaMaccabee*. Jerusalem: Institute for Publication of the Writings of Rabbi Meir Kahane.

Kalechofsky, Roberta. 1998. *Vegetarian Judaism: A Guide for Everyone*. Marblehead: Micah Publications.

Kaplan, Eran. 2005. *The Jewish Radical Right: Revisionist Zionism and Its Ideological Legacy*. Madison: University of Wisconsin Press.

Kaplan, Lawrence. 2000. "Rabbinic Authority and Modernity." In *The Jewish Political Tradition*, edited by Michael Walzer, Menachem Lorberbaum, Noam Zohar, and Yair Lorberbaum, 1: 301–306. New Haven: Yale University Press.

Kaplan, Mordecai Menahem. 1956. *Questions Jews Ask: Reconstructionist Answers*. New York: Reconstructionist Press.

Kasher, Hannah. 2019. "Maimonides on the Intellects of Women and Gentiles." In *Interpreting Maimonides: Critical Essays*, edited by Charles H. Manekin and Daniel Davies, 46–64. Cambridge: Cambridge University Press.

Katri, Ido. 2019. "Trans-Arab-Jew: A Look beyond the Boundaries of In-Between Identities." *TSQ: Transgender Studies Quarterly* 6 (3): 338–357.

Katz, Eric. 1997. "Nature's Healing Power, the Holocaust, and the Environmental Crisis." *Judaism: A Quarterly Journal of Jewish Life and Thought* 46 (1): 79–90.

Kavka, Martin. 2021. "Judaism and Christianity in Jewish Ethics of the 1950s." *Journal of Jewish Ethics* 7 (1–2): 63–81.

Kay, Judith W. 2020. "Jews as Oppressed and Oppressor: Doing Ethics at the Intersections of Classism, Racism, and Antisemitism." In *Judaism, Race, and Ethics: Conversations and Questions*, edited by Jonathan K. Crane, 66–104. University Park: Pennsylvania State University Press.

Kaye/Kantrowitz, Melanie. 1992. *The Issue Is Power: Essays on Women, Jews, Violence, and Resistance.* San Francisco: Aunt Lute Books.

Kaye/Kantrowitz, Melanie. 2007. *The Colors of Jews: Racial Politics and Radical Diasporism.* Bloomington: Indiana University Press.

Kedar, Nir. 2013. "Ben-Gurion's View of the Place of Judaism in Israel." *Journal of Israeli History* 32 (2): 157–174.

Kellner, Menachem Marc. 1990. *Maimonides on Human Perfection.* Atlanta: Scholars Press.

Kellner, Menachem Marc. 2006. *Maimonides' Confrontation with Mysticism.* Oxford: Littman Library of Jewish Civilization.

Kellner, Menachem Marc, and David Gillis. 2020. *Maimonides the Universalist: The Ethical Horizons of the Mishneh Torah.* London: The Littman Library of Jewish Civilization.

Kessler, Gwynn. 2020. "Perspectives on Rabbinic Constructions of Gendered Bodies." In *The Wiley Blackwell Companion to Religion and Materiality*, edited by Vasudha Narayanan, 63–89. Bognor Regis: John Wiley & Sons.

Kiel, Yishai. 2016. "Dynamics of Sexual Desire: Babylonian Rabbinic Culture at the Crossroads of Christian and Zoroastrian Ethics." *Journal for the Study of Judaism in the Persian, Hellenistic, and Roman Period* 47 (3): 364–410.

Klagsbrun, Francine. 2017. *Lioness: Golda Meir and the Nation of Israel.* New York: Schocken.

Klein-Braslavy, Sarah. 2011. *Maimonides as a Biblical Interpreter.* Brighton: Academic Studies.

Klepfisz, Irena. 1990. *Dreams of an Insomniac: Jewish Feminist Essays, Speeches, and Diatribes.* Portland: Eighth Mountain Press.

Koch, Patrick B. 2015. *Human Self-Perfection: A Re-assessment of Kabbalistic Musar-Literature of Sixteenth-Century Safed.* Los Angeles: Cherub Press.

Koffman, David S. 2019. *The Jews' Indian: Colonialism, Pluralism, and Belonging in America.* New Brunswick: Rutgers University Press.

Kohler, George Y. 2012. *Reading Maimonides' Philosophy in 19th Century Germany: The Guide to Religious Reform.* New York: Springer.

Kohler, Kaufmann, Emil G. Hirsch, and Isaac Broyde. 1903. "Ethics." In *The Jewish Encyclopedia*, edited by Isidore Singer, 5: 245–258. New York: Funk and Wagnalls.

Koren, Sharon Faye. 2011. *Forsaken: The Menstruant in Medieval Jewish Mysticism.* Waltham: Brandeis University Press.

Kraemer, David Charles. 1996. *Reading the Rabbis: The Talmud as Literature.* New York: Oxford University Press.

Kraemer, Joel L. 2008. *Maimonides: The Life and World of One of Civilization's Greatest Minds*. New York: Doubleday.

Kreisel, Howard T. 1999. *Maimonides' Political Thought: Studies in Ethics, Law, and the Human Ideal*. Albany: SUNY Press.

Kreisel, Howard T. 2015. *Judaism as Philosophy: Studies in Maimonides and the Medieval Jewish Philosophers of Provence*. Boston: Academic Studies Press.

Kugel, James L. 1997. *The Bible as It Was*. Cambridge: Belknap Press of Harvard University Press.

Kukla, Elliot Rose. 2008. "Created Beings of Our Own: Toward a Jewish Liberation Theology for Men, Women, and Everyone Else." In *Righteous Indignation: A Jewish Call for Justice*, edited by Or N. Rose, Jo Ellen Green Kaiser, and Margie Klein, 214–221. Woodstock: Jewish Lights.

Labendz, Jacob, and Shmuly Yanklowitz, eds. 2019. *Jewish Veganism and Vegetarianism: Studies and New Directions*. Albany: SUNY Press.

Ladin, Joy. 2019. *The Soul of the Stranger: Reading God and Torah from a Transgender Perspective*. Waltham: Brandeis University Press.

LaGrone, Matthew. 2013. "Ethical Theories of Mordecai Kaplan and Abraham Joshua Heschel." In *The Oxford Handbook of Jewish Ethics and Morality*, edited by Elliot N. Dorff and Jonathan K. Crane, 151–164. Oxford: Oxford University Press.

Lamm, Norman. 1966. In *The Condition of Jewish Belief: A Symposium*, edited by Editors of Commentary Magazine, 123–131. New York: Macmillan.

Lappe, Benay. 2009. "The New Rabbis: A Postscript." In *Torah Queeries: Weekly Commentaries on the Hebrew Bible*, edited by Gregg Drinkwater, Joshua Lesser, and David Shneer, 311–314. New York: New York University Press.

Lawson, Sandra. 2021. "Kaddish in Memory of Black Lives." *Interfaith America*. February 2. https://www.interfaithamerica.org/article/kaddish-in-memory-of-black-lives.

Lawson, Sandra. 2023. "Fighting Racism with Jewish Values." *My Musings*. July 25. https://rabbisandra.substack.com/p/fighting-racism-with-jewish-values.

Lazarus, Moritz. 1900 [1898]. *The Ethics of Judaism*. Translated by Henrietta Szold. Vol. 1. Philadelphia: The Jewish Publication Society of America.

Leder, Sharon. 2021. *Three Groundbreaking Jewish Feminists Pursuing Social Justice*. New York: Hybrid Global Publishing.

Levin, Geoffrey. 2023. *Our Palestine Question: Israel and American Jewish Dissent, 1948–1978*. New Haven: Yale University Press.

Levinas, Emmanuel. 1990. *Difficult Freedom: Essays on Judaism*. Translated by Sean Hand. Baltimore: Johns Hopkins University Press.

Levins Morales, Aurora. 1995. "Nadie La Tiene: Land, Ecology and Nationalism." *Bridges* 5 (2): 31–39.

Levins Morales, Aurora. 2012. "Latin@s, Israel and Palestine: Understanding Anti-Semitism." March 15. http://www.auroralevinsmorales.com/blog/la tins-israel-and-palestine-understanding-anti-semitism.

Levins Morales, Aurora. 2017. "Who Am I to Speak?" In *On Antisemitism: Solidarity and the Struggle for Justice*, edited by Jewish Voice for Peace, 103–110. Chicago: Haymarket Books.

Levitt, Laura. 2012. "Interrogating the Judeo-Christian Tradition: Will Herberg's Construction of American Religion, Religious Pluralism, and the Problem of Inclusion." In *The Cambridge History of Religions in America*, edited by Stephen J. Stein, 3: 285–307. New York: Cambridge University Press.

Levy, Lital. 2012. "Partitioned Pasts: Arab Jewish Intellectuals and the Case of Esther Azharī Moyal (1873–1948)." In *The Making of the Arab Intellectual: Empire, Public Sphere and the Colonial Coordinates of Selfhood*, edited by Dyala Hamzah. New York: Routledge.

Linfield, Susie. 2019. *The Lions' Den: Zionism and the Left from Hannah Arendt to Noam Chomsky*. New Haven: Yale University Press.

Litvak, Olga. 2012. *Haskalah: The Romantic Movement in Judaism*. New Brunswick: Rutgers University Press.

Lober, Brooke. 2019. "Everything's Connected: An Interview with Aurora Levins Morales." *Meridians* 18 (2): 372–393.

Longmire-Avital, Buffie. 2023. "It Has Always Been a Shared Story: Finding the Narratives of Diversity, Inclusion, and Racial Equity in Judaism." *Evolve*. June 4. https://evolve.reconstructingjudaism.org/is-it-our-story-ra ce-and-judaism.

Luz, Ehud. 1987. "The Moral Price of Sovereignty: The Dispute about the Use of Military Power within Zionism." *Modern Judaism* 7 (1): 51–98.

Luz, Ehud. 2003. *Wrestling with an Angel: Power, Morality, and Jewish Identity*. Translated by Michael Swirsky. New Haven: Yale University Press.

Magid, Shaul. 2014. "'America Is No Different,' 'America Is Different' – Is There an American Jewish Fundamentalism?" In *Fundamentalism: Perspectives on a Contested History*, edited by Simon A. Wood and David Harrington Watt, 70–107. Columbia: University of South Carolina Press.

Magid, Shaul. 2021a. *Meir Kahane: The Public Life and Political Thought of an American Jewish Radical*. Princeton: Princeton University Press.

Magid, Shaul. 2021b. "The Enforcers." *Tablet Magazine*. July 14. https://www.tabletmag.com/sections/community/articles/enforcers-anti-zionists.

Magid, Shaul. 2023a. "Preface." In *End of Days: Ethics, Tradition, and Power in Israel*, by Mikhael Manekin. Brookline: Academic Studies Press.

Magid, Shaul. 2023b. *The Necessity of Exile: Essays from a Distance*. New York: Ayin Press.

Malino, Frances. 1996. *A Jew in the French Revolution: The Life of Zalkind Hourwitz*. Oxford: Blackwell.

Marcus, Hadas. 2019. "Farm Animal Welfare in Jewish Art and Literature." In *Jewish Veganism and Vegetarianism: Studies and New Directions*, edited by Jacob Labendz and Shmuly Yanklowitz, 67–91. Albany: SUNY Press.

Martin, Craig. 2017. *A Critical Introduction to the Study of Religion*. London: Routledge.

Mbuvi, Amanda Beckenstein. 2016. *Belonging in Genesis: Biblical Israel and the Politics of Identity Formation*. Waco: Baylor University Press.

Mbuvi, Amanda Beckenstein. 2020. "Black Jews Matter: Solidarity Begins Beyond the Limits of Whiteness." *Contending Modernities*. September 16. https://contendingmodernities.nd.edu/theorizing-modernities/black-jews-matter.

Mbuvi, Amanda Beckenstein. 2021. "Avadim Hayinu: An Intersectional Jewish Perspective on the Global Ethic of Solidarity." In *Multi-Religious Perspectives on a Global Ethic: In Search of a Common Morality*, edited by Myriam Renaud and William Schweiker. New York: Routledge.

Meir, Asher. 2005. *Meaning in Mitzvot*. Jerusalem: ACHY.

Melamed, Abraham. 2003. *The Image of the Black in Jewish Culture: A History of the Other*. London: Routledge.

Mendelsohn, Ezra. 1993. *On Modern Jewish Politics*. Oxford: Oxford University Press.

Meyer, Michael A. 1988a. *Response to Modernity: A History of the Reform Movement in Judaism*. New York: Oxford University Press.

Meyer, Michael A. 1988b. "The Emergence of Jewish Historiography: Motives and Motifs." *History and Theory* 27 (4): 160–175.

Michels, Tony. 2005. *A Fire in Their Hearts: Yiddish Socialists in New York*. Cambridge: Harvard University Press.

Miller, Avigdor. 1980. *Awake My Glory: Aspects of Jewish Ideology*. New York: Bais Yisroel of Rugby.

Miller, Michael T. 2021. "Ben Ammi's Adaptation of Veganism in the Theology of the African Hebrew Israelites of Jerusalem." *Interdisciplinary Journal for Religion and Transformation in Contemporary Society* 9 (2): 417–444.

Mittleman, Alan. 2012. *A Short History of Jewish Ethics: Conduct and Character in the Context of Covenant*. Chichester: Wiley-Blackwell.

Montell, Jessica. 2013. "Making Universalism Resonate Locally." *openDemocracy*. August 23. https://www.opendemocracy.net/en/openglobalrights-openpage/making-universalism-resonate-locally.

Morgan, Michael L. 2011. *The Cambridge Introduction to Emmanuel Levinas*. Cambridge: Cambridge University Press.

Morris, Benny. 2004. *The Birth of the Palestinian Refugee Problem Revisited*. Cambridge: Cambridge University Press.

Motzafi-Haller, Pnina. 2001. "Scholarship, Identity, and Power: Mizrahi Women in Israel." *Signs: Journal of Women in Culture and Society* 26 (3): 697–734.

Motzafi-Haller, Pnina. 2014. "Negotiating Difference in Israeli Scholarship: Towards a New Feminist Discourse." In *Israelis in Conflict*, edited by Adriana Kemp, David Newman, Uri Ram, and Oren Yiftachel, 162–187. Brighton: Sussex Academic Press.

Myers, David. 2020. "Knowing the Victim? Reflections on Empathy, Analogy, and Voice from the Shoah to the Present." *Herbert D. Katz Center for Advanced Judaic Studies*. June 25. https://katz.sas.upenn.edu/resources/blog/knowing-victim-reflections-empathy-analogy-and-voice-shoah-present.

Naar, Devin E. 2019. "Our White Supremacy Problem." *Jewish Currents*. April 29. https://jewishcurrents.org/our-white-supremacy-problem.

Nadler, Steven M., and Tamar Rudavsky, eds. 2009. *The Cambridge History of Jewish Philosophy: From Antiquity Through the Seventeenth Century*. Cambridge: Cambridge University Press.

Naḥman of Bratslav. 2010. *Sefer Likkutei Moharan*. 2 vols. Mechon Pituchey Chotam.

Naor, Arye. 2003. "Lessons of the Holocaust Versus Territories for Peace, 1967–2001." *Israel Studies* 8 (1): 130–152.

Netanyahu, Benjamin. 2024. "Statement by PM Netanyahu." *Gov.il*. January 13. https://www.gov.il/en/departments/news/spoke-press130424.

Neumann, Jonathan. 2018. *To Heal the World?: How the Jewish Left Corrupts Judaism and Endangers Israel*. New York: All Points Books.

Newman, Louis E. 1998a. "Constructing a Jewish Sexual Ethic: A Rejoinder to David Novak and Judith Plaskow." In *Sexual Orientation and Human Rights in American Religious Discourse*, edited by Saul M. Olyan and Martha C. Nussbaum, 46–53. New York: Oxford University Press.

Newman, Louis E. 1998b. *Past Imperatives: Studies in the History and Theory of Jewish Ethics*. Albany: SUNY Press.

Newman, Louis E. 2005. *An Introduction to Jewish Ethics*. Upper Saddle River: Pearson Prentice Hall.

Nirenberg, David. 2013. *Anti-Judaism: The Western Tradition*. New York: W.W. Norton & Co.

Novak, David. 1974. *Law and Theology in Judaism*. New York: Ktav.

Novak, David. 1981. "Universal Moral Law in the Theology of Hermann Cohen." *Modern Judaism* 1 (1): 101–117.

Novak, David. 2000. *Covenantal Rights: A Study in Jewish Political Theory*. Princeton: Princeton University Press.

Novak, David. 2005. *The Jewish Social Contract: An Essay in Political Theology*. Princeton: Princeton University Press.

Novak, David. 2007. *The Sanctity of Human Life*. Washington: Georgetown University Press.

Ohana, David. 2010. *Political Theologies in the Holy Land: Israeli Messianism and Its Critics*. London: Routledge.

Omer, Atalia. 2013. *When Peace Is Not Enough: How the Israeli Peace Camp Thinks About Religion, Nationalism, and Justice*. Chicago: University of Chicago Press.

Omer, Atalia. 2019. *Days of Awe: Reimagining Jewishness in Solidarity with Palestinians*. Chicago: The University of Chicago Press.

Ophir, Adi, and Ishay Rosen-Zvi. 2018. *Goy: Israel's Multiple Others and the Birth of the Gentile*. Oxford: Oxford University Press.

Patterson, Charles. 2002. *Eternal Treblinka: Our Treatment of Animals and the Holocaust*. New York: Lantern Books.

Penslar, Derek J. 2005. "Herzl and the Palestinian Arabs: Myth and Counter-Myth." *The Journal of Israeli History* 24 (1): 65–77.

Penslar, Derek J. 2020. "Theodor Herzl, Race, and Empire." In *Making History Jewish: The Dialectics of Jewish History in Eastern Europe and the Middle East, Studies in Honor of Professor Israel Bartal*, edited by Paweł Maciejko and Scott Ury, 185–209. Leiden: Brill.

Penslar, Derek J. 2023. *Zionism: An Emotional State*. New Brunswick: Rutgers University Press.

Peskowitz, Miriam. 1997. *Spinning Fantasies: Rabbis, Gender, and History*. Berkeley: University of California Press.

Petuchowski, Jakob J. 1966. In *The Condition of Jewish Belief: A Symposium*, edited by Editors of Commentary Magazine, 158–165. New York: Macmillan.

Philipson, David. 1905. "The Rabbinical Conferences, 1844–6." *The Jewish Quarterly Review* 17 (4): 656–689.

Philipson, David. 1919. *Centenary Papers and Others*. Cincinnati: Ark Publishing.

Plaskow, Judith. 1990. *Standing Again at Sinai: Judaism from a Feminist Perspective*. New York: Harper & Row.

Plaskow, Judith. 2005. *The Coming of Lilith: Essays on Feminism, Judaism, and Sexual Ethics, 1972–2003*. With Donna Berman. Boston: Beacon Press.

Plevan, William. 2023. "Martin Buber." In *Jewish Virtue Ethics*, edited by Geoffrey D. Claussen, Alexander Green, and Alan L. Mittleman, 369–381. Albany: SUNY Press.

Polner, Murray, and Naomi Goodman, eds. 1994. *The Challenge of Shalom: The Jewish Tradition of Peace and Justice*. Philadelphia: New Society Publishers.

Prescod-Weinstein, Chanda. 2017. "Black and Palestinian Lives Matter: Black and Jewish America in the Twenty-First Century." In *On Antisemitism: Solidarity and the Struggle for Justice*, edited by Jewish Voice for Peace, 103–110. Chicago: Haymarket Books.

Presner, Todd Samuel. 2007. *Muscular Judaism: The Jewish Body and the Politics of Regeneration*. London: Routledge.

Prinz, Joachim. 2007. *Joachim Prinz, Rebellious Rabbi: An Autobiography: The German and Early American Years*. Edited by Michael A. Meyer. Bloomington: Indiana University Press.

Prouser, Joseph H. 1995. "Hesed or Hiyuv? The Obligation to Preserve Life and the Question of Post-Mortem Organ Donations." *Rabbinical Assembly.* https://www.rabbinicalassembly.org/sites/default/files/assets/public/hala khah/teshuvot/19912000/prouser_chesed.pdf.

Rabinovitch, Simon. 2014. *Jewish Rights, National Rites: Nationalism and Autonomy in Late Imperial and Revolutionary Russia.* Stanford: Stanford University Press.

Raucher, Michal. 2016. "Ethnography and Jewish Ethics." *Journal of Religious Ethics* 44 (4): 636–658.

Raucher, Michal. 2020. *Conceiving Agency: Reproductive Authority Among Haredi Women.* Bloomington: Indiana University Press.

Raucher, Michal. 2022. "Jewish Tradition 'Permits' Abortion. If You Believe in Bodily Autonomy, That's Not Enough." *Jewish Telegraphic Agency.* May 10. https://www.jta.org/2022/05/10/ideas/jewish-tradition-permits-abor tion-if-you-believe-in-bodily-autonomy-thats-not-enough.

Raucher, Michal. 2023a. "From Justification to Justice: Calling for a New Conservative Movement Position on Abortion." *Masorti: The New Journal of Conservative Judaism* 67 (1): 55–77.

Raucher, Michal. 2023b. "The Religion of Reproductive Rights Claims: The Jewish Fight to Legalize Abortion." *The Revealer.* October 4. https://there vealer.org/the-religion-of-reproductive-rights-claims-the-jewish-fight-to-legalize-abortion.

Raveh, Inbar. 2014. *Feminist Rereadings of Rabbinic Literature.* Translated by Kaeren Fish. Waltham: Brandeis University Press.

Ravitzky, Aviezer. 1996. *Messianism, Zionism, and Jewish Religious Radicalism.* Translated by Michael Swirsky and Jonathan Chipman. Chicago: University of Chicago Press.

Richman, Julia, and Eugene Heitler Lehman. 1914. *Methods of Teaching Jewish Ethics.* Philadelphia: Jewish Chautauqua Society.

Rock-Singer, Cara. 2020. "Hadassah and the Gender of Modern Jewish Thought: The Affective, Embodied Messianism of Jessie Sampter, Irma Lindheim, and Nima Adlerblum." *American Jewish History* 104 (2–3): 423–456.

Rodinson, Maxime. 1983. *Cult, Ghetto, and State: The Persistence of the Jewish Question.* Translated by Jon Rothschild. London: Al Saqi Books.

Rose, Dawn Robinson. 1999. "Class as Problematic in Jewish Feminist Theology." *Race, Gender and Class* 6 (4): 125–135.

Rosen, Brant. 2016. "On Passover, Israel and 'Demographic Threats'". *Truthout.* April 28. http://www.truth-out.org/opinion/item/35811-on-pa ssover-israel-and-demographic-threats.

Rosenstock, Bruce. 2014. "'God … Has Sent Me to Germany': Salomon Maimon, Friedrich Jacobi, and the Spinoza Quarrel." *The Southern Journal of Philosophy* 52 (3): 287–315.

Ross, Tamar. 2004. *Expanding the Palace of Torah: Orthodoxy and Feminism.* Waltham: Brandeis University Press.

Rovner, Adam. 2014. *In the Shadow of Zion: Promised Lands Before Israel.* New York: NYU Press.

Roy, Sara. 1995. *The Gaza Strip: The Political Economy of De-Development.* Washington: Institute for Palestine Studies.

Roy, Sara. 2002. "Living with the Holocaust: The Journey of a Child of Holocaust Survivors." *Journal of Palestine Studies* 32 (1): 5–12.

Rubenstein, Jeffrey L. 1999. *Talmudic Stories: Narrative Art, Composition, and Culture.* Baltimore: Johns Hopkins University Press.

Sagi, Avi. 1996. "'He Slew the Egyptian and Hid Him in the Sand': Jewish Tradition and the Moral Element." Translated by Batya Stein. *Hebrew Union College Annual* 67: 55–76.

Sagi, Avi. 2021. *Morality and Religion: The Jewish Story.* Translated by Batya Stein. Cham: Springer International Publishing.

Samudzi, Zoé. 2024. "'We Are Fighting Nazis': Genocidal Fashionings of Gaza(ns) After 7 October." *Journal of Genocide Research*, 1–9.

Saperstein, Marc. 2008. *Jewish Preaching in Times of War, 1800–2001.* Oxford: Littman Library of Jewish Civilization.

Satherley, Tessa. 2013. "'The Simple Jew': The 'Price Tag' Phenomenon, Vigilantism, and Rabbi Yitzchak Ginsburgh's Political Kabbalah." *Melilah* 10: 57–91.

Satlow, Michael L. 1995. *Tasting the Dish: Rabbinic Rhetorics of Sexuality.* Atlanta: Scholars Press.

Schofer, Jonathan Wyn. 2004. *The Making of a Sage: A Study in Rabbinic Ethics.* Madison: University of Wisconsin Press.

Scholem, Gershom. 1971. *The Messianic Idea in Judaism and Other Essays on Jewish Spirituality.* New York: Schocken Books.

Schwartz, Daniel B. 2012. *The First Modern Jew: Spinoza and the History of an Image.* Princeton: Princeton University Press.

Schwartz, Daniel R. 2014. *Judeans and Jews: Four Faces of Dichotomy in Ancient Jewish History.* Toronto: University of Toronto Press.

Schwartz, Eilon. 1997. "Bal Tashchit: A Jewish Environmental Precept." *Environmental Ethics* 19 (4): 355–374.

Schwarzschild, Steven S. 1956. "The Democratic Socialism of Hermann Cohen." *Hebrew Union College Annual* 27: 417–438.

Scult, Mel. 2013. *The Radical American Judaism of Mordecai M. Kaplan.* Bloomington: Indiana University Press.

Secunda, Shai. 2012. "The Construction, Composition and Idealization of the Female Body in Rabbinic Literature and Parallel Iranian Texts: Three Excursuses." *Nashim: A Journal of Jewish Women's Studies and Gender Issues* 23: 60–86.

Seeskin, Kenneth. 1997. "Jewish Neo-Kantianism: Hermann Cohen." In *History of Jewish Philosophy*, edited by Daniel H. Frank and Oliver Leaman, 786–798. London: Routledge.

Segal, Raz. 2023. "Here's What the Mass Violence in Gaza Looks Like to a Scholar of Genocide." *Los Angeles Times*. November 19. https://www.la times.com/opinion/story/2023-11-19/israel-hostages-gaza-bombing-civilia ns-genocide-holocaust-studies.

Segev, Tom. 1993. *The Seventh Million: The Israelis and the Holocaust*. Translated by Haim Watzman. New York: Hill and Wang.

Segev, Tom. 2019. *A State at Any Cost: The Life of David Ben-Gurion*. Translated by Haim Watzman. New York: Farrar, Straus and Giroux.

Seidenberg, David Mevorach. 2015. *Kabbalah and Ecology: God's Image in the More-Than-Human World*. New York: Cambridge University Press.

Shapira, Anita. 1990. "Herzl, Ahad Ha-'Am, and Berdichevsky: Comments on Their Nationalist Concepts." *Jewish History* 4 (2): 59–69.

Shapira, Anita. 1992. *Land and Power: The Zionist Resort to Force, 1881–1948*. New York: Oxford University Press.

Shemesh, Yael. 2006. "Vegetarian Ideology in Talmudic Literature and Traditional Biblical Exegesis." *Review of Rabbinic Judaism* 9 (1–2): 141–166.

Shenhav, Yehouda. 2012. "Spineless Bookkeeping: The Use of Mizrahi Jews as Pawns Against Palestinian Refugees." *+972 Magazine*. September 25. http://www.972mag.com/spineless-bookkeeping-the-use-of-mizra hi-jews-as-pawns-against-palestinian-refugees.

Shlaim, Avi. 2012. "Zionism, the Founding Fathers and the Palestine Arabs." In *Pretending Democracy: Israel, an Ethnocratic State*, edited by Na'eem Jeenah, 53–68. Johannesburg, South Africa: AMEC.

Shohat, Ella. 1988. "Sephardim in Israel: Zionism from the Standpoint of Its Jewish Victims." *Social Text* 19/20: 1–35.

Shohat, Ella. 2017. *On the Arab-Jew, Palestine, and Other Displacements: Selected Writings*. London: Pluto Press.

Shuldiner, David Philip. 1999. *Of Moses and Marx: Folk Ideology and Folk History in the Jewish Labor Movement*. Westport: Bergin & Garvey.

Sienna, Noam. 2019. *A Rainbow Thread: An Anthology of Queer Jewish Texts from the First Century to 1969*. Philadelphia: Print-O-Craft.

Simon-Shoshan, Moshe. 2021. "'These and Those Are the Words of the Living God, but …': Meaning, Background, and Reception of an Early Rabbinic Teaching." *AJS Review* 45 (2): 382–410.

Slabodsky, Santiago. 2014. *Decolonial Judaism: Triumphal Failures of Barbaric Thinking*. New York: Palgrave Macmillan.

Slifkin, Natan. 2021. *Rationalism vs. Mysticism: Schisms in Traditional Jewish Thought*. Jerusalem: Gefen Publishing.

Soloveitchik, Joseph Dov. 2005. *The Emergence of Ethical Man*. Jersey City: Ktav.

Steinfeld, Rebecca. 2015. "Wars of the Wombs: Struggles Over Abortion Policies in Israel." *Israel Studies* 20 (2): 1–26.

Steinmetz, Devora. 2008. *Punishment and Freedom: The Rabbinic Construction of Criminal Law*. Philadelphia: University of Pennsylvania Press.

Stern, Josef. 2013. *The Matter and Form of Maimonides' Guide*. Cambridge: Harvard University Press.

Stern, Sacha. 1994. *Jewish Identity in Early Rabbinic Writings*. Leiden: Brill.

Stern, Yedidia, and Karen Friedman-Stern. 2017. "Ma'aseh Imahot Siman Le-Banot." *Musaf Shabbat (Makor Rishon)*. January 20. https://musaf-sha bbat.com/2017/01/22/מעשה-אמהות-סימן-לבנות-ידידיה-צ-שטר.

Strassfeld, Max K. 2022a. *Trans Talmud: Androgynes and Eunuchs in Rabbinic Literature*. Oakland: University of California Press.

Strassfeld, Max K. 2022b. "Turning to the Talmud to Find Gender Diversity That Speaks to Today." *The Revealer*. October 6. https://therevealer.org/turning-to-the-talmud-to-find-gender-diversity-that-speaks-to-today.

Stroumsa, Sarah. 2009. *Maimonides in His World: Portrait of a Mediterranean Thinker*. Princeton: Princeton University Press.

Sufrin, Claire E. 2011. "Telling Stories: The Legal Turn in Jewish Feminist Thought." In *Gender and Jewish History*, edited by Marion A. Kaplan and Deborah Dash Moore, 233–248. Bloomington: Indiana University Press.

Teutsch, David A. 2009. *Community, Gemilut Hesed, and Tikun Olam*. Wyncote, PA: Reconstructionist Rabbinical College Press.

Tirosh-Samuelson, Hava. 2003. *Happiness in Premodern Judaism: Virtue, Knowledge, and Well-Being*. Cincinnati: Hebrew Union College Press.

Tirosh-Samuelson, Hava. 2014. "Judith Plaskow: An Intellectual Portrait." In *Judith Plaskow: Feminism, Theology, and Justice*, edited by Hava Tirosh-Samuelson and Aaron W. Hughes, 1–25. Leiden: Brill.

Tirosh-Samuelson, Hava. 2023. "Jewish Environmentalism." In *Jewish Virtue Ethics*, edited by Geoffrey D. Claussen, Alexander Green, and Alan L. Mittleman, 483–496. Albany: SUNY Press.

Tishby, Isaiah. 1989. *The Wisdom of the Zohar*. Translated by David Goldstein. 3 vols. Oxford: Oxford University Press.

Torres, Anna Elena. 2024. *Horizons Blossom, Borders Vanish: Anarchism and Yiddish Literature*. New Haven: Yale University Press.

Walzer, Michael, *et al.* eds. 2000. *The Jewish Political Tradition*. Vol. 1. New Haven: Yale University Press.

Waskow, Arthur I. 1978. *Godwrestling*. New York: Schocken.

Wasserman, Mira Beth. 2017. *Jews, Gentiles, and Other Animals: The Talmud After the Humanities*. Philadelphia: University of Pennsylvania Press.

Wasserman, Mira Beth. 2019. "Noahide Law, Animal Ethics, and Talmudic Narrative." *Journal of Jewish Ethics* 5 (1): 40–67.

Wegner, Judith Romney. 1998. "The Image and Status of Women in Classical Rabbinic Judaism." In *Jewish Women in Historical Perspective*, 2nd ed., edited by Judith R. Baskin, 73–100. Detroit: Wayne State University Press.

Wein, Berel. 2007. "Beginnings." *The Jerusalem Post*. October 2. https://www.jpost.com/jewish-world/judaism/beginnings.

Weisberg, Anne, and Rachel Landsberg. 2021. "It's Time for Jews to Mobilize for Climate Action." *The Forward*. July 27. https://forward.com/community/473588/its-time-for-jews-to-mobilize-for-climate-action.

Weiss, Raymond L. 1991. *Maimonides' Ethics: The Encounter of Philosophic and Religious Morality*. Chicago: University of Chicago Press.

Weiss, Roslyn. 1989. "Maimonides on 'Shilluaḥ Ha-Qen'." *The Jewish Quarterly Review* 79 (4): 345–366.

Weiss, Shira. 2021. "Paradise and the Fall." In *Maimonides' Guide of the Perplexed: A Critical Guide*, edited by Daniel Frank and Aaron Segal, 51–59. Cambridge: Cambridge University Press.

Wenig, Margaret Moers. 2003. "Their Lives a Page Plucked from a Holy Book." In *The Women's Passover Companion: Women's Reflections on the Festival of Freedom*, edited by Sharon Cohen Anisfeld, Tara Mohr, and Catherine Spector, 119–127. Woodstock: Jewish Lights.

Wenig, Margaret Moers. 2009. "Male and Female God Created Them: Parashat Bereshit." In *Torah Queeries: Weekly Commentaries on the Hebrew Bible*, edited by Gregg Drinkwater, Joshua Lesser, and David Shneer, 11–18. New York: New York University Press.

Westreich, Miri. 2022. "This One Will Be Called Woman." In *Dirshuni: Contemporary Women's Midrash*, edited by Tamar Biala, 6–8. Waltham: Brandeis University Press.

Wiese, Christian. 2007. "Samuel Holdheim's 'Most Powerful Comrade in Conviction': David Einhorn and the Debate Concerning Jewish Universalism in the Radical Reform Movement." In *Redefining Judaism in an Age of Emancipation: Comparative Perspectives on Samuel Holdheim (1806–1860)*, edited by Christian Wiese, 306–373. Leiden: Brill.

Wiesel, Elie, and Richard D. Heffner. 2001. *Conversations with Elie Wiesel*. New York: Schocken Books.

Wine, Sherwin T. 1995. *Judaism Beyond God*. KTAV, Society for Humanistic Judaism, and Milan Press.

Wolfson, Elliot R. 1987. "Circumcision, Vision of God, and Textual Interpretation: From Midrashic Trope to Mystical Symbol." *History of Religions* 27 (2): 189–215.

Wolfson, Elliot R. 1994. "Woman—The Feminine as Other in Theosophic Kabbalah: Some Philosophical Observations on the Divine Androgyne." In *The Other in Jewish Thought and History: Constructions of Jewish Culture and*

Identity, edited by Laurence J. Silberstein and Robert L. Cohn, 166–204. New York: New York University Press.

Wolfson, Elliot R. 2002. "The Cut That Binds: Time, Memory, and the Ascetic Impulse." In *God's Voice from the Void: Old and New Studies in Bratslav Hasidism*, edited by Shaul Magid. Albany: SUNY Press.

Wolfson, Elliot R. 2006. *Venturing Beyond: Law and Morality in Kabbalistic Mysticism*. New York: Oxford University Press.

Wolfson, Elliot R. 2009. *Open Secret: Postmessianic Messianism and the Mystical Revision of Menaḥem Mendel Schneerson*. New York: Columbia University Press.

Wollenberg, Rebecca Scharbach. 2023. *The Closed Book: How the Rabbis Taught the Jews (Not) to Read the Bible*. Princeton: Princeton University Press.

Woocher, Jonathan S. 1986. *Sacred Survival: The Civil Religion of American Jews*. Bloomington: Indiana University Press.

Wyse, Raelene Camille. 2021. "Aurora Levins Morales." *Jewish Women's Archive, Shalvi/Hyman Encyclopedia of Jewish Women*. https://jwa.org/encyclopedia/article/morales-aurora-levins.

Yaffe, Martin D., ed. 2001. *Judaism and Environmental Ethics: A Reader*. Lanham: Lexington Books.

Yanai, Nathan. 1989. "Ben-Gurion's Concept of Mamlahtiut and the Forming Reality of the State of Israel." *Jewish Political Studies Review* 1 (1–2): 151–177.

Yanklowitz, Shmuly. 2020. *The Book of Jonah: A Social Justice Commentary*. New York: CCAR Press.

Yefet, Karin Carmit. 2016. "Born to Be a Mother: Anatomy, Autonomy, and Substantive Citizenship for Women in Israel." *Harvard Journal of Law and Gender* 39 (1): 257–315.

Yefet, Karin Carmit. 2022. "The Womb Monologues: Toward a Mizrahi Feminist Theory of Israeli Law." *The American Journal of Comparative Law* 70 (4): 816–857.

Yoreh, Tanhum. 2019. *Waste Not: A Jewish Environmental Ethic*. Albany: SUNY Press.

Yuchtman-Yaar, Ephraim, and Tamar Hermann. 2000. "Shas: The Haredi-Dovish Image in a Changing Reality." *Israel Studies* 5 (2): 32–77.

Yuval-Davis, Nira. 1989. "National Reproduction and the 'Demographic Race' in Israel." In *Woman, Nation, State*, edited by Nira Yuval-Davis, Floya Anthias, and Jo Campling. London: Macmillan.

Zertal, Idith. 2005. *Israel's Holocaust and the Politics of Nationhood*. Cambridge: Cambridge University Press.

Zipperstein, Steven J. 2018. *Pogrom: Kishinev and the Tilt of History*. New York: Liveright.

Zohar, Noam. 1997. *Alternatives in Jewish Bioethics*. Albany: SUNY Press.

Zohar, Noam. 2007. "War and Peace." In *Judaism and the Challenges of Modern Life*, edited by Moshe Halbertal and Donniel Hartman. London: Continuum.

Zoloth, Laurie. 1999. *Health Care and the Ethics of Encounter: A Jewish Discussion of Social Justice*. Chapel Hill: University of North Carolina Press.

Zoosman, Michael. 2022. "'Pikuach Nefesh' – Jewish Abolitionists Help Save the Life of Melissa Lucio." *The Times of Israel*. May 3. https://blogs.timesofisrael.com/pikuach-nefesh-jewish-abolitionists-help-save-the-life-of-melissa-lucio.

INDEX

·

Printed in the United States
by Baker & Taylor Publisher Services